The Bathroom
Golf Almanac

Compiled and Edited by: Steve Heldt

Contributors: Jack Kreismer
Geoff Scowcroft

RED-LETTER PRESS, INC.
SADDLE RIVER, NEW JERSEY

The Bathroom Golf ALMANAC

A DAILY ROLL CALL
OF QUIPS, QUOTES
AND TRIVIA
FOR THE 19TH HOLE

The Bathroom Library™

JANUARY

TODAY'S THOUGHT:

"A game in which one endeavors to control a ball with implements ill adapted for the purpose."

—Woodrow Wilson, on golf

ON THIS DATE—

In 1938, a rule went into effect limiting the number of clubs allowed in tournament competition. The USGA, in an effort to speed up play, decreed that a player could use no more than 14 clubs.

CHIP SHOT

A golf ball with no dimples will fly approximately 60 to 80 yards, taking off like an ordinary dimpled ball, but dropping quickly back to earth.

TRIVIA QUIZ—

Name the first golfer to win the U.S. Open and the British Open in the same year.

TODAY'S TIP—

First tee jitters cause most golfers to take hurried swings. To get off to a good start, plan to swing the club at about half of your normal speed.

THE 19TH HOLE
"The woods are full of long hitters."
——Harvey Penick

Quiz Answer: Bobby Jones, who won both tournaments in 1926.

JANUARY

TODAY'S THOUGHT:
"If profanity had an influence on the flight of the ball, the game would be played far better than it is."
    —Horace Hutchinson, "Hints on the Game of Golf", 1886

ON THIS DATE—
In 1995, amateur golfer Sonya Osugi scored two holes-in-one during the same round at the Chung Shan Hot Springs Golf Club in southern China. Osugi was playing with a 24-stroke handicap.

CHIP SHOT
The odds against an amateur golfer recording a single hole-in-one are approximately 43,000 to one.

TRIVIA QUIZ—
What is Fuzzy Zoeller's real name?

TODAY'S TIP—
Golf courses are designed so that rainwater drains away from the greens. So if there's water to the right of the green, expect your putt to break in that direction.

—— THE 19TH HOLE ——
"Water holes are sacrificial waters where you make a steady gift of your pride and high-priced balls."
    —Tommy Bolt

Quiz Answer: The personable pro's full name is Frank Urban Zoeller, hence the nickname Fuzzy.

J A N U A R Y

TODAY'S THOUGHT:

"Golf is an awkward set of bodily contortions designed to produce a graceful result."   —Tommy Armour

ON THIS DATE—

In 1991, Paul Azinger shot a bogey-free round of 67 to win the Pebble Beach National Pro-Am and the $198,000 first prize. Brian Claar and Corey Pavin tied for second, four strokes back.

CHIP SHOT

In 1457, the Scottish Parliament banned golf. The august body felt the time would be better spent practicing archery for defense against the English.

TRIVIA QUIZ—

Who holds the record for most PGA tournaments won in a year?

TODAY'S TIP—

When attempting a chip shot, let the club do the work. Play the shot back in your stance and hit down on the ball. Skulled shots are caused by hitting up.

—THE 19TH HOLE—

"The wind was so strong, there were whitecaps in the Porta-John."   —Joyce Kasmierski, at the 1983 Women's Kemper Open

Quiz Answer: Byron Nelson won 18 times in 1945.

 **JANUARY**

TODAY'S THOUGHT:

"If you aspire to be a champion, it's up to you to find a way to get the ball in the cup on the crucial holes on the last day."
—Tom Watson

ON THIS DATE—

In 1973, the LPGA began its most ambitious season to date with a total purse of more than $1.5 million for 36 scheduled tournaments.

CHIP SHOT

The highest score for one hole in a pro tournament is the 23 Tommy Armour carded on the 17th hole in the 1927 Shawnee Open.

TRIVIA QUIZ—

The PGA Tour record for winning the same event the most times is eight. Who holds the record?

TODAY'S TIP—

When chipping from a downhill lie, keep your head still and your hands forward to prevent skulling the ball. Leave your hands in that position throughout the swing.

THE 19TH HOLE

"If a lot of people gripped a knife and fork like they do a golf club, they'd starve to death." —Sam Snead

Quiz Anwer: Sam Snead won the Greater Greensboro Open eight times.

JANUARY

TODAY'S THOUGHT:
"Golf is absurd, stupid, ridiculous, impossible, unfair, and wonderful."
—Art Spander, writer

ON THIS DATE—
In 1990, 21-year old Robert Gamez was given the last spot in the Northern Telecom Open field. Gamez took advantage, winning his first-ever pro event the following weekend.

CHIP SHOT
The first time admission was charged for the U.S. Open was in 1922, when the price of a ticket was one dollar.

TRIVIA QUIZ—
Who was the first American to win the British Open?

TODAY'S TIP—
Deep divots mean you could be standing too close to the ball at address, causing you to take a steep swing. Back away from the ball a little and take a flatter swing.

THE 19TH HOLE
"One of the troubles with a very high handicap is that the owner is either looked upon as a poor golfer or a possible cheat."   —George Plimpton, writer
---

Quiz Answer: Walter Hagen, who first won the tournament in 1922. Hagen captured the crown three more times in his career.

JANUARY

TODAY'S THOUGHT:
"It is this constant and undying hope for improvement that makes golf so exquisitely worth the playing."
—Bernard Darwin, writer

ON THIS DATE—
In 1957, Nancy Lopez was born. Lopez dazzled the golf world in 1978, winning 9 tournaments. Also born: Cary Middlecoff (1921); Paul Azinger (1960).

CHIP SHOT
Golf is a game in which the slowest people in the world are in front of you, and the fastest are those behind you.

TRIVIA QUIZ—
Lee Trevino has won three of the four majors in his long career. Can you name the only title to elude him?

TODAY'S TIP—
Try this drill to eliminate your slice: Keep your feet together and swing naturally. It will force you to practice the full range of motion in the swing.

THE 19TH HOLE
"One of the advantages bowling has over golf is that you seldom lose a bowling ball."
—Don Carter, Hall of Fame Bowler

Quiz Answer: Trevino has never won The Masters.

JANUARY

TODAY'S THOUGHT:

" Golf is not, on the whole, a game for realists. By its exactitudes of measurement it invites the attention of perfectionists."
—Heywood Hale Broun, writer

ON THIS DATE—

In 1993, Fred Couples won his second consecutive award as the PGA Tour's Player of the Year. The Senior PGA Tour's honor went to Lee Trevino.

CHIP SHOT

1954 was the first year that women players could wear shorts in USGA-sponsored championships.

TRIVIA QUIZ—

Only two golfers have won tournaments on the PGA Tour in four different decades. Name them.

TODAY'S TIP—

Widening your stance on a windy day will restrict your swing. Use your normal stance and adjust your club selection instead.

THE 19TH HOLE

"I don't even drive that far when I go on vacation."
—Raymond Floyd, on John Daly's driving prowess

Quiz Answer: Sam Snead ('30's, '40's, '50's & '60's) and Raymond Floyd ('60's, '70's, '80's, & '90's).

JANUARY

TODAY'S THOUGHT:

"The sport isn't like any other where a player can take out all that is eating him on an opponent. In golf, it's strictly you against your clubs." —Bob Rosburg

ON THIS DATE—

In 1972, Brandie Burton was born. Burton joined the LPGA Tour in 1991 and won her first major tournament at the duMaurier Classic in 1993.

CHIP SHOT

Charles Sands of the United States won the first Olympic gold medal in men's golf at the 1900 Paris Olympics.

TRIVIA QUIZ—

Who was the first golfer from Great Britain to win The Masters?

TODAY'S TIP—

If you're in the rough and under trees, play the ball back in a square stance. Keeping your weight on the left foot, hold the club firmly and use a short swing.

THE 19TH HOLE

"I call my sand wedge my half-Nelson, because I can always strangle the opposition with it."

—Byron Nelson

Quiz Answer: Sandy Lyle, a Scot, won it in 1988.

JANUARY

TODAY'S THOUGHT:

"Serenity is knowing that your worst shot is still going to be pretty good." —Johnny Miller

ON THIS DATE—

In 1994, Phil Mickelson beat Fred Couples in a playoff, but Jack Nicklaus stole the spotlight at the Mercedes Championships. Nicklaus came from three strokes back to win the senior section of the event.

CHIP SHOT

Golfing great Tommy Armour came up with the term "yips" to describe the tension afflicting the nervous putter.

TRIVIA QUIZ—

Who was the first amateur to win the U.S. Women's Open?

TODAY'S TIP—

Teeing the ball up on a par-3 will create more backspin as well as giving you a cleaner hit on the ball.

THE 19TH HOLE

"Mulligan: invented by an Irishman who wanted to hit one more twenty-yard grounder."

—Jim Bishop, writer

Quiz Answer: Catherine Lacoste of France, in 1967.

JANUARY

TODAY'S THOUGHT:

"Golf does strange things to other people, too. It makes liars out of honest men, cheats out of altruists, cowards out of brave men, and fools out of everybody."   —Milton Gross, writer

ON THIS DATE—

In 1992, modern technology cost Paul Azinger a two-stroke penalty at the Tournament of Champions. TV instant replay caught Azinger removing a leaf, a loose impediment, moments before his ball rolled into a bunker.

CHIP SHOT

President Dwight D. Eisenhower had a putting green installed outside the Oval Office at the White House.

TRIVIA QUIZ—

During the 1980's, I was the only player to win two PGA Championships. Who am I?

TODAY'S TIP—

If you're topping the ball, take a smooth backswing and keep your eye on the back of the ball.

THE 19TH HOLE

"You'll never get anywhere fooling around those golf courses."   —Claire Hogan, to son Ben

---

Quiz Answer: Larry Nelson, who won in 1981 and 1987.

JANUARY

TODAY'S THOUGHT:

"No man living can make a player keep his eye on the ball, and still this is the underlying secret of successful play."
—Francis Ouimet, U.S. Open champion

ON THIS DATE—

In 1970, Billy Casper became the second golfer in history to win one million dollars in his career with a victory at the LA Open. Until then, only Arnold Palmer had cracked the lofty barrier. Born: Ben Crenshaw (1952); Larry Laoretti (1939).

CHIP SHOT

The United States named their Ryder Cup squad in 1942 in case the war would end before the next scheduled match in 1943.

TRIVIA QUIZ—

What pro golfer is known as "The Walrus?"

TODAY'S TIP—

When putting from the fringe, you don't want to make contact with the grass before the ball. Play the ball slightly back in your stance and shift your weight forward.

THE 19TH HOLE

"When I make a bad shot, your job is to take the blame."
—Seve Ballesteros, to his caddies

Quiz Answer: Craig Stadler.

JANUARY

TODAY'S THOUGHT:
"If you travel first class, you think first class and you're more likely to play first class." —Raymond Floyd

ON THIS DATE—
In 1992, Steve Elkington sank a 10-foot birdie putt on the first extra hole to win the Tournament of Champions. Brad Faxon had rallied from two strokes down to force the playoff, only to fall short in the end.

CHIP SHOT
The sand wedge was invented by Gene Sarazen in 1932.

TRIVIA QUIZ—
Name the father and son who won 8 of the first 12 British Opens.

TODAY'S TIP—
Make sure your chin is lifted a few inches from your chest. If it's too close to the chest, your swing will be restricted.

THE 19TH HOLE
"When a pro hits it left to right, it's called a fade. When an amateur hits it left to right, it's called a slice."
—Peter Jacobsen

Quiz Answer: Tom Morris Sr. and Tom Morris Jr.

JANUARY

TODAY'S THOUGHT:

"Golf, like measles, should be caught young, for, if postponed to riper years, the results may be serious."

—P.G. Wodehouse, writer

ON THIS DATE—

In 1985, Otto Bucher became the oldest golfer to score a hole-in-one when he aced the 12th hole of the La Manga Golf Course in Spain. Bucher was 99 years old! Born: Mark O'Meara (1957).

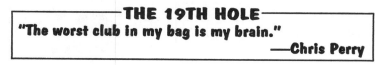

CHIP SHOT

Arnold Palmer, the general of "Arnie's Army," served in the Coast Guard from 1951 to 1954.

TRIVIA QUIZ—

What is the name of the trophy given to the LPGA player with the lowest scoring average for the year?

TODAY'S TIP—

Take advantage of modern technology. Have someone video-tape you from behind while you practice. You'll be able to check your alignment, and see how your club follows the target line.

THE 19TH HOLE

"The worst club in my bag is my brain."

—Chris Perry

Quiz Answer: The Vare Trophy, named after Glenna Collett Vare, winner of six U.S. Amateur titles in the 1920's.

JANUARY

TODAY'S THOUGHT:
"Golf is not a game of great shots. It's a game of the most accurate misses. The people who win make the smallest mistakes."
—Gene Littler

ON THIS DATE—
In 1941, Senior PGA Tour player Gibby Gilbert was born. Gilbert earned over one million dollars on the PGA Tour before turning his attention to the Senior Tour in 1991.

CHIP SHOT
A golf hole should be four inches deep.

TRIVIA QUIZ—
What four events did Bobby Jones win when he captured the Grand Slam in 1930?

TODAY'S TIP—
Heels apart about the width of your shoulders is a balanced stance. Narrow the stance gradually as the clubs you use shorten.

THE 19TH HOLE
"Being pretty, ugly, or semi has no effect on the golf ball. It doesn't help your 5-iron if you're pretty."
—Laura Baugh

Quiz Answer: Jones won the U.S. Open, British Open, U.S. Amateur, and the British Amateur.

JANUARY

TODAY'S THOUGHT:
"All men are created equal and I am one shot better than the rest." —Gene Sarazen

ON THIS DATE—
In 1991, Beth Daniel was named The Associated Press' Female Athlete of the Year for 1990. Daniel was the LPGA Tour's leading money-winner for the year and won the first major tournament of her career at the LPGA Championship. Born: Howard Twitty (1949)

CHIP SHOT
When municipal course pro Jack Fleck beat Ben Hogan in a playoff to win the 1955 U.S. Open, he was using a set of Ben Hogan golf clubs.

TRIVIA QUIZ—
Name the only major won by Tom Weiskopf in his PGA career.

TODAY'S TIP—
Building up your arm or chest muscles will restrict your swing. Concentrate on the back, legs, and abdomen.

THE 19TH HOLE
"Too tired for golf? You're kidding, right?"
—Michael Jordan

Quiz Answer: Weiskopf won the British Open in 1973.

JANUARY

TODAY'S THOUGHT:
"Golf is a way of testing ourselves while enjoying ourselves."
—Arnold Palmer

ON THIS DATE—
In 1994, Brett Ogle overtook Davis Love III to win the Hawaiian Open by one stroke. Ogle's birdie, coupled with Love's bogey, on the 17th hole gave the Australian his second victory in the United States.

CHIP SHOT
Golfers have to be 50 years old to play in the U.S. Senior Open, but they must be 55 to enter the U.S. Senior Amateur.

TRIVIA QUIZ—
What do Al Geiberger and Chip Beck have in common?

TODAY'S TIP—
If you're putting on a wet green, hit your putts more firmly than usual and aim for the back of the hole.

THE 19TH HOLE
"If I can last out here until I'm 65, I'll be able to retire without ever having held a real job."
—John Brodie, Senior Tour player
& former NFL quarterback

Quiz Answer: Both have shot rounds of 59. Geiberger did it in 1977 and Beck tied the record in 1991.

JANUARY

TODAY'S THOUGHT:

"Golf is the only sport where the object is to play as little as possible." —Charles G. McLoughlin, writer

ON THIS DATE—

In 1916, the Professional Golfers Association was established in New York City. An organizing committee was formed to draw up the by-laws for the association.

CHIP SHOT

A survey by the National Golf Foundation revealed that the average, not pro, golfer averages a 97 for 18 holes. To make you feel even better, it said only one-third of all golfers regularly break 90.

TRIVIA QUIZ—

Four golfers have had 10 or more wins on the PGA Tour before reaching their 30th birthdays. Jack Nicklaus had 30 and Arnold Palmer had 10. Who are the other two?

TODAY'S TIP—

To get a better idea of how the wind might affect your shot, look up at the tops of the trees, not at the flag.

THE 19TH HOLE

"I find it to be the hole-in-one."
—Groucho Marx, on golf's toughest shot

Quiz Answer: Johnny Miller had 17 wins and Tom Watson collected 16.

JANUARY

TODAY'S THOUGHT:

"Golf is a friend. A friend is an antidote for despair."

—Bob Toski

ON THIS DATE—

In 1992, Pat Bradley became the 12th player inducted into the LPGA Hall of Fame. Bradley had won her required 30th tournament during the previous season.

CHIP SHOT

Pat Bradley once worked as a ski instructor before joining the LPGA Tour.

TRIVIA QUIZ—

Sam Snead holds the record for most career wins on the PGA Tour. How many tournaments did Snead win?

TODAY'S TIP—

If your tee shots fly so high that the infield fly rule is called, tee the ball a little lower. Play it back slightly in your stance and take the club back low to the ground.

THE 19TH HOLE

"I don't know why that putt hung on the edge. I'm a clean liver. It must be my caddie." **—JoAnne Carner**

Quiz Answer: Snead collected 84 wins in his career.

JANUARY

TODAY'S THOUGHT:
"If you think the game is just a matter of getting it close and letting the law of averages do your work for you, you'll find a different way to miss every time."   —Jack Nicklaus

ON THIS DATE—
In 1969, Miller Barber won the Kaiser International for his fourth victory on the PGA Tour. The tournament, now known as the Anheuser-Busch Golf Classic, was won by Barber for a second time eight years later.

CHIP SHOT
The first time galleries were kept off the fairways and behind ropes at a tournament was in 1954 at the U.S. Open at Baltusrol Golf Club.

TRIVIA QUIZ—
What course was the site of Arnold Palmer's only U.S. Open victory?

TODAY'S TIP—
Don't be discouraged by downhill lies. Play the ball back in your stance, keep your weight on your rear foot, and hold it there throughout your swing.

—THE 19TH HOLE—
"Putting and dancing are the two things I hate most."
—President George W. Bush

Quiz Answer: Cherry Hills Country Club in Denver, Colorado.

JANUARY

TODAY'S THOUGHT:
"Victory is everything. You can spend the money, but you can never spend the memories." —Ken Venturi

ON THIS DATE—
In 1928, Lionel Hebert was born. Hebert made his mark in golf with a win in the 1957 PGA Championship.

CHIP SHOT
The record for playing in the most consecutive events on the PGA Tour without missing the cut is 113, held by Byron Nelson. Second is Jack Nicklaus with 105.

TRIVIA QUIZ—
Name the first golfer to win four U.S. Open titles.

TODAY'S TIP—
When watching your partner putt, don't just watch the ball. Checking out his backswing and stroke will give you an idea of how the ball is rolling on that green.

THE 19TH HOLE
"It took me seventeen years to get three thousand hits. I did it in one afternoon on the golf course."
—Hank Aaron, baseball Hall-of-Famer

Quiz Answer: Willie Anderson. Anderson won the Open in 1901, '03, '04, and '05.

J A N U A R Y

TODAY'S THOUGHT:

"We borrowed golf from Scotland as we borrowed whiskey. Not because it is Scottish, but because it is good."
—Horace G. Hutchinson, golf historian

ON THIS DATE—

In 1940, Jack Nicklaus was born. Nicklaus is the golfer with the most major tournament wins in history, including back-to-back Masters titles.

CHIP SHOT

Nicklaus made his debut on the PGA Tour at the 1962 Los Angeles Open. He finished last in the money, earning $33.33.

TRIVIA QUIZ—

1988 was the first year that a player won more than a million dollars in one season on the PGA Tour. Who was it?

TODAY'S TIP—

When faced with a bunker shot, strike the club in the sand one full ball length behind your ball. Make sure you swing through the ball and finish high.

THE 19TH HOLE

"My wife's got a broken wrist, we've got a 10-week old baby, and our dog's pregnant. I came out here to rest."
—Lee Trevino, at the 1969 Byron Nelson Classic

Quiz Answer: Curtis Strange. Strange earned $1,147,644 that year.

 **JANUARY**

TODAY'S THOUGHT:

"Golf is built around, and always will be built around, the amateur." —Phil Mickelson, 1990 U.S. Amateur champion

ON THIS DATE—

In 1995, Phil Mickelson became the first man to win the same tournament as an amateur and a professional when he captured the Northern Telecom Open. Four years earlier, Mickelson beat the pros as a collegian, unable to collect a cent. This time, though, he pocketed the first prize of $225,000.

CHIP SHOT

The 365 acres that house the Augusta National Golf Club were purchased by Bobby Jones and fellow investors for $70,000 in 1931.

TRIVIA QUIZ—

Byron Nelson holds the PGA Tour record for consecutive victories. Who set the mark for the LPGA Tour?

TODAY'S TIP—

For confidence, remember your best shot with that club in your hand. Replay it in your mind, then swing.

THE 19TH HOLE

"Golf is based on honesty. Where else would someone admit to a seven on an easy par-three?
—Jimmy Demaret

Quiz Answer: Nancy Lopez won five tournaments in a row in 1978.

J A N U A R Y

TODAY'S THOUGHT:
"The harder you work, the luckier you get." —Gary Player

ON THIS DATE—
In 1994, Andrew Magee ended a two-year victory drought with a win at the Northern Telecom Open. His errorless final round produced a two-shot margin between Magee and his closest challengers.

CHIP SHOT
The Walker Cup was donated in 1921 by George Herbert Walker, president of the USGA in 1920 and grandfather of President George Walker Bush.

TRIVIA QUIZ—
These two University of Texas teammates finished tied for the individual collegiate championship in 1972. Who are they?

TODAY'S TIP—
If you're a golfer regularly shooting in the 90's, practicing your short game is the fastest way to the 80's.

THE 19TH HOLE
"Give me a man with big hands, big feet, and no brains and I will make a golfer out of him."
                                        —Walter Hagen

Quiz Answer: Ben Crenshaw and Tom Kite.

JANUARY

TODAY'S THOUGHT:
"If you keep shooting par at them, they all crack sooner or later."
—Bobby Jones

ON THIS DATE—
In 1992, Mark Calcavecchia's 8-iron shot hit the flagstick on the 169-yard 4th hole and dropped in for an ace during the second round of the Phoenix Open. Calcavecchia's second career hole-in-one must have been an omen. He won the tournament by five strokes.

CHIP SHOT
Playing in the pro-am for the 1986 Chrysler Cup, Arnold Palmer holed-in-one on the third hole of the TPC at Avenel two days in a row.

TRIVIA QUIZ—
What was Arnold Palmer's last win on the regular PGA Tour?

TODAY'S TIP—
If your left elbow and shoulder aren't pointing at the target when you're on the tee, don't count on a straight drive. Make sure they're aligned.

THE 19TH HOLE
"The rough was so tough it takes a search warrant to get in, and a wedge and a prayer to get out."
—Harold Henning

Quiz Answer: Palmer won the Bob Hope Desert Classic in 1973.

JANUARY

TODAY'S THOUGHT:
"Putting is the greatest psychological arena on the golf course, and many are the mighty who have fallen there."
—Dr. David C. Morley

ON THIS DATE—
In 1964, PGA Tour player Billy Andrade was born. Victories in the 1991 Kemper Open and Buick Classic made him the only Tour player to win back-to-back tournaments that year.

CHIP SHOT
In 1962, Australian meteorologist Nils Lied hit a golf ball 2,640 yards across ice in Antarctica. That's approximately a one and a half mile tee shot!

TRIVIA QUIZ—
True or false: The PGA Championship was once decided by match play.

TODAY'S TIP—
When using long irons, make sure your head is not too far forward at address. Moving your hands back to the center will square up the clubface, allowing you to hit the ball straighter.

THE 19TH HOLE
"The income tax has made more liars out of the American people than golf has."   —Will Rogers

Quiz Answer: True. The 1958 championship was the first decided by stroke play.

JANUARY

TODAY'S THOUGHT:
"Golf is a negative sport, telling yourself over and over all the things that can go wrong, then not letting them."
—Tom Watson

ON THIS DATE—
In 1992, Bruce Lietzke scored a "freak of golf" when he followed an eagle on the third hole with an ace on the par-three fourth at the Phoenix Open. The back-to-back eagles weren't enough, though, to stop him from finishing nine strokes back of the leader.

CHIP SHOT
In 1953, Ben Hogan played in only six tournaments, winning five of them. His victories that year included The Masters, the U.S. Open, and the British Open.

TRIVIA QUIZ—
What tournament did Jack Nicklaus win for his first victory as a pro?

TODAY'S TIP—
If you're topping your chip shots, set up with a narrow, slightly open stance with more weight on your left foot. Keep your left hand firm as you go through the ball.

THE 19TH HOLE
"I don't have any handicap. I am all handicap."
—President Lyndon B. Johnson

Quiz Answer: The 1962 U.S. Open.

JANUARY

TODAY'S THOUGHT:

"You don't hit anything with your backswing. So don't rush it."
—Doug Ford

ON THIS DATE—

In 1939, Mike Hill was born. An average player on the PGA Tour, Hill blossomed when he joined the Senior PGA Tour, winning five tournaments in both 1990 and '91.

CHIP SHOT

The first British Open was originally called a "General Golf Tournament for Scotland" and was "open" to only eight invited professionals. It was played at Prestwick in 1860.

TRIVIA QUIZ—

I was the first player to win a Senior PGA Tour event, without ever winning on the regular tour. Who am I?

TODAY'S TIP—

When attempting a short putt it's important not to decelerate at impact. Shorten your backswing and strike the ball firmly.

THE 19TH HOLE

"Never have so many spent so much to sit in relative comfort to brag about their failures."
—Keith Jackson, sports announcer

Quiz Answer: Walt Zembriski, who won the Newport Cup Tournament in 1988.

JANUARY

TODAY'S THOUGHT:
"Golf is like art. It's impossible to be perfect."   —Sandra Palmer

ON THIS DATE—
In 1957, Nick Price was born. When Price won the British Open and PGA Championship in 1994, he became the first golfer to win the two tournaments in the same year in 70 years.

CHIP SHOT
Gene Littler has the dubious distinction of playing in The Masters the most times without winning it. Littler entered 26 Masters between 1954 and 1980.

TRIVIA QUIZ—
Who was the golfer who won both the British Open and PGA Championship in 1924?

TODAY'S TIP—
Stuck in a fairway bunker? Get back to the fairway by playing the ball inside your right foot. Using a well-lofted club, strike the ball with a firm, descending blow.

THE 19TH HOLE
"Augusta National is the only course I know where you choke when you come in the gate."
—Lionel Hebert, on The Masters

Quiz Answer: Walter Hagen.

JANUARY

TODAY'S THOUGHT:

"A club is like an automobile. Performance can make it look either ugly or beautiful." —Gary Hallberg

ON THIS DATE—

In 1995, Raymond Floyd won the richest hole in skins history. Playing in the Senior Skins Game, Floyd birdied the 17th hole and walked away with $290,000. His $420,000 total was the most won in skins competition on either the Senior or PGA Tour.

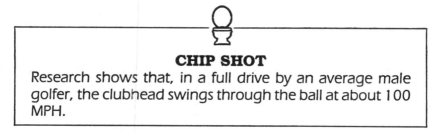

CHIP SHOT

Research shows that, in a full drive by an average male golfer, the clubhead swings through the ball at about 100 MPH.

TRIVIA QUIZ—

What's my penalty if I'm closer to the hole than you are, but I hit first anyway?

TODAY'S TIP—

When addressing the ball, always focus on finishing the shot with your chest facing the target.

—THE 19TH HOLE—

"Golf is more fun than walking naked in a strange place, but not much." —Buddy Hackett, comedian

Quiz Answer: There is no penalty. The ball shall be played where it lies.

JANUARY

TODAY'S THOUGHT:
"I don't have any big secret about putting. Just hit at it . . . it's either going to miss or go in."   —Ben Crenshaw

ON THIS DATE—
In 1995, Curtis Strange was born. The first golfer to win more than a million dollars in a year, Strange also won back-to-back U.S. Open titles in 1988 and '89. Also born: Payne Stewart (1957).

CHIP SHOT
Local rule at the Jinja Golf Course in Uganda: If a ball comes to rest in dangerous proximity to a crocodile, another ball may be dropped.

TRIVIA QUIZ—
This golfer set the record when he shot a 257 over 72 holes at the 1955 Texas Open. Who was it?

TODAY'S TIP—
Keep your knees flexed and wrists firm when chipping. Sweep the ball off the ground and don't look up until the ball has landed.

THE 19TH HOLE
"It is a law of nature that everybody plays a hole badly when going through."   —Bernard Darwin, writer

Quiz Answer: Mike Souchak.

JANUARY

TODAY'S THOUGHT:

"The arc of your swing doesn't have a thing to do with the size of your heart." —Carol Mann

ON THIS DATE—

In 1993, 63-year old Arnold Palmer successfully defended his title in the Senior Skins Game. The highlight was a 22-foot birdie putt which earned Palmer $140,000 of his $190,000 total.

CHIP SHOT

Harry Vardon, J.H. Taylor, and Gary Player are the only golfers to win the British Open in three different decades.

TRIVIA QUIZ—

What golf course has the famous Road Hole as its seventeenth?

TODAY'S TIP—

If your backswing is too short off the tee, remember to turn the right hip and shoulder back together.

THE 19TH HOLE

"I would like to knock it on every green and two-putt, but that's not my style of play or my style of living."
—Muffin Spencer-Devlin

Quiz Answer: The Old Course at St. Andrews in Scotland.

FEBRUARY

TODAY'S THOUGHT:
"The hardest thing to learn about golf is keeping quiet about it."
—George Houghton, writer

ON THIS DATE—
In 1968, W. Lawson Little died. Little was the 1940 U.S. Open winner, and captured the U.S. and British Amateur titles in 1934 and '35.

CHIP SHOT
In 1934 and '35, Little won 31 consecutive matches in the U.S. and British Amateur championships.

TRIVIA QUIZ—
This golfer won back-to-back British Opens in 1961 and '62. Who was it?

TODAY'S TIP—
Take advantage of a tailwind by teeing the ball up a little higher and playing it farther up in your stance. This will encourage hitting it on the upswing, producing a higher shot that can ride the wind for extra distance.

THE 19TH HOLE
"My putting is so bad I could putt it off a tabletop and leave it short, halfway down a leg."   —J.C. Snead

Quiz Answer: Arnold Palmer.

FEBRUARY

TODAY'S THOUGHT:
"If you've got to remind yourself to concentrate during competition, you've got no chance to concentrate."
—Bobby Nichols

ON THIS DATE—
In 1949, Ben Hogan suffered near-fatal injuries when his car was hit head-on by a bus. Hogan recovered enough to be back on the tour in less than a year, winning the 1950 U.S. Open.

CHIP SHOT
According to the USGA, if your driver is out of line by one degree, the ball will be off target by ten yards.

TRIVIA QUIZ—
Where was the first Ryder Cup played in 1927?

TODAY'S TIP—
Check your lie before using a driver on the fairway. The ball should be either sitting up or in light rough so you have a better chance of getting the clubface squarely on it.

THE 19TH HOLE
"Selecting a stroke is like selecting a wife. To each his own."   —Ben Hogan

Quiz Answer: The United States and Great Britain locked horns at the Worcester Country Club in Massachusetts.

FEBRUARY

TODAY'S THOUGHT:
"It's a compromise between what your ego wants you to do, what experience tells you to do, and what your nerves let you do." —Bruce Crampton, on tournament play

ON THIS DATE—
In 1941, Carol Mann was born. Mann won the U.S. Women's Open in 1965 and was inducted into the LPGA Hall of Fame in 1977.

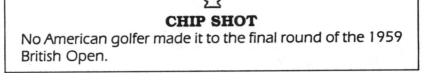

CHIP SHOT
No American golfer made it to the final round of the 1959 British Open.

TRIVIA QUIZ—
True or false: Jack Nicklaus and Tom Watson both attended Ohio State University.

TODAY'S TIP—
Swinging your hands up over your right shoulder on the backswing will allow you to swing the club on a good plane while making a strong turn away from the ball.

THE 19TH HOLE
"I've heard it's boring to play golf 365 days a year, but I'd like to find out for myself." —Bob Newhart
---

Quiz Answer: False. Nicklaus did attend Ohio State, but Watson went to school at Stanford.

F E B R U A R Y

TODAY'S THOUGHT:
"Make the hard ones look easy and the easy ones look hard."
—Walter Hagen

ON THIS DATE—
In 1979, JoAnne Carner bested Pat Bradley, 4 and 3, to take the Colgate Triple Crown at Mission Hills Country Club. Carner pocketed the first prize of $23,000.

CHIP SHOT
The brothers Turnesa (Mike, Frank, Joe, Phil, Doug, and Jim) all played professional golf in the '30's and '40's. A seventh brother, Willie, won the U.S. Amateur in 1938.

TRIVIA QUIZ—
Name the golfer who was nicknamed "Champagne Tony."

TODAY'S TIP—
Before putting, check the grass on the green. If it looks shiny, the grain is with you causing your ball to roll faster. If it's dark, the grain is against you.

THE 19TH HOLE
"Before, I couldn't make any important putts. Now I miss more than I did, but I also make more than I did."
—Mike Hulbert, on putting with only his right hand

Quiz Answer: Tony Lema.

FEBRUARY

TODAY'S THOUGHT:

"Golf is one of the last refuges of real sport. You're your own policeman, and the behavior of its athletes is quite remarkable when you compare it to other sports."
—Jim McKay, announcer

ON THIS DAY—

In 1995, Peter Jacobsen ended a five-year victory drought with a win in the AT&T National Pro-Am in Pebble Beach. Born: Jose Maria Olazabal (1966); Jane Geddes (1960).

CHIP SHOT

The youngest golfer to win the U.S. Open was Johnny McDermott, who was 19 years old when he won the title in 1911.

TRIVIA QUIZ

What four events make up the Women's Grand Slam?

TODAY'S TIP—

If your lie has little or no grass, play the ball slightly back in your stance. Gripping the club a little tighter than usual, make an upright swing.

THE 19TH HOLE

"I don't have any particular hang-ups about superstitions. I did try them all, but they didn't work."
—Kathy Whitworth

Quiz Answer: The U.S. Women's Open, the LPGA Championship, the Nabisco Dinah Shore, and the duMaurier Classic.

FEBRUARY

TODAY'S THOUGHT:

"I don't know of any game that makes you so ashamed of your profanity. It is a game full of moments of self-abasement, with only a few moments of self-exaltation."

—President William Howard Taft, on golf

ON THIS DATE—

In 1971, Alan Shepard took a mulligan . . . on the moon! His backpack shortened his first swing, but the astronaut connected solidly with a 6-iron on his second shot.

CHIP SHOT

The purpose of Shepard's golf swing on the lunar surface was to demonstrate the moon's reduced gravity.

TRIVIA QUIZ—

True or false: Charley Seaver, a member of the 1932 US Walker Cup team, is the father of Tom Seaver, Baseball Hall of Fame pitcher.

TODAY'S TIP—

If your hitting the ball fat, fix your eyes on a spot an inch in front of the ball. Try to hit the ball low, keying on hitting that spot.

THE 19TH HOLE

"People talking about their golf games is as bad as having them show you films of their last vacation."

—Rick Schwab, writer

Quiz Answer: True.

FEBRUARY

TODAY'S THOUGHT:
"Golf is a game played on a five-inch course between the ears."
—Bobby Jones

ON THIS DATE—
In 1993, Tammie Green beat Hall of Famer JoAnne Carner in a playoff to win the Palm Beach Classic championship. It was the first victory for Green since capturing the 1989 duMaurier Classic.

CHIP SHOT
Between 1936 and 1979, Art Wall scored 42 holes-in-one, more than any other professional golfer.

TRIVIA QUIZ—
Of all the players to ever win a major title, who comes first alphabetically?

TODAY'S TIP—
When you're leading in a match, continue to play your own game, avoiding any fancy shots.

———THE 19TH HOLE———
"Some players think that the rake by the side of the trap is a hazard itself and it is a two-stroke penalty if you touch it."   —Jay Cronley, writer

Quiz Answer: Tommy Aaron, who won the 1973 Masters.

FEBRUARY

TODAY'S THOUGHT:

"How well you play golf depends on how well you control that left hand of yours."   —Tommy Armour

ON THIS DATE—

In 1987, Nancy Lopez qualified for the LPGA Hall of Fame by winning the Sarasota Classic, her 35th career victory.

CHIP SHOT

The first win of Lopez' professional career came in 1978. . . at the Sarasota Classic.

TRIVIA QUIZ—

If your driver breaks after hitting a ball during a match, are you allowed to replace it?

TODAY'S TIP—

If you're topping your chips and pitches, you're probably lifting your upper body during the downswing. Flexing your knees a little more and maintaining that flex will allow you to hit the ball solidly.

THE 19TH HOLE

"Lay off for three weeks and then quit for good."
—Sam Snead, giving advice to a pupil

Quiz Answer: Yes, if you do not delay play. However, if you've broken it in a fit of anger, you can't replace it.

FEBRUARY

TODAY'S THOUGHT:
"To watch a first-class field drive off must convince everyone that a golf ball can be hit in many ways."
—Henry Cotton, 1934 British Open champion

ON THIS DATE—
In 1992, the courageous Shelley Hamlin fired a final round of 66 to win the Phar-Mor at Inverrary. The victory, her first in 14 years, came seven months after she underwent a mastectomy.

CHIP SHOT
Despite losing an eye in World War I, Tommy Armour still won three major titles: the U.S. Open in 1927, the PGA Championship in 1930, and the British Open in 1931.

TRIVIA QUIZ—
Who is the only golfer to win six British Opens?

TODAY'S TIP—
Believe it or not, putting against the wind can cause problems for some. Solve them by widening your stance for balance and take a shorter, but firmer, stroke.

THE 19TH HOLE
"I've never once seen the cup move towards the ball."
—Henry Longhurst, writer

Quiz Answer: Harry Vardon, who won it in 1896, '98, '99, 1903, '11, and '14.

F E B R U A R Y

TODAY'S THOUGHT:

"The thing with golf is, it's like a cat chasing its tail. You're never going to catch it. The day you think you've got your swing down pat, something goes awry and you've got to go back to the driving range." —Greg Norman

ON THIS DATE—

In 1955, Greg Norman was born. Norman's long and accurate tee shots helped him win British Open titles in 1986 and 1993.

CHIP SHOT

During a tournament week, a PGA Tour field will use approximately 2,500 practice balls a day.

TRIVIA QUIZ—

Name the golfer who chipped in from 35 yards on the second sudden-death hole of the 1987 Masters to seize victory from Greg Norman.

TODAY'S TIP—

Remember, the time to try out a new shot is on the practice tee, not in the middle of a match.

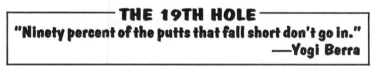

THE 19TH HOLE
"Ninety percent of the putts that fall short don't go in."
—Yogi Berra

Quiz Answer: Larry Mize.

F E B R U A R Y

TODAY'S THOUGHT:
"The difference between Hogan and Palmer was that with Hogan, when he reached a green, the people stood up and applauded. When Palmer got there, they all whooped and hollered." —Nick Faldo

ON THIS DATE—
In 1973, Arnold Palmer won his 60th, and final, PGA Tour title when he led the field at the Bob Hope Desert Classic.

CHIP SHOT
The 1965 U.S. Open was the first to be played in a four-day format of 18 holes each day. Before that, golfers played 18 holes the first two days and a 36-hole final day.

TRIVIA QUIZ—
What golfer holds the record for most career Tour victories?

TODAY'S TIP—
It's easier to roll the ball than to loft it, plus there's more chance of error when you add velocity. So, putt when you can and chip when you can't putt.

THE 19TH HOLE
"My goal is to become filthy rich. But obviously, that isn't going to be in golf." —Gary McCord

Quiz Answer: Kathy Whitworth, who won 88 tournaments in her LPGA career.

F E B R U A R Y

TODAY'S THOUGHT:

"It's always been my contention that the winners of major tournaments are the true champions, although at times some luck may play a part in the victory." —Tony Jacklin

ON THIS DATE—

In 1995, Peter Jacobsen continued his torrid playing, winning consecutive tournaments for the first time in his 19-year pro career. Jacobsen won the Buick Invitational a week after finishing first at the National Pro-Am.

CHIP SHOT

Jacobsen spends his spare time as lead singer for his band, Jake Trout and the Flounders.

TRIVIA QUIZ—

1990 was the first year a member of the Senior PGA Tour earned more money than the PGA Tour's leading money-winner. Who was it?

TODAY'S TIP—

Putting more weight on your right foot can sometimes keep you from bouncing the ball instead of rolling it smoothly across the green.

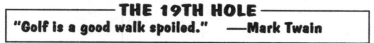

THE 19TH HOLE

"Golf is a good walk spoiled." —Mark Twain

Quiz Answer: Lee Trevino, who made $1,190,518.

FEBRUARY

TODAY'S THOUGHT:

"I hate to watch tennis, where you have the McEnroes and Connors and the language they use. Golf is bigger than that."
—Tom Watson

ON THIS DATE—

In 1971, Vice President Spiro Agnew teed off at the Bob Hope Desert Classic. His drive ricocheted off the arms of a man and his wife. After apologizing, Agnew tried again. And hit them again!

CHIP SHOT

Presidents Truman, Ford, Bush, and Clinton played golf right-handed but were natural lefties.

TRIVIA QUIZ—

Who was our first golfing President?

TODAY'S TIP—

If, at the top of your swing, you can see the clubhead out of the corner of your eye, you're overswinging. Firm up your left hand and don't go beyond parallel at the top.

THE 19TH HOLE

"I know I'm getting better at golf because I'm hitting fewer spectators." —President Gerald R. Ford

Quiz Answer: William Howard Taft, who played golf once a week.

FEBRUARY

TODAY'S THOUGHT:
"A great golf hole is one which puts a question mark into the player's mind when he arrives on the tee to play it."
—Mackenzie Ross, golf course architect

ON THIS DATE—
In 1912, golfing great Byron Nelson was born. Nelson took the golf world by storm in 1945 when he won 18 tournaments, 11 of them in a row. Also born: Mickey Wright (1935); Bob Murphy (1943).

CHIP SHOT
Nelson actually won 12 tournaments consecutively, but the event wasn't counted as official since its purse fell below the PGA minimum of $3,000.

TRIVIA QUIZ—
The 3-hole stretch from the 11th to 13th holes at Augusta National is affectionately known by what nickname?

TODAY'S TIP—
Never attempt to play through the treetops. Play over, under, or around a tree, never through it.

THE 19TH HOLE
"What are you doing, copying my swing?"
—Babe Zaharias, on being outdriven by Mickey Wright

Quiz Answer: Amen Corner.

FEBRUARY

TODAY'S THOUGHT:
"It's a helluva lot easier to make money with an education than it is with a golf club."   —Jack Burke, Jr.

ON THIS DATE—
In 1987, Chi Chi Rodriguez won the PGA Seniors Championship. It proved to be a very good year for Rodriguez, winning seven titles in all.

CHIP SHOT
Don January won the first Senior PGA Tour event in 1980 at the Atlantic City (NJ) Senior International.

TRIVIA QUIZ—
What is Chi Chi Rodriguez' real name?

TODAY'S TIP—
Take your glove off when putting to enhance your touch on the green. You may be surprised by the difference it makes.

THE 19TH HOLE
"This is a mulligan in life. We're already doing what most people spend their whole life trying to be able to do."   —George Archer, on the Senior PGA Tour

---

QUIZ ANSWER: Juan Rodriguez.

FEBRUARY

TODAY'S THOUGHT:
"If you try to fight the course, it will beat you. "   —Lou Graham

ON THIS DATE—
In 1992, Craig Parry slipped by six-time champ Greg Norman to win the Australian Masters. Norman bogeyed the 15th, 16th, and 17th holes after Parry had tied him for the lead, finishing three strokes back.

CHIP SHOT
PGA golfer Jay Haas' uncle is 1986 Masters champion Bob Goalby.

TRIVIA QUIZ—
Name the only American golfer to win the British Open five times.

TODAY'S TIP—
Take advantage of hard fairways. Tee the ball low and play it toward the center of your stance. The idea is to hit low drives that will roll a long distance.

THE 19TH HOLE
"Lee's got more lines than the Illinois Railroad."
—Fuzzy Zoeller, on Lee Trevino

Quiz Answer: Tom Watson, who won it in 1975, '77, '80, '82, and '83.

FEBRUARY

TODAY'S THOUGHT:

"I hit a hook that went so far out of bounds I almost killed a horse in some stables a cab ride from the first fairway."
—Mike Souchak, on his first pro tournament

ON THIS DATE—

In 1955, a sizzling 27 on the back nine enabled Mike Souchak to shoot a first round of 60 in the Texas Open. His scoring record included 2 pars, 6 birdies, and an eagle.

CHIP SHOT

Willie Anderson beat Alex Smith in the first playoff in the U.S. Open. The year was 1901.

TRIVIA QUIZ—

Three players have hit 8 straight birdies in a round. Two of them are Bob Goalby and Dewey Arnette. Who's the third?

TODAY'S TIP—

When putting downhill, imagine the hole is closer to you. It will alter your stroke, and, if you do miss, the ball will not roll well past the hole.

THE 19TH HOLE

"I'd do better if the ball were two feet off the ground and moving."
—Stan Musial, Baseball Hall-of-Famer

Quiz Answer: Fuzzy Zoeller, who did it in the 1976 Quad Cities Open.

FEBRUARY

TODAY'S THOUGHT:
"Everyone gets wounded in a game of golf. The trick is not to bleed." —Peter Dobereiner, writer

ON THIS DATE—
In 1962, Louise Suggs picked up the final win of her career at the St. Petersburg Open. The LPGA co-founder and Hall-of-Famer finished with 50 career victories. Born: Judy Rankin (1945).

CHIP SHOT
The Irish Golfing Union is the oldest such organization in the world. It was founded in 1891.

TRIVIA QUIZ—
I never won a major title on the PGA Tour, yet I was the winner in three of the first six US Senior Opens. Who am I?

TODAY'S TIP—
Don't drive for yardage alone. Nearness to the hole isn't any good if that means the woods. Drive for the best approach angles and the most level lies.

THE 19TH HOLE
"Golf, a game kings and presidents play when they get tired of running countries."   —Charles Price, writer

Quiz Answer: Miller Barber, who won in 1982, '84, and '85.

FEBRUARY

TODAY'S THOUGHT:
"Sometimes you'd like to just stand there in the middle of the green and scream as loud as you can. But we're the perfect gentlemen." —Raymond Floyd

ON THIS DATE—
In 1995, Kenny Perry held on to win the Bob Hope Classic by one stroke over David Duval. Perry won despite shooting par from the seventh hole on at the Bermuda Dunes golf course.

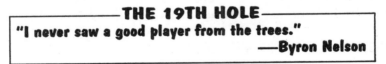

CHIP SHOT
Golf carts are prohibited in all PGA and LPGA Tour events and all USGA tournaments, including senior events.

TRIVIA QUIZ—
This NJ course is continually ranked as one of the best in the world. Although two Walker Cup matches have been held there, the course has never hosted a U.S. Open. Name it.

TODAY'S TIP—
The tempo of your swing should be the same regardless of the club. For most golfers the ideal tempo should be the one you use when swinging your driver.

THE 19TH HOLE
"I never saw a good player from the trees."
—Byron Nelson

Quiz Answer: Pine Valley Golf Club in Clementon, NJ.

F E B R U A R Y

TODAY'S THOUGHT:

"Golf is neither a microcosm of nor a metaphor for life. It is a sport, a bloodless sport, if you don't count ulcers."

—Dick Schaap, writer

ON THIS DATE—

In 1994, Mike Hill successfully defended his title at the Senior PGA Tour's IntelliNet Challenge. Back spasms didn't stop Hill from shooting a course-record 63 in the final round. Born: Jeff Maggert (1964).

CHIP SHOT

1920's trick-shot artist Jack Redmond once asked the King of Samoa what his handicap was. "Six wives," said the king.

TRIVIA QUIZ—

True or false: Former Colorado defensive back Hale Irwin played one year of professional football before joining the PGA Tour.

TODAY'S TIP—

In a fairway bunker don't let the sand slow the clubface. Play the ball forward and sweep the ball off the sand.

THE 19TH HOLE

"Good thing I had a good drive on that hole or I'd have really made a mess of it."

—Ben Crenshaw, after shooting a 13

Quiz Answer: False.

FEBRUARY

TODAY'S THOUGHT:
"I don't care what anybody says. The first tournament is not the hardest one to win. It's always the second one."   —John Daly

ON THIS DATE—
In 1993, 22-year old Phil Mickelson conducted a putting clinic over the back nine to pull away to a four-shot victory at the Buick Invitational, his first win as a pro.

CHIP SHOT
Between 1923 and his retirement in 1930, Bobby Jones finished first or second in the U.S. Open every year except 1927.

TRIVIA QUIZ—
In the nineteenth century, most golf shafts were made of what type of wood?

TODAY'S TIP—
Image is everything. To help build your confidence, mentally replay your best performance on each hole before heading to the course.

—THE 19TH HOLE—
"Give me a millionaire with a bad backswing and I can have a very pleasant afternoon."   —George Low

Quiz Answer: Hickory.

FEBRUARY

TODAY'S THOUGHT:
"If you're going to miss 'em, miss 'em quick."
—George Duncan, British Open champ, on putting

ON THIS DATE—
In 1992, 96 golfers were invited to play in that year's Masters. But for the first time in 17 years, Tom Kite did not qualify. Born: Tommy Aaron (1937); Wayne Levi (1952); Amy Alcott (1956); Vijay Singh (1963).

CHIP SHOT
The only time a golfer tells the truth is when he calls another golfer a liar.

TRIVIA QUIZ—
In the 1980's, only one golfer won more than five PGA Tour events in a year. Who was it?

TODAY'S TIP—
Don't always take preferrred lies when practicing. Create realistic situations, set goals, and practice playing to a target.

THE 19TH HOLE
"My best score ever is 103. But I've only been playing fifteen years."
—Alex Karras, actor and former football player

Quiz Answer: Tom Watson, who won six tournaments in 1980.

FEBRUARY

TODAY'S THOUGHT:

"If you're not prepared, somewhere in the quiz there are going to be some questions you can't answer."

—Charles Coody

ON THIS DATE—

In 1992, a 16-foot birdie on the final hole gave Steve Pate a one-stroke win at the Buick Invitational. Born: Cindy Figg-Currier (1960).

CHIP SHOT

According to the National Hole-in-One Association, more than 31 thousand aces were scored in 1988. Of those, 27 were scored after the player's ball hit a tree.

TRIVIA QUIZ—

In what event were Lee Trevino, Bobby Nichols, and Jerry Heard playing when they were struck by lightning?

TODAY'S TIP—

To get your hands to release in the hitting zone, hold your wrist break until your shoulders, hips, and legs have uncoiled.

THE 19TH HOLE

"Doc, your reputation is on the line. Blow this one and you can use those scalpels to eat your dinner."
—Lee Trevino, before undergoing back surgery

Quiz Answer: The 1975 Western Open.

FEBRUARY

TODAY'S THOUGHT:
"If you watch a game, it's fun. If you play it, it's recreation. If you work at it, it's golf."   —Bob Hope

ON THIS DATE—
In 1990, Beth Daniel shot 6-under par to win the Hawaiian Ladies Open. It was the first of two straight victories for Daniel, and one of seven events she won that year.

CHIP SHOT
In 1986, Wayne Grady was disqualified from both the Phoenix Open and the LA Open for hitting someone else's ball.

TRIVIA QUIZ—
My final round of 63, including eight birdies in the first 13 holes, propelled me to victory in the 1973 U.S. Open. Who am I?

TODAY'S TIP—
To prevent slicing your long irons, accelerate, not decelerate your hands through the impact area. Slowing down is a common error.

THE 19TH HOLE
"If you think it's hard to meet new people, try picking up the wrong golf ball."   —Jack Lemmon

Quiz Answer: Johnny Miller.

 # FEBRUARY

TODAY'S THOUGHT:
"The object of a bunker or trap is not only to punish a physical mistake, to punish lack of control, but also to punish pride and egotism." —Charles Blair MacDonald, writer

ON THIS DATE—
In 1951, Babe Zaharias and George Bolesta won the Orlando, Florida 2-Ball tournament. The win gave Zaharias three straight victories to start the LPGA season.

CHIP SHOT
To win the 1920 British Open, George Duncan had to make up a 13-stroke deficit. He won the tournament by two strokes.

TRIVIA QUIZ—
What golfer won four consecutive PGA Championships between 1924 and 1927?

TODAY'S TIP—
When faced with a narrow fairway use an iron or 5-wood off the tee and focus on a landing area. Save the longer club for your second shot.

THE 19TH HOLE
"I never really dreamed of making many putts. Maybe that's why I haven't made many."   —Calvin Peete

Quiz Answer: Walter Hagen.

F E B R U A R Y

TODAY'S THOUGHT:
"No matter how hard I try, I just can't seem to break sixty-four."
—Jack Nicklaus

ON THIS DATE—
In 1978, Jack Nicklaus put on a show at the Inverrary Classic, dazzling the crowd with five birdies on the last five holes on his way to a one-stroke victory over Grier Jones.

CHIP SHOT
77-year old John Protti played a round of golf at the Vancouver Golf Club in 1994 after presenting a rain check dated April 7, 1948.

TRIVIA QUIZ—
Only one man has ever won a major tournament by birdieing five of the last six holes. Who was it?

TODAY'S TIP—
When shooting from wet sand allow for more resistance. Play the shot with a square clubface and hit into the sand closer behind the ball than usual.

THE 19TH HOLE
"If it weren't for golf, I'd be waiting on this table instead of sitting at it." —Judy Rankin

Quiz Answer: Art Wall, in the 1959 Masters.

FEBRUARY

TODAY'S THOUGHT:

"Bad golf is played with the shoulders and the body; good golf is played with the hands."   —Gene Sarazen

ON THIS DATE—

In 1901, Gene Sarazen was born. Sarazen was the first golfer to win each of the four modern Grand Slam championships.

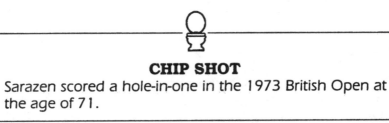

CHIP SHOT

Sarazen scored a hole-in-one in the 1973 British Open at the age of 71.

TRIVIA QUIZ—

Besides Gene Sarazen, three other golfers have won all four major championships. Who are they?

TODAY'S TIP—

A descending blow of the clubhead and clean contact between the ball and clubface will result in a good backspin. Get better backspin by emphasizing a strong lead with the left hand through impact, helping you make a sharp, descending blow.

THE 19TH HOLE

"I can't win anything but money."   —**Frank Beard**

Quiz Answer: Ben Hogan, Jack Nicklaus, and Gary Player.

FEBRUARY

TODAY'S THOUGHT:

"It is this constant and undying hope for improvement that makes golf so exquisitely worth the playing."

—Bernard Darwin, writer

ON THIS DATE—

In 1971, Jack Nicklaus won his second PGA Championship by two strokes over Billy Casper. The victory meant Nicklaus possessed a second set of the four major titles.

CHIP SHOT

The tee at the first hole of the Homestead in White Sulfur Springs, West Virginia has been in continuous use since 1892.

TRIVIA QUIZ—

This golf course is the home of the Los Angeles Open. Name it.

TODAY'S TIP—

Your glove can give you a clue as to how you're hitting the ball. A worn spot near the left thumb could mean you're gripping the club too tightly.

THE 19TH HOLE

"The food at this restaurant is like Jack Nicklaus. Very good, and very slow."   —Roberto de Vicenzo

---

Quiz Answer: The Riviera Country Club.

 **FEBRUARY**

TODAY'S THOUGHT:
"Spring was designed like an old set of MacGregor irons - to rejuvenate the soul." —Deane Beman

ON THIS DATE—
In 1992, Dawn Coe won the Women's Kemper Open on the Wailea Golf Club Blue Course in Kihei, Maui, Hawaii. Her first win since joining the LPGA Tour in 1982, Coe earned $75,000.

CHIP SHOT
According to the Guinness Book of Records, the longest drive on a standard course is 515 yards, by Michael Hoke Austin in 1974.

TRIVIA QUIZ—
What LPGA player is nicknamed "Big Mama?"

TODAY'S TIP—
If your tee shots are Superman drives, but wild, back off. It's time to go with your 3-wood off the tee. The loftier club will give you less distance but more accuracy.

THE 19TH HOLE
"I can airmail the golf ball, but sometimes I don't put the right address on it." —Jim Dent

Quiz Answer: JoAnne Carner.

MARCH

TODAY'S THOUGHT:
"The cause of stress during a golf match, or anywhere else for that matter, is largely within yourself."   —Thomas N. Dorsel

ON THIS DATE—
In 1992, Fred Couples won the LA Open for the second time in three years. Couples rolled in a birdie putt on the second playoff hole to beat Davis Love III. Born: Dave Barr (1952).

CHIP SHOT
Only two players have won the U.S. Open and U.S. Amateur in the same year. Chick Evans, Jr. did it in 1916 while Bobby Jones won both events in 1930.

TRIVIA QUIZ—
The USGA recommends that the flagstick be a certain height. How high?

TODAY'S TIP—
Staying level in your backswing and downswing will help keep you from shanking the ball. To keep from dropping, picture a string attached to your head and someone pulling it up.

THE 19TH HOLE
"In golf, when we hit a foul ball, we got to go out and play it."
—Sam Snead, comparing golf with baseball

Quiz Answer: Seven feet.

M A R C H

TODAY'S THOUGHT:
"Golf is a total obsession: the chess of sports, the only sport that requires total intelligence."   —James Woods, actor

ON THIS DATE—
In 1958, Ian Woosnam was born. The Welshman won the green jacket at The Masters in 1991 for his first major title.

CHIP SHOT
The most consecutive years a player has led the PGA Tour money list is four. Tom Watson was the biggest money-winner between 1977 and 1980.

TRIVIA QUIZ—
If Tommy Aaron is first on the alphabetical list of players who have ever won a major, who's last?

TODAY'S TIP—
Balancing your weight between the heels and toes is important. If you put too much weight in one area, you might have trouble shifting weight during your swing.

THE 19TH HOLE
"The dollars aren't so important - once you have them."
—Johnny Miller, on big tour purses

Quiz Answer: Fuzzy Zoeller, who won the 1979 Masters and the 1984 U.S. Open.

M A R C H

TODAY'S THOUGHT:
"The place of the father in the modern suburban family is a very small one - particularly if he plays golf." —Bertrand Russell

ON THIS DATE—
In 1920, Julius Boros was born. The PGA Hall-of-Famer won the U.S. Open in 1952 and 1963 and added a PGA Championship title to his belt at the age of 48 in 1968.

CHIP SHOT
The first playoff between American players at the British Open was in 1933. Denny Shute beat Craig Wood.

TRIVIA QUIZ—
I never won The Masters. However, I did finish second four times in my career. Who am I?

TODAY'S TIP—
To hit under branches, begin with the ball back in your stance and your hands ahead of it. Your hands leading the club into the ball will reduce the effective loft of the clubface.

THE 19TH HOLE
"I really enjoy doing corporate outings because there are no cuts and I'm low pro every day."
—Dave Stockton

Quiz Answer: Tom Weiskopf, who finished as the runner-up in 1969, '72, '74, and'75.

M A R C H

TODAY'S THOUGHT:
"Golf is not a funeral, although both can be very sad affairs."
—Bernard Darwin, writer

ON THIS DATE—
In 1950, Judy Dickinson was born. During the 1985 U.S. Women's Open, Dickinson's round of 65 tied the record for the lowest round under par ever recorded in USGA history. Also born: Peter Jacobsen (1954).

CHIP SHOT
Greg Norman and Craig Wood share the dubious honor of having lost all four majors in playoffs.

TRIVIA QUIZ—
Can you name the first golfer to break 70 in all four rounds of a major championship?

TODAY'S TIP—
To generate more power off the tee, remember to allow the shoulders to lead the hips as you go into your backswing.

THE 19TH HOLE
"Oh, God, Gardiner. Sometimes I think you married me just so you could see your name on the leaderboard."
—Judy Dickinson, to husband Gardiner

Quiz Answer: Arnold Palmer, who shot 68, 68, 69, and 69 at the 1964 PGA Championship.

M A R C H

TODAY'S THOUGHT:
"Putting is three things: the line, the length and the stroke."
—Nick Faldo

ON THIS DATE—
In 1995, Nick Faldo won his first tournament on U.S. soil in almost five years. Faldo's victory at the Doral Ryder Open was his first since winning The Masters in 1990. Born: Dale Douglass (1936).

CHIP SHOT
The only brothers to win the PGA Championship were Lionel (1957) and Jay (1960) Herbert.

TRIVIA QUIZ—
What's the modern-day name for the "niblick?"

TODAY'S TIP—
Reminding yourself of putting fundamentals, and seeing the ball go into the hole before you putt, will help smooth your stroke.

THE 19TH HOLE
"For most amateurs, the best wood in the bag is the pencil." —Chi Chi Rodriguez

Quiz Answer: The 9-iron.

M A R C H

TODAY'S THOUGHT:

"A man's true colors will surface quicker in a five-dollar nassau than in any other form of diversion." —Grantland Rice

ON THIS DATE—

In 1988, Orville Moody blistered the field at the Vintage International. Moody set a Senior PGA Tour record with a final round 63 to finish the tournament 25 shots under par.

CHIP SHOT

The 1954 World Championship, won by Bob Toski, was golf's first $50,000 first prize.

TRIVIA QUIZ—

Excluding the British Isles, what country had the first golf course?

TODAY'S TIP—

To play a run-up shot, take one more club than usual and choke down on the grip. Play the ball back in your stance and use a firm, slightly shorter swing.

THE 19TH HOLE

"My putter had a heart attack the last nine holes and just died on me." —Lanny Wadkins

Quiz Answer: India. The Royal Calcutta Golf Club was established in 1829.

M A R C H

TODAY'S THOUGHT:
"The guy who chokes least wins the most." —Hubert Green

ON THIS DATE—
In 1993, Greg Norman set a tournament record on his way to victory at the Doral Open. Norman's 265 total broke the record set by Hubert Green by five strokes. Born: Tom Lehman (1959).

CHIP SHOT
The first British monarch to attend the British Open was King George VI. The king appeared at the 1948 Open.

TRIVIA QUIZ—
From 1960 to 1968, the Vardon Trophy for best scoring average was shared by only two players. Who were they?

TODAY'S TIP—
If your ball lies in a fairway divot, play the ball towards the center of your stance with a little more weight on your left side. The swing will bring the club down sharply on the ball, so take less club than usual. The shot will fly low and land with a lot of run.

THE 19TH HOLE
"Golf's not that hard. The ball doesn't move."
—Ted Williams, baseball Hall of Famer

Quiz Answer: Billy Casper, who won the trophy 5 times, and Arnold Palmer who won it the other four years.

MARCH

TODAY'S THOUGHT:
"A lot of times putting comes down to the guts of the putter - not being afraid to lose." —Curtis Strange

ON THIS DATE—
In 1992, Raymond Floyd became the second man to win PGA Tour titles in four different decades with a two-stroke victory in the Doral Open. Sam Snead was the first.

CHIP SHOT
A golf cart is started and stopped an average of 150 times during a round of golf.

TRIVIA QUIZ—
True or false: Lee Trevino is one of a long line of golfers who attended the University of Texas.

TODAY'S TIP—
After hitting a good practice shot, remember the feel of the swing. It'll take your mind off the mechanical aspects if you remember that feeling while on the course.

THE 19TH HOLE
"I'm hitting the woods just great, but I'm having a terrible time getting out of them."   —Harry Toscano

Quiz Answer: False. Trevino never attended college.

M A R C H

TODAY'S THOUGHT:

"I'm going to miss at least seven shots in every 18 holes, so if I'm going to be angry, I might as well start right on the first tee."
—Walter Hagen

ON THIS DATE—

In 1941, Jim Colbert was born. Colbert won Rookie of the Year honors on the Senior PGA Tour when he won three tournaments in 1991.

CHIP SHOT

The 630-yard, par-5 17th hole at Baltusrol GC is the longest ever played in a men's major championship.

TRIVIA QUIZ—

In which James Bond movie does Bond play golf against the villain?

TODAY'S TIP—

Swinging with only the upper body will send your shot to the right of the target. Push off your back foot in the downswing and slide onto the front foot.

THE 19TH HOLE

"When I was walking down the fairway, I saw a bunch of USGA guys down on their hands and knees parting the rough trying to find my ball. I knew I was in trouble." —Jim Colbert

Quiz Answer: *Goldfinger.*

MARCH

TODAY'S THOUGHT:
"Relax? How can anybody relax and play golf? You have to grip the club, don't you?"   —Ben Hogan

ON THIS DATE—
In 1991, 35 mph wind gusts sent scores sailing at the Honda Classic. Curtis Strange posted a 14-over-par 86, and Steve Pate's 3-over-par 75 was enough to give him the win.

CHIP SHOT
In 1971, Lee Trevino captured three national titles over a 20-day period. Trevino won the U.S. Open, the Canadian Open, and the British Open in succession.

TRIVIA QUIZ—
Name the golfer who's been the leading money-winner on the PGA Tour the most times.

TODAY'S TIP—
Don't putt from rough areas around the green. Use a club that will lift the ball over the high grass and onto the putting surface.

THE 19TH HOLE
"He quit playing when I started outdriving him."
—JoAnne Carner, on husband Don

Quiz Answer: Jack Nicklaus, who led the way eight times including three years in a row between 1971 and '73.

M A R C H

TODAY'S THOUGHT:

"When one wants to play golf, one wants to be alone with nature." —Alister MacKenzie, course designer

ON THIS DATE—

In 1945, Byron Nelson began his record winning streak with a victory at the Miami Four Ball Tournament. That streak reached 11 wins before it ended in August.

CHIP SHOT

Nelson and Harold McSpaden became known as the "Gold Dust Twins" that year because the tournaments Nelson didn't win, McSpaden usually did. McSpaden was runner-up numerous times.

TRIVIA QUIZ—

Only one player with exactly three letters in his last name has ever won a major title. Name him.

TODAY'S TIP—

When chipping downhill on a fast green, leave the pin in. Only take it out if you're chipping uphill or if the green is slow.

THE 19TH HOLE

"Sam was born with a natural ability to keep his bar bills as low as his golf scores."
—Jimmy Demaret, on Mr. Snead

Quiz Answer: Edward "Ted" Ray, who won the U.S. Open in 1920 for his only victory in a major championship.

M A R C H

TODAY'S THOUGHT:
"There's no better game in the world when you are in good company, and no worse game when you are in bad company."
—Tommy Bolt

ON THIS DATE—
In 1961, Mickey Wright defended her LPGA Championship crown with a nine-stroke win over Lousie Suggs. For Wright, it was her third title in the last four years.

CHIP SHOT
During World War II, British golfers were asked to pick up bomb and shell fragments off the course to help the greenkeeper spare damage to the lawnmowers.

TRIVIA QUIZ—
In 1981, the US Post Office came out with a stamp honoring this male Hall of Fame Golfer. Who was it?

TODAY'S TIP—
Hands high in the air at the top of your swing will add an upright arc and give you more power and greater accuracy.

THE 19TH HOLE
"I hit a 341-yard drive in Hawaii once. It was downhill, downwind, down everything."   —Laura Davies

Quiz Answer: Bobby Jones.

M A R C H

TODAY'S THOUGHT:
"Golf is an easy game . .. it's just hard to play."   —Anonymous

ON THIS DATE—
In 1994, Nick Price captured the Honda Classic. But the spotlight was focused on John Daly, who was returning to the Tour after a suspension for quitting in the middle of a round the previous fall. Daly finished fourth, four strokes behind Price.

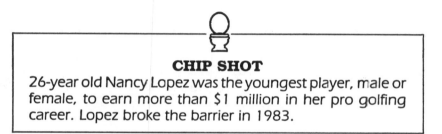

CHIP SHOT
26-year old Nancy Lopez was the youngest player, male or female, to earn more than $1 million in her pro golfing career. Lopez broke the barrier in 1983.

TRIVIA QUIZ—
Can you name the only major title Sam Snead never won in his illustrious career?

TODAY'S TIP—
Draping your left forefinger over the last three fingers of your right hand when putting will take the wrists out of your stroke and improve your control over direction and distance.

THE 19TH HOLE
"I have three-putted in over forty countries."
                                   —Fred Corcoran

Quiz Answer: Snead never won the U.S. Open.

M A R C H

TODAY'S THOUGHT:
"It is easier to tell a man that there's something wrong with his wife and child than with his golf course."   —Frank Hannigan

ON THIS DATE—
In 1993, Meg Mallon edged Betsy King by one stroke to win the Ping-Welch's Championship. Mallon's tournament included three bogey-free rounds. Born: Bob Charles (1936).

CHIP SHOT
Bob Charles is the only lefthanded golfer to ever win the British Open. The New Zealander did it in 1963.

TRIVIA QUIZ—
Legal or illegal: Just before putting, I use my club to flatten a few spike marks which are on my line.

TODAY'S TIP—
Place a tee in the hole of the grip of your club, swing back to waist high and stop. If the tee is not pointing at the target, there's too much hand movement.

——— THE 19TH HOLE ———
"Being left-handed is a big advantage. No one knows enough about your swing to mess you up with advice."
—Bob Charles

Quiz Answer: Illegal. As a result I am assessed a two-stroke penalty.

M A R C H

TODAY'S THOUGHT:
"The average expert player, if he is lucky, hits six, eight or ten real shots in a round. The rest are good misses."

—Tommy Armour

ON THIS DATE—
In 1987, fortune smiled on Don Pooley. Pooley aced the 192-yard 17th hole at the Hertz Bay Classic and collected a half-million dollar bonus, the largest single-hole prize in golf history.

CHIP SHOT
Kathy Whitworth and Mickey Wright combined for 170 victories on the LPGA Tour. They also finished second 140 times between them.

TRIVIA QUIZ—
What was Babe Zaharias' real name?

TODAY'S TIP—
To gain more accuracy, clear out your left side as you begin your downswing. This will allow your arms to swing freely down and through the ball.

THE 19TH HOLE
"Look like a woman, but play like a man."

—Jan Stephenson

Quiz Answer: Mildred Ella Zaharias. Mildred got the nickname, Babe, when she hit five home runs in a baseball game as a kid.

M A R C H

TODAY'S THOUGHT:
"When I play my best golf, I feel as if I'm in a fog, standing back watching the earth in orbit with a golf club in your hands."
—Mickey Wright

ON THIS DATE—
In 1957, Patty Berg won her record-setting seventh Titleholders Championship. It was the third time in five years that Berg had won the title. Born: Hollis Stacey (1954).

CHIP SHOT
Sam Snead had to be persuaded by fellow pro, Johnny Bulla, to enter the 1946 British Open. Snead won, while Bulla finished tied for second.

TRIVIA QUIZ—
Who was the first foreigner to pass the million dollar mark in her career on the LPGA Tour?

TODAY'S TIP—
Gain control over your long irons by choking down about one inch on the grip.

THE 19TH HOLE
"The only time I talk on a golf course is to my caddie - and only then to complain."   —Seve Ballesteros

Quiz Answer: Australian Jan Stephenson, who accomplished the feat in 1985.

M A R C H

TODAY'S THOUGHT:

"It's a shame, but he'll never make a golfer. Too much temper."
—Alex Smith, golf pro, on 13-year old Bobby Jones

ON THIS DATE—

In 1902, golfing legend Bobby Jones was born. Known as the best amateur player ever, Jones won 13 tournaments, including the Grand Slam, before retiring at the age of 28.

CHIP SHOT

The portrait of Bobby Jones that hangs in the Jones Cabin at Augusta National Golf Club was painted by Dwight D. Eisenhower.

TRIVIA QUIZ—

Quick! Which state has the most golf courses?

TODAY'S TIP—

Trying to steer your drives leads to poor shots. Select a target, line up properly, and then put the trust in your swing.

THE 19TH HOLE

"I did my best, but chasing Nicklaus is like chasing a walking record book." **—Tom Weiskopf**

Quiz Answer: Florida, with California close behind.

MARCH

TODAY'S THOUGHT:
"That little white ball won't move until you hit it, and there's nothing you can do after it has gone."   —Babe Zaharias

ON THIS DATE—
In 1951, amateur Pat Sullivan won the Titleholders Championship despite shooting nine-over-par. Her win also stopped Babe Zaharias' consecutive victory streak at three.

CHIP SHOT
The first time an LPGA Tour event was televised was in 1963. ABC carried the final round of the U.S. Women's Open from Cincinnati.

TRIVIA QUIZ—
In 1986, this golfer shot a final-round 63, but still finished second to Jack Nicklaus in The Masters. Who was it?

TODAY'S TIP—
In any given match you'll probably hit a couple of bad shots. Accept that fact so you don't allow one bad shot to immediately lead to another.

THE 19TH HOLE
"Winged Foot has the toughest eighteen finishing holes in golf."   —Dave Marr

Quiz Answer: Nick Price.

M A R C H

TODAY'S THOUGHT:
"Fifty percent of the fairways we play on today are better than ninety percent of the greens we played on thirty years ago."
—Jim Ferree, Senior PGA Tour player

ON THIS DATE—
In 1950, Babe Zaharias won her second U.S. Women's Open. Eleven years later, Bob Goalby set a PGA record with eight birdies in a row at the St. Petersburg Open.

CHIP SHOT
Golfers on the PGA Tour are not allowed to play more than one ball during a practice round.

TRIVIA QUIZ—
The oldest golf club in North America is located in what Canadian city?

TODAY'S TIP—
If a stone is against the back of your ball, take a well-lofted club and hit down sharply.

THE 19TH HOLE
"Are you asking me if I wear girdles and bras and the rest of that junk? What do you think I am? A sissy?"
—Babe Zaharias

Quiz Answer: Montreal. The Royal Montreal Golf Club was founded in 1873.

MARCH

TODAY'S THOUGHT:
"Golf is a typical capitalist lunacy of upperclass Edwardian England." —George Bernard Shaw

ON THIS DATE—
In 1937, golfing great Harry Vardon died. Vardon won the British Open a record six times, and was known for the grip that bears his name.

CHIP SHOT
The U.S. Open was first televised in 1947, the British Open in 1955, and The Masters in 1956.

TRIVIA QUIZ—
What's the oldest event on the PGA Tour?

TODAY'S TIP—
The Vardon grip locks the last finger of the right hand between the index and middle fingers of the left hand. It closes the gap between the hands and allows the wrists to work as a unit.

THE 19TH HOLE
"I used to play golf with a guy who cheated so badly, that he once had a hole-in-one and wrote down zero on the scorecard." —Bob Brue, Senior PGA Tour player

Quiz Answer: The U.S. Open, which was first held in 1895.

M A R C H

TODAY'S THOUGHT:

"Golf is an indispensable adjunct to high civilization."
—Andrew Carnegie

ON THIS DATE—

In 1982, Jerry Pate won the Tournament Players Championship at the new, and difficult, TPC at Sawgrass. Pate celebrated by dragging commissioner Deane Beman, designer Pete Dye, and himself into the lake next to the 18th green.

CHIP SHOT

Harvey Penick's Little Red Book is the best selling sports book in history with more than one million copies sold.

TRIVIA QUIZ—

Two players have won the Vardon Trophy five times in their careers. One of them is Billy Casper. Who's the other golfer?

TODAY'S TIP—

If you're opening the blade at impact while putting, play the ball slightly farther away from you.

─THE 19TH HOLE─

"I threw Deane in because he wanted this course, I threw Pete in because he built it, and I went in because I wanted to drown both of 'em." **—Jerry Pate**

Quiz Answer: Lee Trevino, who won it in 1970, '71, '72, '74, and 1980.

M A R C H

TODAY'S THOUGHT:
"I could make a pretty fair appraisal of the worth of an opponent simply by speaking to him on the first tee and taking a good measuring look into his eyes." —Bobby Jones

ON THIS DATE—
In 1992, the race was for second place at the Nestle Invitational. Fred Couples led from start to finish to win the event by nine strokes.

CHIP SHOT
One of Jack Nicklaus' victims on his march to the 1959 U.S. Amateur title was Robert T. Jones III, son of Bobby Jones.

TRIVIA QUIZ—
At the 1982 U.S. Open, Tom Watson's pitch from the rough on the seventeenth hole helped him win the title. Name the course.

TODAY'S TIP—
Can't remember that "tempo" is the key to a good drive? Write it on a piece of tape and fix it on the top of your driver.

THE 19TH HOLE
"I'd give up golf if I didn't have so many sweaters."
—Bob Hope

Quiz Answer: Pebble Beach Golf Links.

M A R C H

TODAY'S THOUGHT:

"Hickory golf was a game of manipulation and inspiration; steel golf is a game of precision and calculation."
—Peter Dobereiner, writer

ON THIS DATE—

In 1980, Lee Trevino won the Tournament Players Championship. The event was one of three victories for Trevino that year on his way to winning the Vardon Trophy for best scoring average.

CHIP SHOT

The Rules of Golf prevent a caddie from shielding a player from the elements while playing a stroke.

TRIVIA QUIZ—

In 1986, I led each major after three rounds, but only won one of the championships. Who am I?

TODAY'S TIP—

After addressing the ball, turn your head only to check the target. Moving up and down to check your target will throw your alignment off.

THE 19TH HOLE

"Usually, I play golf with the kind of people who rob banks, not own them." —Jim Murray, writer

Quiz Answer: Greg Norman. His only win came at the British Open.

MARCH

TODAY'S THOUGHT:
"They were real golfers, for real golf is a thing of the spirit, not of mere mechanical excellence of stroke."
—P.G. Wodehouse, *A Woman Is Only A Woman*

ON THIS DATE—
In 1974, Johnny Miller won his fourth tournament of the year, leading the field at the Heritage Classic. Born: Pat Bradley (1951); Jim Gallagher, Jr. (1961).

CHIP SHOT
Teyateyaneng GC in South Africa has a par three of 67 yards. It also has a par five measuring 619 yards.

TRIVIA QUIZ—
If a Walker Cup match is tied, which team (United States or Great Britain and Ireland) keeps the Cup?

TODAY'S TIP—
To prevent hitting a downhill lie fat, place your hands well ahead of the ball and keep them ahead of the clubhead throughout the stroke. Keep your left side firm.

THE 19TH HOLE
"I don't like to watch golf on television. I can't stand whispering."   —David Brenner, comedian

Quiz Answer: In the event of a tie, the Cup is retained for another two years by the previous winner.

M A R C H

TODAY'S THOUGHT:

"Good corn whiskey. It was a fun sort of tournament, that first one. They had 50 gallons and ran out by mid-morning of the third day of the tournament."

—Paul Runyan, memories of the first Masters

ON THIS DATE—

In 1934, play concluded at the first Masters at Augusta National. Horton Smith held on to defeat Craig Wood by one stroke to become the inaugural winner.

CHIP SHOT

Craig Wood finished second in the first two Masters. He finally won the championship in 1941.

TRIVIA QUIZ—

This golfer lost two Masters playoffs, one each to Byron Nelson and Sam Snead. Name him.

TODAY'S TIP—

Play within yourself when faced with an opponent who is a long hitter off the tee. Don't look when he hits because it will cause you to try to hit harder and alter your swing and tempo.

THE 19TH HOLE

"Coaches who shoot par in the summer are the guys I want on my schedule in the winter."

—Abe Lemons, college basketball coach

Quiz Answer: Ben Hogan. Hogan lost to Nelson in 1942 and to Snead in 1954.

MARCH

TODAY'S THOUGHT:
"When our putting is sour, then we are in honest, interminable, miserable trouble." —Arnold Palmer

ON THIS DATE—
In 1961, Lou Kretlow aced the par-4, 427-yard 16th hole at Oklahoma City's Lake Hefner golf course. Kretlow's tremendous drive hit in front of the green and rolled up into the hole.

CHIP SHOT
Arnold Palmer and Jack Nicklaus won at least one tournament on the PGA Tour for 17 consecutive years, a record.

TRIVIA QUIZ—
What is an "albatross?"

TODAY'S TIP—
If your putts are quitting on you, take a shorter backswing and accelerate through the ball.

THE 19TH HOLE
"That putt was so good, I could feel the baby applaud."
—Donna Horton-White, 7 months
pregnant, after holing a long putt

Quiz Answer: "Albatross" is the British term for a double-eagle.

M A R C H

TODAY'S THOUGHT:
"I never knew what top golf was like until I turned professional - then it was too late." —Steve Melnyk

ON THIS DATE—
In 1994, Donna Andrews captured the first major title of her career, winning the Nabisco Dinah Shore. Andrews celebrated, a la Jerry Pate, by jumping into the murky waters alongside the 18th green.

CHIP SHOT
The movie *Caddyshack* was filmed at the Rolling Hills Golf Resort in Ft. Lauderdale, Florida.

TRIVIA QUIZ—
What's the penalty in stroke play for carrying an extra club?

TODAY'S TIP—
Don't be afraid to use a 3 or 4-iron for a long chip. The ball will drop quickly and roll instead of bouncing.

THE 19TH HOLE
"Most people retire to play golf and fish. I do that now."
—Julius Boros, on his reluctance to retire

Quiz Answer: You're penalized two strokes for every hole you had the extra club with a maximum penalty of four strokes. You're disqualified if you don't discard it after realizing the mistake.

M A R C H

TODAY'S THOUGHT:
"In every tournament there are a few rounds of super golf; without a doubt they are played subconsciously."
—Chick Evans, Jr.

ON THIS DATE—
In 1993, Nick Price cruised to victory in the Players Championship at the TPC at Sawgrass. Price's 270 total was three strokes better than the course record set by Mark McCumber in 1988.

CHIP SHOT
In golf, nothing counts like your opponent.

TRIVIA QUIZ—
Who was the first golfer to win the U.S. Open and the U.S. Senior Open?

TODAY'S TIP—
If your game is plagued by duckhooks, try a heavier driver. It will slow down your swing and keep your hands in front of the clubhead.

THE 19TH HOLE
"If you birdie the 18th, do you win a free game?"
—John Mahaffey, on the TPC at Sawgrass

Quiz Answer: Arnold Palmer. Palmer won the U.S. Open in 1960 and the U.S. Senior Open in 1981, the second year in which the event was held.

M A R C H

TODAY'S THOUGHT:

"Golf is like a razor. You get just so sharp and then it begins to dull a little the more you use it." —Doug Sanders

ON THIS DATE—

In 1992, Dottie Mochrie won the LPGA's first major tournament of the year. Mochrie stopped Julie Inkster's bid for a third Nabisco Dinah Shore title on the first hole of a playoff.

CHIP SHOT

A golfer cannot participate in any PGA Tour event until he's paid the $100 annual membership fee.

TRIVIA QUIZ—

Quick! Who's known as "Super Mex?"

TODAY'S TIP—

Letting the fingers of your left hand to come off the grip at the top of your backswing leads to inconsistent shots. Place a tee between the club and the pad of the left hand. If it falls out during backswing, you've opened your grip.

THE 19TH HOLE

"Some guys get so nervous playing for their own money, the greens don't need fertilizing for a year."
                                                    —Dave Hill

Quiz Answer: Lee Trevino.

M A R C H

TODAY'S THOUGHT:
"The only thing that you should force in a golf swing is the club back into the bag."   —Byron Nelson

ON THIS DATE—
In 1889, after months of delay caused by the "Blizzard of '88," the first mixed foursome teed off at the St. Andrews Golf Club in Yonkers, NY. Born: Joey Sindelar (1958).

CHIP SHOT
Seve Ballesteros was disqualified from the 1980 U.S. Open after a traffic tie-up caused Ballesteros to arrive late at the first tee.

TRIVIA QUIZ—
Where is the Oakland Hills Country Club located?

TODAY'S TIP—
If you're faced with an uphill putt, don't try to pop it over the hill. Play the ball a little more forward and let the blade follow the contour of the slope.

——— THE 19TH HOLE ———
"The last time I birdied the first hole, I tried to lay up for the next seventeen."   —Charles Price, writer

Quiz Answer: The Oakland Hills Country Club is located in Birmingham, Michigan.

M A R C H

TODAY'S THOUGHT:
"Competitors take bad breaks and use them to drive themselves just that much harder. Quitters take bad breaks and use them as reasons to give up." —Nancy Lopez

ON THIS DATE—
In 1991, Amy Alcott won her record third Nabisco Dinah Shore Classic. In doing so she rewrote her own tournament record with a 15-under-par 273. Born: Miller Barber (1931).

CHIP SHOT
The first golf instruction book printed was *The Golfer's Manual*. Written by Henry B. Farnie in 1857, it discussed the mechanics of the swing and proper use of equipment.

TRIVIA QUIZ—
When the US Post Office came out with a stamp in 1981 honoring Bobby Jones, it also came out with one honoring a female Hall of Famer. Do you know her?

TODAY'S TIP—
Too hyper on the course? Walk slower, relax your arms, and take deep breaths.

THE 19TH HOLE
"Don't blame me. Blame the foursome ahead of me."
—Lawrence Taylor, pro football player, on why he was late for practice

Quiz Answer: Babe Zaharias.

APRIL

TODAY'S THOUGHT:

"Golf is a matter of ethical communication with yourself. A true golfer is never going to cheat because he is only cheating himself." —Frank Chirkinian, TV producer

ON THIS DATE—

In 1957, PGA Tour player Donnie Hammond was born. Hammond, who usually plays in fewer than 25 events a year, made a run at the '92 British Open title before a 74 dropped him to fifth.

CHIP SHOT

Rocky Thompson won two Senior PGA Tour events in 1991. But on the PGA Tour, Thompson endured 28 years and 600 events without a victory.

TRIVIA QUIZ—

Can you name the Australian golfer who won three consecutive British Opens during the 1950's?

TODAY'S TIP—

Always remember to keep your head down until after putting the ball. If you lift your head too soon your shoulders will rotate, and your sure putt will turn into a sure miss.

THE 19TH HOLE

"Even the men's room has a double dogleg."
—Dave Stockton, on the Poppy Hills Golf Course

Quiz Answer: Peter Thomson, who won the Open in 1952, '53, and '54.

A P R I L

TODAY'S THOUGHT:

"It's number one for me, pure and simple, because it's golf. The other events have become tented villages and circuses. When you go to The Masters, the focus is golf." —Greg Norman

ON THIS DATE—

In 1939, Ralph Guldahl, coming off back-to-back wins in the U.S. Open, won The Masters. Guldahl's 279 total was one stroke better than runner-up Sam Snead.

CHIP SHOT

If you're an average 150-pound male who walks the course and pulls golf clubs while playing 18 holes, expect to burn about 1,060 calories.

TRIVIA QUIZ—

Who was the first African-American golfer to play in The Masters?

TODAY'S TIP—

When attempting the pitch and run, choke down about three inches on the club. Bring your feet closer together with the ball in the middle of your stance. To swing, turn away from the ball and turn back. Make sure you hit through the ball.

THE 19TH HOLE
"We could make them so slick we'd have to furnish ice skates on the first tee."
   —Horn Hardin, on the greens at Augusta National

Quiz Answer: Lee Elder, who competed in the 1975 tournament.

APRIL

TODAY'S THOUGHT:

"It's just a matter of patience. It's a matter of whether it's your week or not. If the putts go in, it's your week. If they don't go in, it's not your week. It's that simple."   —Ian Woosnam

ON THIS DATE—

In 1992, Chip Beck set a two-round tournament record at the $1 million Freeport McMoRan Golf Classic. Beck's 36-hole total of 132 broke the 1989 record by one stroke.

CHIP SHOT

Built in 1895, the Van Cortlandt Park Golf Course in the Bronx (NY) was the first public golf course in the US.

TRIVIA QUIZ—

What LPGA golfer won The Vare Trophy, for lowest scoring average, a record seven times in her career?

TODAY'S TIP—

The rules say you can't wipe your ball clean while it's in play. So, if there's mud on your ball use one more club than necessary. That little bit of mud will limit the flight of your ball even with your normal swing.

THE 19TH HOLE

"If it wasn't for golf, I'd probably be a caddie today."
—George Archer

Quiz Answer: Kathy Whitworth.

A P R I L

TODAY'S THOUGHT:
"The job of a finishing hole is as clearly defined as that of a dance hall bouncer. It has to maintain order, clear out the amateurs, preserve the dignity of the game." —Jim Murray, writer

ON THIS DATE—
In 1937, Byron Nelson won the first of his two Masters titles. Exactly one year later, Henry Picard took home the green jacket. Born: JoAnne Carner (1939).

CHIP SHOT
Between the Japanese attack on Pearl Harbor and the end of World War II, only four major championships were played: the '42 Masters and the '42, '44, and '45 PGA Championships.

TRIVIA QUIZ—
True or false: Arnold Palmer and Curtis Strange attended the same university.

TODAY'S TIP—
If you find yourself in trouble more often than not on the golf course, spend some time practicing recovery shots. Learn how to get out of trouble on the links.

THE 19TH HOLE
"I was three over - one over a house, one over a patio, and one over a swimming pool."
—George Brett, pro baseball player
but amateur golfer

Quiz Answer: True. Both went to Wake Forest University.

APRIL

TODAY'S THOUGHT:
"It's nice to have the opportunity to play for so much money, but it's nicer to win it." —Patty Sheehan

ON THIS DATE—
In 1959, Art Wall came from six strokes down, firing a 66 in the final round at Augusta to win The Masters. Wall's round included eight birdies. Born: Billy Ray Brown (1963).

CHIP SHOT
Masters champions do not use the same locker room as the rest of the competitors. They have their own facility in another part of the clubhouse, which is off-limits to everyone else.

TRIVIA QUIZ—
Name the only two South African golfers to win the U.S. Open.

TODAY'S TIP—
To encourage a smoother takeaway on the tee, don't put the clubhead of the driver on the ground. Keep it slightly off the ground behind your ball.

THE 19TH HOLE
"I have a tip that can take five strokes off anyone's golf game. It's called an eraser." —Arnold Palmer

Quiz Answer: Gary Player, who won his title in 1965, and Ernie Els, who won the championship in 1994.

A P R I L

TODAY'S THOUGHT:
"There are two kinds of golf - golf and tournament golf. The latter is an aging game." —Bobby Jones

ON THIS DATE—
In 1936, Horton Smith battled a wet Augusta National golf course to win his second Masters tournament in three years. Defending champ Gene Sarazen finished two strokes back.

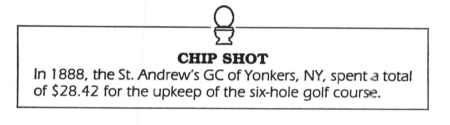

CHIP SHOT
In 1888, the St. Andrew's GC of Yonkers, NY, spent a total of $28.42 for the upkeep of the six-hole golf course.

TRIVIA QUIZ—
Before the invention of wooden tees, what did golfers use to tee up the ball?

TODAY'S TIP—
Closing your eyes when hitting the ball is not a good idea, but a few practice swings with your eyes closed is. It will give you a better sense of balance and timing.

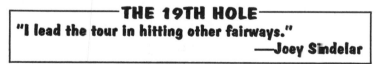

THE 19TH HOLE
"I lead the tour in hitting other fairways."
—Joey Sindelar

Quiz Answer: Sand. A sand box was located near the tee area from which the golfer or his caddy would grab a pinch of wet sand and form a makeshift pyramid on the ground. He would then place his ball on it.

APRIL

TODAY'S THOUGHT:
"Nicklaus will never be a hungry golfer as Palmer and Player and Sanders and Snead and Hogan and all the other successful ones have been in their time." —*Sports Illustrated*, 1962

ON THIS DATE—
In 1963, 23-year old Jack Nicklaus became the youngest golfer to wear the green jacket when he edged Tony Lema by one stroke to win The Masters. It was the first of six Masters championships for Nicklaus.

CHIP SHOT
Sam Snead's PGA Tour victories span a record 29 years, from his first win in 1936 to his last in 1965.

TRIVIA QUIZ—
What golfing great was nicknamed "The Hawk?"

TODAY'S TIP—
Place five balls in a line and attempt to hit them all without regripping your club. You won't be able to if your hands have slipped at some time during the swing. Looseness during the takeaway and at the top of the backswing can cause inconsistency in your game.

THE 19TH HOLE
"You don't necessarily have to bring your clubs to play golf - just lie about your score."
—Lon Simmons, announcer

Quiz Answer: Ben Hogan.

A P R I L

TODAY'S THOUGHT:

"Golf is really two games. One is the game in the air. The golfer can lick that part of the game." —Claude Harmon

ON THIS DATE—

In 1990, Nick Faldo defeated Raymond Floyd in a playoff to become the second player to defend his Masters title. Jack Nicklaus had won back-to-back titles in 1965 and '66.

CHIP SHOT

The Masters was the first major to switch from an 18-hole playoff to sudden death, making the change in 1976.

TRIVIA QUIZ—

The first defeat on home soil for the United States Ryder Cup team occurred at the Muirfield GC in Dublin, Ohio, a course designed by Jack Nicklaus. What was the year?

TODAY'S TIP—

A good swing form will lead to good timing. So, if you think your timing is off examine your form. Break down areas like your tempo in the takeaway and the switch from the backswing to swinging through the ball. Good timing will return.

THE 19TH HOLE

"There's no pressure. Mediocrity knows no pressure."
—Gary McCord

Quiz Answer: 1987.

APRIL

TODAY'S THOUGHT:
"Putting is simple. You need a sound putting stroke, confidence, patience, feel, and visualization." —Seve Ballesteros

ON THIS DATE—
In 1978, Gary Player rose to the challenge at The Masters. Trailing by seven strokes on the final day, Player shot a record-tying 64 to win his third green jacket at Augusta. Born: Seve Ballesteros (1957); Helen Alfredsson (1965).

CHIP SHOT
The Puntas Arenas GC in Chile is the southernmost course in the world. Because of strong winds, the greens are set below the fairway level.

TRIVIA QUIZ—
Only one golfer won two Masters titles in the 1980's. Who was it?

TODAY'S TIP—
Don't actually pause at the top of your backswing. You want your lower body to start the downswing just before the upper body finishes the backswing. Pausing prevents that from happening.

THE 19TH HOLE
"I wear black. I loved Westerns and the cowboys always looked good in black." —Gary Player
---

Quiz Answer: Seve Ballesteros, who won in 1980 and '83.

A P R I L

TODAY'S THOUGHT:
"You never get golf. You play well one day, at least you play well for you, and you think you've got it. But you go out the next day and you haven't got it. Instead, it's got you."
—John Madden, announcer

ON THIS DATE—
In 1916, Englishman Jim Barnes won the first PGA Championship. The event was staged at the Siwanoy Golf Course in Bronxville, NY.

CHIP SHOT
Walter Hagen reached the finals of the PGA Championship five straight times when the event was played at match play. He also had four consecutive victories.

TRIVIA QUIZ—
What foreign-born player won the first U.S. Senior Open?

TODAY'S TIP—
Need a low shot with your wedge? Point your feet slightly left of target and play the ball slightly behind center in your stance. Swing through and extend your arms to the target. Don't let your arms get above your shoulders on follow-through.

THE 19TH HOLE
"I've made a million, but I don't have a million."
—Walt Zembriski

Quiz Answer: Argentinean Roberto DeVicenzo, at Winged Foot GC in 1980.

APRIL

TODAY'S THOUGHT:
"He's the best there ever was in the game, and if a man doesn't want to play the best, he doesn't like ice cream."
—Lee Trevino, on competing with Nicklaus

ON THIS DATE—
In 1966, Jack Nicklaus successfully defended his Masters title with a playoff win over Tommy Jacobs and Gay Brewer. Brewer's title hopes were dashed when he three-putted the final hole of the tournament, thereby setting up the playoff.

CHIP SHOT
The first recorded hole-in-one is credited to Young Tom Morris in the 1868 British Open.

TRIVIA QUIZ—
Legal or illegal: I ask you what club you just hit.

TODAY'S TIP—
To hit a wedge shot high, take advantage of the club's loft. With a square stance and the ball ahead of center, swing through and pretend to reach for the sky on your follow through. The ball will take a higher, softer flight.

THE 19TH HOLE
"If there's anything to this astrology business, Jack Nicklaus must have been born under every sign."
—Gibby Gilbert

Quiz Answer: Illegal. It's a two-stroke penalty for me, but, if you answer me you also get a two-stroke penalty.

A P R I L

TODAY'S THOUGHT:

"Arnold Palmer is the king of kings. Anybody who resents Arnold getting more attention than the rest of us doesn't deserve to use his head for more than a hat rack." —Doug Sanders

ON THIS DATE—

In 1964, Arnold Palmer became the first golfer to win The Masters four times. Palmer had six strokes to spare over Dave Marr. Born: Donna Andrews (1967).

CHIP SHOT

Arnold Palmer broke 70 on the golf course before he hit the age of 12.

TRIVIA QUIZ—

Name the president who was a member of the Augusta National Golf Club.

TODAY'S TIP—

How important is hitting the "sweet spot" when driving off the tee? Hitting the ball squarely with a club speed of 100 mph produces a 240-yard drive. A hit ¾ of an inch off-center will result in a drive 30 yards shorter.

THE 19TH HOLE

"I drew a big gallery today. I was paired with Arnold Palmer." —Gene Littler

Quiz Answer: Dwight D. Eisenhower.

A P R I L

TODAY'S THOUGHT:
"You can be the greatest iron player in the world or the greatest putter, but if you can't get the ball in position to use your greatness, you can't win." —Ben Hogan

ON THIS DATE—
In 1980, Spaniard Seve Ballesteros became the youngest golfer to win The Masters. Ballesteros was nearly three months younger than Jack Nicklaus was when Nicklaus won his first championship. Born: Davis Love III (1964).

CHIP SHOT
The course at Augusta National GC was designed by Alister MacKenzie and Bobby Jones.

TRIVIA QUIZ—
To the nearest hundred, how many dimples are on the modern golf ball?

TODAY'S TIP—
Here's a way to find out if you're hitting the ball squarely. Place a piece of masking tape on the face of your club. After hitting a shot, look for the mark left on the tape by the ball.

THE 19TH HOLE
**"This guy has been in more bunkers than Eva Braun."
—Phil Harris, comedian, on the play of Jack Lemmon**

Quiz Answer: 400.

APRIL

TODAY'S THOUGHT:

"Most pros quietly admit they'd rather win The Masters than our Open because you almost have to beat the ghosts of Jones and Roberts - beat nature, perhaps even God - to win the green jacket." —Skip Bayless, writer

ON THIS DATE—

In 1968, the last day of The Masters was not a happy birthday for Roberto De Vicenzo. His signing of an incorrect scorecard gave the title to Bob Goalby. Born: Roberto De Vicenzo (1923); Bobby Nichols (1936); Mike Hulbert (1958); Meg Mallon (1963).

CHIP SHOT

Tommy Aaron, DeVicenzo's playing partner, put down a four on the Argentine's card instead of a three on the 71st hole.

TRIVIA QUIZ—

Name the first president of the Augusta National GC.

TODAY'S TIP—

When faced with a sand shot, grip the wedge at the end and make a smooth, slow swing. Choking down on the club will only produce skulled shots.

THE 19TH HOLE

"I am a stupid."
                    —Roberto DeVicenzo, after the '68 Masters

Quiz Answer: Bobby Jones.

A P R I L

TODAY'S THOUGHT:

"The biggest liar in the world is the golfer who claims he plays the game merely for the exercise." —Tommy Bolt

ON THIS DATE—

In 1979, Fuzzy Zoeller became the first player to win The Masters in his initial appearance at Augusta. Zoeller survived a playoff with Tom Watson and Ed Sneed to grab the green jacket.

CHIP SHOT

Zoeller is the only golfer to win playoffs in majors under two different formats. He won The Masters in sudden death, and beat Greg Norman over 18 holes at the 1984 U.S. Open.

TRIVIA QUIZ—

When I won The Masters in 1971, little did I know that would be the only major tournament win of my career. Who am I?

TODAY'S TIP—

First reads of the line of a putt are usually correct. Don't shift your feet after setting up. Square the club to the line, take your stance, and stroke the ball.

THE 19TH HOLE

"How did I four-putt? I missed the hole. I missed the hole. I missed the hole. I made it."

—Fuzzy Zoeller

Quiz Answer: Charles Coody.

A P R I L

TODAY'S THOUGHT:

"Watching golf on TV is one thing. Trying to watch a golf tournament in person is like trying to cover a war on foot."
—Jay Cronley, writer

ON THIS DATE—

In 1958, Arnold Palmer won the first of his eight major championships with a one-stroke victory over defending champion Doug Ford in The Masters. Palmer, at 28, was the youngest Masters winner since Byron Nelson in 1937.

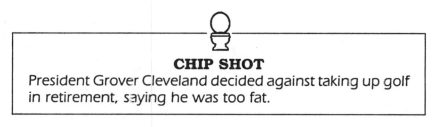

CHIP SHOT

President Grover Cleveland decided against taking up golf in retirement, saying he was too fat.

TRIVIA QUIZ—

Three golfers have won The Masters exactly three times. Two of them are Sam Snead ('49, '52, & '54) and Gary Player ('61, '74, & '78). Who's the third?

TODAY'S TIP—

Your mother was right when she told you to mind your posture. At address, your back should be straight. A stance too far away from the ball will have you leaning over and forward.

THE 19TH HOLE

"Bob Hope has a beautiful short game. Unfortunately, it's off the tee." —Jimmy Demaret

Quiz Answer: Jimmy Demaret won in 1940, '47, & '50.

APRIL

TODAY'S THOUGHT:

"There's no such thing as a bad course. Courses are like people - each course has its own personality. You have to challenge each one as it comes along." —Barbara Mizrahie

ON THIS DATE—

In 1994, Raymond Floyd hit three balls into the water on the final four holes, virtually handing Lee Trevino the PGA Seniors Championship. Trevino won by a stroke.

CHIP SHOT

Eldrick "Tiger" Woods was the first golfer to repeat as U.S. Junior Amateur champion, winning the event in 1991 and '92. Woods made it three in a row when he won in 1993.

TRIVIA QUIZ—

The Inverness Club was the site of two playoff losses by Greg Norman in the PGA Championship. Where's it located?

TODAY'S TIP—

Losing consistency with the long irons has always been a matter of confidence. Using a tee when practicing with long irons allows you to get the ball, and your confidence, up quickly without having to scoop the ball.

THE 19TH HOLE

"He'll be tougher than a 50-cent steak."
—Lee Trevino, on Floyd joining the Senior Tour

Quiz Answer: Toledo, Ohio.

APRIL

TODAY'S THOUGHT:
"It's all right to put all your eggs in one basket - if you've got the right basket." —Sam Snead

ON THIS DATE—
In 1993, former steel worker Tom Wargo came out of nowhere to win the PGA Seniors Championship on the second hole of sudden death. Wargo defeated Bruce Crampton for the victory. Born: David Edwards (1956).

CHIP SHOT
Wargo, who taught himself how to play golf, didn't take up the game until he was 25 years old.

TRIVIA QUIZ—
What's the modern-day name for the "mashie?"

TODAY'S TIP—
A sidehill shot with the ball high above your feet has a tendency to hook. Choke down on the club, keep your weight more on your toes for balance, and stand a little more upright. Sweep at the ball with a smooth swing and, remember, aim to the right of the target.

THE 19TH HOLE
"I tell myself that Jack Nicklaus probably has a lousy curve ball." —Bob Walk, Major League pitcher

Quiz Answer: The 5-iron.

APRIL

TODAY'S THOUGHT:
"Excessive golfing dwarfs the intellect. And is this to be wondered at when we consider that the more fatuously vacant the mind is, the better the play."
— Sir Walter Simpson, writer, 1887

ON THIS DATE—
In 1992, Davis Love III became the first golfer to win the Heritage Classic three times with a four-stroke victory over Chip Beck at the Harbour Town Golf Links.

CHIP SHOT
The 9th hole at St. Andrews Old Course is named Bobby Jones. The 18th hole is named Old Tom Morris.

TRIVIA QUIZ—
Name one of the four players who aced the sixth hole in the same round of the 1989 U.S. Open at Oak Hill.

TODAY'S TIP—
Over-cautious swings result in chip shots left short of the hole. You'll find yourself making more of those shots if you strike the ball firmly so, if you do miss, it will go past the hole a few feet.

THE 19TH HOLE
"The safest place would be on the fairway."
— Joe Garagiola, on where to stand at a celebrity tournament

Quiz Answer: Jerry Pate, Nick Price, Doug Weaver, and Mark Wiebe each used a 7-iron on the 167-yard, par-3 hole.

A P R I L

TODAY'S THOUGHT:

"There is nothing that will get your mind off everything like golf will. They say you can get so sore at yourself that you forget you hate your enemies."   —Will Rogers

ON THIS DATE—

In 1958, Louise Suggs shot three-under par for her second win in the Babe Zaharias Open. Defending champion Marlene Hagge was the runner-up to Suggs.

CHIP SHOT

Babe Zaharias was voted Woman Athlete of the First Half of the 20th Century in an Associated Press poll.

TRIVIA QUIZ—

You're on the first tee, ready to make your first shot of the day. What's the ruling if you accidentally knock the ball off the tee at address?

TODAY'S TIP—

Don't base your club selection on what other players are using. Use your practice time to get an idea of how far you can hit certain clubs. Know your own game, not others'.

THE 19TH HOLE
"My wife hates to cook, so I've started cooking a little more. I'm a great microwaver."   —Ken Green

Quiz Answer: No stroke, so no penalty. Tee it up again.

APRIL

TODAY'S THOUGHT:
"Golfers used to check the grass on the greens; today they study the roots under the blade." —Jimmy Demaret

ON THIS DATE—
In 1991, Jack Nicklaus continued his hot start on the Senior PGA Tour. Winning the PGA Seniors Championship gave Nicklaus his fourth victory in six starts in his initial season on the Tour.

CHIP SHOT
Brandie Burton reached $1 million in career earnings in her third year on the LPGA Tour. Mickey Wright earned slightly more than $368,000 in her career - and she won 82 events!

TRIVIA QUIZ—
This 1970 NFL MVP now makes his living on the Senior PGA Tour. Who is it?

TODAY'S TIP—
Make this a part of your warm-up routine: Take practice swings, letting go with the right hand near impact of an imaginary ball. This will be a reminder not to let go with the last three fingers of your left hand at impact on the course.

THE 19TH HOLE
"I've injured both my hands playing golf and they're okay now, but my brain has always been somewhat suspect." —Bob Murphy

Quiz Answer: Former 49ers quarterback John Brodie.

A P R I L

TODAY'S THOUGHT:

"I really don't like playoffs. I feel sorry for the other guy if I win and I feel worse if I lose."   —Chi Chi Rodriguez

ON THIS DATE—

In 1979, Tom Watson rebounded from a playoff loss in The Masters to win the Tournament of Champions. Watson ended the month of April with two first and two second-place finishes.

CHIP SHOT

The 19th hole at Royal Troon, Scotland is called the "dirty bar" because players are permitted to drink in their golf attire rather than in jacket and tie.

TRIVIA QUIZ—

Name the only golfer to win back-to-back British Opens in the 1970's.

TODAY'S TIP—

Practice strokes before a pressure putt not only help your mechanics, but also your confidence. Use them to settle your nerves and calm your hands so the putt itself becomes the final step of your success.

THE 19TH HOLE

"I've gone through more putters than Carter has pills."
—Tom Watson, on putting problems

Quiz Answer: Lee Trevino won the tournament in 1971 and '72. Trevino also won the U.S. Open in 1971.

A P R I L

TODAY'S THOUGHT:
"I like golf because when somebody tells the gallery to be quiet, they get quiet. Try that in baseball and they get louder."
—Mark McGwire, baseball player

ON THIS DATE—
In 1944, Marty Fleckman was born. In 1967, Fleckman won the Cajun Classic, his first professional tournament. The following year the Texan finished third in the PGA Championship.

CHIP SHOT
Former PGA Tour Commissioner and one-time Tour player Deane Beman is the only man to become commissioner of the major sport he played.

TRIVIA QUIZ—
What is the diameter of a golf ball:
      a) 1.62 inches   b) 1.68 inches   c) 1.72 inches?

TODAY'S TIP—
Straighten out your slice by widening your stance a bit. It will give you better balance and prevent you from swaying back and putting weight on your back foot, one of the causes of a slice.

THE 19TH HOLE
"If you think you can, or if you think you can't you're right." —Deane Beman

---

Quiz Answer: B. 1.68 inches .

A P R I L

TODAY'S THOUGHT:

"You're only here for a short visit. Don't hurry, don't worry. And be sure to smell the flowers along the way."

—Walter Hagen

ON THIS DATE—

In 1994, Mike Springer won for the first time on the PGA Tour. Springer led the final round from start to finish for a three-stroke victory at the Greater Greensboro Open.

CHIP SHOT

Jack Burke, Jr. is the only golfer since 1945 to win more than three straight events. Burke won four in a row in 1952.

TRIVIA QUIZ—

From 1949 to 1972, colleges from this state won 19 of the 24 NCAA Golf Championships. Name it.

TODAY'S TIP—

Woods down the left? Teeing the ball lower will force you to hit the ball with a slightly open clubface, reducing the hock spin, and keeping the ball to the right.

THE 19TH HOLE

"I'm not an intellectual person. I don't get headaches from concentration. I get them from double bogeys."

—Tom Weiskopf

Quiz Answer: Texas. Titles were won by Houston, North Texas State, SMU, and Texas.

A P R I L

TODAY'S THOUGHT:
"Gentlemen play golf. And if you aren't a gentleman when you start, after the crushing events of the game, you surely become one." —Bing Crosby

ON THIS DATE—
In 1993, it took four playoff holes before a winner emerged at the Greater Greensboro Open. Rocco Mediate came from four strokes down to edge Steve Elkington with a birdie putt.

CHIP SHOT
The first British Open played in England was in 1894. John H. Taylor won the silver jug at Royal St. George's.

TRIVIA QUIZ—
When was the last time an amateur won the U.S. Open, 1931 or 1933?

TODAY'S TIP—
Regain composure on the spur of the moment by choosing a club that will give you the safest productive shot. Concentrate on hitting the back of the ball, looking nowhere else until the finish of your swing. The emphasis is on ball contact.

THE 19TH HOLE
"I play with friends, but we don't play friendly games."
—Ben Hogan

Quiz Answer: John Goodman became the last amateur to win the U.S. Open when he took the title in 1933.

A P R I L

TODAY'S THOUGHT:

"The game was easy for me as a kid, and I had to play a while to find out how hard it is." —Raymond Floyd

ON THIS DATE—

In 1992, Lee Trevino and Mike Hill held off all challengers to win the Legends of Golf. The defending champs did so despite two bogies on the front nine. Born: Nancy Scranton (1961).

CHIP SHOT

The 18th hole at Barton Creek Club in Austin, Texas has a natural cave located just short of the green.

TRIVIA QUIZ—

In 1969, this golfer won the U.S. Women's Amateur, two years after walking away with the U.S. Women's Open title. Who was it?

TODAY'S TIP—

Freezing over the ball at address will result in a jerky swing. Staying in motion in some part of the body as you get ready to swing will prevent that. One example is to slightly shift your weight from foot to foot as you get set to swing.

THE 19TH HOLE

"I am the most over-taught and under-learned golfer in the USA." ——Herb Graffis, writer

Quiz Answer: Catherine Lacoste.

APRIL

TODAY'S THOUGHT:
"Golf is 90 percent inspiration, and 10 percent perspiration."
—Johnny Miller

ON THIS DATE—
In 1992, 68-year old Joe Graney, who hit a hole-in-one only six days after a cataract was removed from his right eye, did it again. Graney knocked down an ace six days after cataract surgery on his left eye!

CHIP SHOT
The first water hazards were streams running across Scottish links on their way to the sea.

TRIVIA QUIZ—
True or false: Nathanial Crosby, son of singer Bing Crosby, once won the U.S. Amateur.

TODAY'S TIP—
If faced with a shot where the ball is below your feet, don't bend your back to get down to the ball. Instead, flex your knees and hold that position through impact. Also, hold your club at the end of the grip.

THE 19TH HOLE
"This is blase now. I can see the ball now. I was walking around blind for years." —Joe Graney

Quiz Answer: True. Crosby won the men's championship in 1981.

A P R I L

TODAY'S THOUGHT:

"You start to choke when you drive through the front gate. On the first hole, you just want to make contact with the ball."
—Hale Irwin

ON THIS DATE—

In 1966, John Daly was born. Daly burst onto the golf scene in fairy-tale fashion with a win in the 1991 PGA Championship. Also born: Hal Sutton (1958).

CHIP SHOT

The record for the longest putt holed in a major belongs to Nick Faldo. Faldo dropped in a 100-foot birdie on the second hole of the 1989 Masters.

TRIVIA QUIZ—

Name the one major championship Ben Crenshaw has won twice.

TODAY'S TIP—

Don't practice when you're tired. It will only lead to poorly hit shots and, possibly, a loss of confidence. That's something you don't need.

—THE 19TH HOLE—

"There are no straight lines on my courses. The good Lord never drew a straight line."   —Jack Nicklaus

Quiz Answer: The Masters. Crenshaw won the green coat in 1984 and 1995.

APRIL

TODAY'S THOUGHT:

"I say this without any reservations whatsoever. It is impossible to outplay an opponent you can't out-think." —Lawson Little

ON THIS DATE—

In 1927, Glenna Collett Vare turned down a $50,000 contract to play golf professionally, saying she only wanted to play golf for the love of the game.

CHIP SHOT

Vare won a record six U.S. Women's Amateur championships between 1922 and 1935. Call it "love."

TRIVIA QUIZ—

This golfer set a record for the lowest stroke total ever in an American major championship when he shot 269 at the 1994 PGA Championship. Who was it?

TODAY'S TIP—

If the greens are hard on a particular day, use one less club than usual and play the ball toward the front of your stance. You should get a high shot that will land softly.

THE 19TH HOLE

"I'll be playing center for the Bulls before he's on the Tour."
—Peter Jacobsen, on Michael Jordan's golf game

Quiz Answer: Nick Price. Price's 11-under-par total was six strokes ahead of runner-up Corey Pavin.

A P R I L

TODAY'S THOUGHT:

"Winning one tournament doesn't do it. That was why I was happy when I won my second. Hell, anyone can win one tournament. I proved that." —Kenny Knox

ON THIS DATE—

In 1972, Kathy Whitworth rang up another victory on the LPGA Tour. Whitworth shot ten-under par at the Alamo Ladies Open, her first of five wins that year.

CHIP SHOT

What do you do when your playing partner claims to have found his ball in the rough, but you know he's lying because his ball is in your pocket?

TRIVIA QUIZ—

Kathy Whitworth won 88 tournaments in her career, but cannot count this major championship among them. Which one?

TODAY'S TIP—

Another way to restore confidence in using your long irons is to practice uphill shots. You'll get that feeling of sweeping the ball off the grass.

THE 19TH HOLE

"The putter is a club designed to hit the ball partway to the hole." —Rex Lardner, humorist

Quiz Answer: Whitworth never won the U.S. Women's Open.

M A Y

TODAY'S THOUGHT:
"When it's going good, you love your putter. When it's going bad, it's like it has betrayed you and you want to throw the sucker into a lake."   —Ken Green

ON THIS DATE—
In 1994, the Houston Open produced a first-time winner on the PGA Tour for the fifth straight year. Rookie Mike Heinen took his turn, edging Hal Sutton by three strokes.

CHIP SHOT
Calvin Peete led the PGA Tour in driving accuracy ten straight years, 1981-90.

TRIVIA QUIZ—
The diameter of a golf hole is:
> a) 3.75"   b) 4.25"   c) 4.50".

TODAY'S TIP—
A shot from deep greenside rough should be treated like a buried lie in the sand. Open your stance, play the ball off your front foot, and open the blade. The idea is to get as little grass as possible between your clubhead and the ball. Come down on the ball and don't decelerate as you go through the ball.

THE 19TH HOLE
"You know the old rule: He who have fastest cart never had to play bad lie.'"
> —Mickey Mantle, baseball Hall of Famer

Quiz Answer: B) 4.25 inches.

M A Y

TODAY'S THOUGHT:

"Baseball player, football player, hockey player retires, he takes up golf. I've never heard of a golfer retiring and taking up hockey. This is the greatest game." —Lee Trevino

ON THIS DATE—

In 1976, JoAnne Carner finished ten-under-par to win the Lady Tara Classic, her second victory of the year. Carner won over $100,000 that year for the first time in her career.

CHIP SHOT

Senior PGA Tour player Orville Moody is nicknamed "Sarge" because of the 14 years he spent in the Army.

TRIVIA QUIZ—

Who was the first South African golfer to win the British Open?

TODAY'S TIP—

Make sure that you center the clubface against the ball at address. Failure to do so will lead to toe or heel contact and a bad shot.

THE 19TH HOLE

"I'm going to sleep with my putter tonight. My husband Don is going to have to sleep in the other bed."
—JoAnne Carner, after a hot putting round

Quiz Answer: Bobby Locke, who won the championship in 1949. Locke also won the Open in 1950, '52, and '57.

M A Y

TODAY'S THOUGHT:
"Golf is temporary insanity practiced in a pasture."
—Dave Kindred, writer

ON THIS DATE—
In 1987, Paul Azinger took home the richest prize in PGA Tour history when he won the Panasonic Las Vegas tournament. Azinger pocketed $250,000 with the triumph. Born: Peter Oosterhuis (1949).

CHIP SHOT
During that same tournament, Scott Hoch won a $118,000 Rolls Royce when he aced the 17th hole.

TRIVIA QUIZ—
This famous seaside course with its feared 107-yard, par-3 7th hole was designed by amateur golfer Jack Neville in 1919, his first and last effort as a golf architect. Name it.

TODAY'S TIP—
Practicing your putting with a wedge will lead to more concentration on the green. Using the edge of the wedge will force you to focus more on hitting the center of the ball.

THE 19TH HOLE
"I'm working as hard as I can to get my life and my cash to run out at the same time. If I can just die after lunch Tuesday, everything will be fine."
—Doug Sanders

Quiz Answer: Pebble Beach Golf Links in California.

M A Y

TODAY'S THOUGHT:

"Give me golf clubs, fresh air, and a beautiful partner . . . and she better be able to putt."   —Anonymous

ON THIS DATE—

In 1928, LPGA Hal of Famer Betsy Rawls was born. Rawls owns 55 LPGA victories, including eight major championships. Also born: Bob Tway (1959).

CHIP SHOT

Rawls graduated Phi Beta Kappa from the University of Texas with a degree in mathematics and physics.

TRIVIA QUIZ—

During the 1960's two golfers from the PGA Tour were honored by *Sports Illustrated* as that magazine's Sportsman of the Year. Who were they?

TODAY'S TIP—

To prevent topping the ball from a fairway bunker place most of your weight on the front foot and leave it there through the swing. You won't fall back on your right foot and top the ball.

THE 19TH HOLE

"The way I hit the ball today, I need to go to the range. Instead, I think I'll go to the bar."   —Fuzzy Zoeller

Quiz Answer: Arnold Palmer won the award in 1960 and Ken Venturi was honored in 1964.

M A Y

TODAY'S THOUGHT:

"If you have a bad grip, you don't want a good swing."
—Harvey Penick

ON THIS DATE—

In 1991, instant-replay was used for the first time in a tournament. Tom Kite lost a stroke at the Byron Nelson Classic when videotape showed that a tee shot into the water should have been replayed from the tee, not a penalty drop.

CHIP SHOT

The practice range at Muirfield Village in Dublin, Ohio is circular so golfers can practice with the wind of their choice.

TRIVIA QUIZ—

In 1933, I lost the British Open in a playoff. In 1935, I lost The Masters in a playoff. In 1939, I lost the U.S. Open in, yes, a playoff. But in 1941, I won both The Masters and the U.S. Open. Who am I?

TODAY'S TIP—

Speeding up a good round can lead to a disappointing finish. Golfers who can't wait to hit that next shot will lose the swing that helped get them that low score. Slow down.

THE 19TH HOLE

"His future is ahead of him."
—Steve Melnyk, on the prospects of Phil Mickelson

Quiz Answer: Craig Wood.

M A Y

TODAY'S THOUGHT:

"I play this game because my sole ambition is to do well enough to give it up." —David Feherty, on professional golf

ON THIS DATE—

In 1979, Nancy Lopez, on her way to Vare Trophy honors, won the Women's International. The tournament was one of eight victories for Lopez that year, earning her the Player of the Year award for the second straight year.

CHIP SHOT

A tap-in for par on the final hole of the 1970 British Open would have clinched the championship for Doug Sanders. Instead, he missed, and lost in an 18-hole playoff the next day to Jack Nicklaus.

TRIVIA QUIZ—

Name the native country of Ian Baker-Finch.

TODAY'S TIP—

Develop a routine for taking your grip, and perform it the same way before every swing. Taking the same grip each time is critical for consistency.

THE 19TH HOLE

"I play in the low 80's. If it's any hotter than that, I won't play." —Joe E. Lewis, comedian

Quiz Answer: Baker-Finch was born in Australia.

M A Y

TODAY'S THOUGHT:

"It's good sportsmanship to not pick up lost golf balls while they are still rolling." —Mark Twain

ON THIS DATE—

In 1995, Michelle McGann ended a seven-year victory drought, edging Laura Davies by one stroke at the Sara Lee Classic. McGann had earned over one million dollars in seven years on the LPGA Tour without a win.

CHIP SHOT

Playing golf on Sunday instead of attending church was a crime in 16th-century Scotland. The fine? 40 shillings.

TRIVIA QUIZ—

Who's the oldest man to win the PGA Championship?

TODAY'S TIP—

If your ball is near a tree or bush and your swing is restricted, don't despair. Take a longer iron and choke down on the club. The result will be a shot that flies long and low and out of harm's way.

—THE 19TH HOLE—

"A cardinal rule for the club breaker is never to break your putter and driver in the same match or you are dead." —Tommy Bolt

Quiz Answer: Julius Boros was 48 years old when he won the PGA in 1968.

M A Y

TODAY'S THOUGHT:

"Golf is a dumb game. Hitting the ball is the fun part of it, but the fewer times you hit the ball, the more fun you have. Does this make any sense?"   —Lou Graham

ON THIS DATE—

In 1994, it took a four-foot birdie putt on the final hole to assure victory for John Daly in the BellSouth Classic. It was Daly's first win since the 1992 B.C. Open.

CHIP SHOT

Golf's oldest trophy is the silver club belonging to The Honourable Company of Edinburgh Golfers. It was first awarded in 1744 to the winner of the Company's annual tournament.

TRIVIA QUIZ—

Who was the first player to win a million dollars while playing on the Senior PGA Tour?

TODAY'S TIP—

John Daly may be the exception, but longer swings do not necessarily produce longer shots. A swing that's too long usually gives you inconsistent contact instead of longer drives.

THE 19TH HOLE

"I owe everything to golf. Where else could a guy with an IQ like mine make this much money?"
                                                        —Hubert Green

Quiz Answer: Don January crossed that threshold in 1985.

M A Y

TODAY'S THOUGHT:
"There are many ways of performing the operation successfully. I can claim, however, to be in a position to explain how not to putt. I think I know as well as anybody how not to do it."

—Harry Vardon

ON THIS DATE—
In 1870, Harry Vardon was born in Great Britain. One of the greatest early 20th century golfers, Vardon won six British Opens and one U.S. Open. Also born: Jim Dent (1939).

CHIP SHOT
Nothing increases your golf score like witnesses.

TRIVIA QUIZ—
What's the difference between match play and medal play?

TODAY'S TIP—
If, for some reason, you have to hit away from the hole, pick out a target several feet ahead of the ball to use when lining up your shot. That will keep you from realigning back toward the hole as you set up.

THE 19TH HOLE
"The way I putted, I must have been reading the greens in Spanish and putting them in English."

—Homero Blancas

Quiz Answer: The winner at match play is determined by the total holes won, while medal play is by total strokes.

M A Y

TODAY'S THOUGHT:

"Golf and sex are about the only things you can enjoy without being good at it."   —Jimmy Demaret

ON THIS DATE—

In 1910, the man who introduced sartorial splendor to the PGA Tour, Jimmy Demaret, was born. The Hall of Famer was also the first golfer to win three Masters championships.

CHIP SHOT

In 1954, Demaret said he owned 71 pairs of slacks, 55 shirts, 39 sportcoats, 20 sweaters, and 43 hats.

TRIVIA QUIZ—

Arnold Palmer lost three playoffs at the U.S. Open in the '60's. Can you name any of the three golfers who beat Arnie?

TODAY'S TIP—

How you tee up the ball can make a difference in your drive. Teeing the ball low means more backspin and less roll. Tee the ball so its center is even with the top edge of the driver. That way you'll sweep the clubhead through on a level path at impact for more carry and more roll.

THE 19TH HOLE

"Most of us would give up our wives, our first-born and our favorite putters just to finish in the top ten in a major."   —Lee Trevino

Quiz Answer: Jack Nicklaus in 1962; Julius Boros in 1963; and Billy Casper in 1966.

M A Y

TODAY'S THOUGHT:
"If I ever needed an eight-foot putt and everything I owned depended on it, I would want Arnold Palmer to putt it for me."
—Bobby Jones

ON THIS DATE—
In 1959, Arnold Palmer finished 15-under-par to win the Oklahoma City Open. For Palmer, it was the 12th victory of his professional career.

CHIP SHOT
Americans won all but one British Open between 1921 and 1933. Briton Arthur Havers won it in 1923. 1925 champ Jim Barnes was a British citizen, but was an expatriate living in America.

TRIVIA QUIZ—
What is the most common 18-hole par on golf courses around the world?

TODAY'S TIP—
Never use the tee markers to line up your shot. To get a better perspective of your tee shot, stand behind your ball and look down the target line.

THE 19TH HOLE
"That's a bagful of indecision."
—Jack Burke, when Palmer brought eight putters to a tournament

Quiz Answer: 72.

M A Y

TODAY'S THOUGHT:

"Don't let the bad shots get to you. Don't let yourself become angry. The true scramblers are thick-skinned. And they always beat the whiners." —Paul Runyan

ON THIS DATE—

In 1985, Kathy Whitworth won the United Virginia Bank Classic. Whitworth didn't know it at the time, but the title would be her 88th, and final, victory of her career.

CHIP SHOT

The difference between learning to play golf and learning to drive a car is that, in golf, you never hit anything.

TRIVIA QUIZ—

Legal or illegal: With my ball in a bunker, I touch the sand with my club to determine its condition.

TODAY'S TIP—

Hit one or more club lengths than usual if you are playing into a strong wind. What you don't want to do is hit the ball high. Sweep the ball off the fairway, trying not to take a divot, and keep your clubhead low during the follow-through.

THE 19TH HOLE

"The number one thing in trouble is: Don't get into more trouble!" —Dave Stockton

Quiz Answer: Illegal. I am assessed a two-stroke penalty.

M A Y

TODAY'S THOUGHT:
"I realize that's why we play golf, to hit the ball into the hole. But it's such a strange feeling when you hit an iron shot and it actually goes in." —Hollis Stacy

ON THIS DATE—
In 1952, long-hitting Mickey Wright slipped past Babe Zaharias on the alltime victory list. Wright's win at the Western Open was the 32nd of her career.

CHIP SHOT
The first known women's tournament took place in Scotland in 1810. First prize was a fish basket.

TRIVIA QUIZ—
Five amateurs have won the U.S. Open, none since 1933. How many can you name?

TODAY'S TIP—
When pitching to an elevated green, aim at a spot near the green where the ball will need only one bounce to get on and start rolling.

THE 19TH HOLE
"How do I address the ball? I say, Hello there, ball. Are you going to go in the hole or not?'"
—Flip Wilson, comedian

Quiz Answer: Francis Ouimet (1913), Jerry Travers (1915), Chick Evans (1916), Bobby Jones (1923, '26, '29 & '30), and John Goodman (1933).

M A Y

TODAY'S THOUGHT:

"The one stroke marks the difference between fame and oblivion."
—Samuel L. Parrish, USGA official

ON THIS DATE—

In 1978, Nancy Lopez began her record-setting streak by capturing the Greater Baltimore Classic. Lopez went on to win five straight tournaments that she entered before Pat Bradley stopped the streak more than a month later.

CHIP SHOT

Robert Trent Jones is given credit as the first golf course architect to use water hazards in his course designs.

TRIVIA QUIZ—

The first twelve British Opens were contested at this course in Scotland. Name it.

TODAY'S TIP—

If you miss your birdie putt, don't just turn away in disgust. Watch how your ball rolls past the hole. That just might give you an idea of how your next putt will break, helping you save par.

THE 19TH HOLE

"My swing is no uglier than Arnold Palmer's, and it's the same ugly swing every time." —Nancy Lopez

Quiz Answer: Prestwick Golf Club.

M A Y

TODAY'S THOUGHT:
"Golf was never meant to be an exact science, it's an art form. Einstein was a great scientist but a lousy golfer."   —Bob Toski

ON THIS DATE—
In 1991, the LPGA announced an anti-discrimination policy, saying that as of the following year, tournaments would no longer be held at golf clubs that excluded minorities.

CHIP SHOT
The worst loss in playoff history was suffered by Al Espinosa, who finished 23 strokes behind Bobby Jones over 36 holes in the 1929 U.S. Open.

TRIVIA QUIZ—
What Hall of Famer has won the most major championships on the LPGA Tour?

TODAY'S TIP—
Always remember that a putt will not break as much on a wet green as opposed to a dry green. Do not read slight breaks near the hole and aim for the back of the cup.

THE 19TH HOLE
"It wasn't much fun being an amateur. I got tired of polishing the silverware."   —Patty Sheehan

Quiz Answer: Patty Berg, who won 16 majors in her career.

M A Y

TODAY'S THOUGHT:
"In football, some coaches have stated, when you throw a pass, three things can happen, two of them are bad. In golf, there is no limit." —Mario Parascenzo, writer

ON THIS DATE—
In 1993, Scott Simpson saved par on the final hole for a one-stroke victory in the Byron Nelson Classic. Simpson had bogeyed three straight holes to shave a four-stroke lead to one.

CHIP SHOT
PGA Tour pro Billy Andrade was named all-state in basketball at Providence (RI) Country Day School. Andrade, all five feet, eight inches of him, was a point guard.

TRIVIA QUIZ—
This Texan won the 1965 PGA Championship and was named the PGA Player of the Year. Later in his career he captained the US to a Ryder Cup victory over Europe in 1981. Who is it?

TODAY'S TIP—
Don't let a narrow fairway frighten you. Focus on one spot, aim at it, and block out any thoughts of trouble along the sides.

THE 19TH HOLE
"Some days I felt like Superman and other days I found I was made of Jell-O." —Dave Marr

Quiz Answer: Dave Marr.

M A Y

TODAY'S THOUGHT:
"There is nothing like winning the Ryder Cup. It beats everything else because you are playing for someone else besides yourself and it means more." —Tom Watson

ON THIS DATE—
In 1992, Betsy King laid claim to her first LPGA Championship with the largest margin of victory in the tournament's history. The 11-stroke win gave King her fifth major title.

CHIP SHOT
Railroad president Walter Ross first came up with the idea for matches between the US and Great Britain. But he didn't want to spend the money for a trophy. English seed merchant Samuel Ryder did.

TRIVIA QUIZ—
If you cut a golf ball with your stroke, are you allowed to immediately replace it?

TODAY'S TIP—
Don't try to steer your short iron shots when close to the green. Instead of guiding the ball and the club, swing the irons like you would a driver.

THE 19TH HOLE
"I never thought I'd live to shoot my age. I thought somebody would shoot me first." —Dale Morey

Quiz Answer: Yes.

M A Y

TODAY'S THOUGHT:

"I don't have any big secret about putting. Just hit at it. It's either going to miss or go in."   —Ben Crenshaw

ON THIS DATE—

In 1986, Pat Bradley didn't win the Chrysler-Plymouth Classic, but her earnings did push her over the $2 million mark in her career, the first woman golfer to do so.

CHIP SHOT

Visitors aren't allowed to play the championship course at Royal Melbourne GC, host of every major Australian championship.

TRIVIA QUIZ—

Only one golfer was able to win the U.S. Open twice during the 1970's. Who was it?

TODAY'S TIP—

Tracking your golf game every time you go out will help you identify trends and problems in your game. Keep track of fairways and greens hit, putts, the direction of your shots, and how successful each shot was. After a while you will be able to identify your problems and work to improve those areas.

THE 19TH HOLE

"Some guys hope to shoot their age. Craig Stadler hopes to shoot his waist."   —Jim Murray, writer

Quiz Answer: Hale Irwin, who won it in 1974 and '79.

M A Y

TODAY'S THOUGHT:
"Golf is a young man's vice and an old man's penance."
—Irving Cobb, humorist

ON THIS DATE—
In 1991, Kenny Perry thwarted Hale Irwin's comeback bid with a birdie on the first playoff hole to win the Memorial. Irwin had made up five shots over the final round to force sudden death. Born: Betty Jameson (1919); Mike Standly (1964).

CHIP SHOT
The first golf magazine, *Golf: A Weekly Record of 'Ye Royal and Ancient' Game*, appeared in Great Britain in 1890. It's still published today as *Golf Illustrated Weekly*.

TRIVIA QUIZ—
The U.S. Open, first held in 1895, is the oldest tournament on the PGA Tour. What event is the second oldest?

TODAY'S TIP—
A good backswing will allow you to develop a good downswing pattern. Since the downswing is reflexive, any faults coming down can be traced to how you take your swing back.

THE 19TH HOLE
"My turn-ons? Big galleries, small scores, long drives, short rough, fat paychecks, and skinny trees."
—Peter Jacobsen

Quiz Answer: The Western Open, first contested in 1899.

M A Y

TODAY'S THOUGHT:

"I once played with Henry Ford II and told him you can buy a country, but you can't buy a golf swing. It's not on the shelf."
—Gene Sarazen

ON THIS DATE—

In 1962, Patty Berg won the 57th title of her career, finishing four-under-par at the Muskogee Civitan Open. Born: Dave Hill (1937).

CHIP SHOT

Patty Berg's hole-in-one in the 1959 U.S. Women's Open made her the first woman to record an ace in USGA competition.

TRIVIA QUIZ—

By what nickname did golfing legend Bobby Jones call his putter?

TODAY'S TIP—

Avoid lifting the heel of your front foot too high when swinging. Doing so could cause you to slightly lift your entire body and throw off the arc of your swing.

THE 19TH HOLE

"It's hard to take a chance when you can't reach the green in the first place." —Tom Kite

Quiz Answer: Calamity Jane.

M A Y

TODAY'S THOUGHT:

"I wouldn't hurt a chicken crossing the road, but if I got a man in trouble on the golf course I'd kick the hell out of him. I don't care if he's my best friend."   —Sam Snead

ON THIS DATE—

In 1961, the Sam Snead Golf Festival tournament in White Sulphur Springs, West Virginia, was won by . . . Sam Snead.

CHIP SHOT

In 1958, Snead won $14,000 in PGA purses. In 1959, his take from the TV show, *All-Star Golf*, was $29,500.

TRIVIA QUIZ—

1966 was the first year the British Open was played over four days. What American came home with the title?

TODAY'S TIP—

A good stance and a good set-up are keys to good putting. Moving either your head or your body will cause you to putt off-line. To help you stay still, watch the putter blade hit the ball before moving.

THE 19TH HOLE

"Why do people panic in bunkers? First of all, a bunker is defined as a hazard by rules, and anything that's called a hazard must be hazardous, right?"

—Nancy Lopez

Quiz Answer: Jack Nicklaus.

M A Y

TODAY'S THOUGHT:
"On tour, you've got to realize that if you take an eight on a hole, ninety percent of the other pros don't care and the other ten percent wish it had been a nine." —Mason Rudolph

ON THIS DATE—
In 1994, Tom Lehman shot his fourth straight round of 67 in an easy five-stroke win at The Memorial. It was Lehman's first win on the PGA Tour. Born: Andrew Magee (1962).

CHIP SHOT
It's not that I cheat at golf. I play for my health, and a low score makes me feel better.

TRIVIA QUIZ—
What tournament was Chip Beck playing in when he shot his record-tying round of 59?

TODAY'S TIP—
"Worm-burners" are often caused by a poor address. Setting up with your front shoulder slightly higher than your back shoulder will give you a swing arc that will hit the ball upward, lifting it in the air and not along the ground.

THE 19TH HOLE
"I'll take a two-shot penalty, but I'll be damned if I'm going to play the ball where it lies."
　　　　　—Elaine Johnson, after her shot hit a tree and caromed into her bra

Quiz Answer: The 1991 Las Vegas International.

M A Y

TODAY'S THOUGHT:
"You can shoot lions in the dark and yet you can quiver like a leaf and fall flat over a two-foot putt."   —Johnny Farrell

ON THIS DATE—
In 1993, Bob Charles became the first golfer to earn $4 million on the Senior PGA Tour, winning the Bell Atlantic Classic.

CHIP SHOT
Twice as many people visit Florida for a golf vacation as any other two states combined.

TRIVIA QUIZ—
Who won the Vardon Trophy for best scoring average in 1977, '78, and '79?

TODAY'S TIP—
The more you can keep your weight on the insides of your feet while you swing, the more balanced you will be. At the top of your swing more weight should be placed on your back foot, switching to your front foot at impact, and eventually all the weight moving to the outer edge of that foot as you follow through.

THE 19TH HOLE
"Golf is a game in which the ball lies poorly and the players well."   —Art Rosenblum, comedian

Quiz Answer: Tom Watson.

M A Y

TODAY'S THOUGHT:
"A secret disbelief in the enemy's play is very useful for match play."
—Sir Walter Simpson

ON THIS DATE—
In 1987, Jane Geddes won the LPGA Championship and $52,500. Five years later, Pat Bradley earned $200,000 . . . on one hole! Bradley sank a birdie putt in a skins game to win her paycheck. Born: Walt Zembriski (1935).

CHIP SHOT
Gary Player remains the last golfer to win three tournaments in a row. But those three wins in 1978 were his last on the PGA Tour.

TRIVIA QUIZ—
Who is the oldest winner of the British Open?

TODAY'S TIP—
To ensure that you're following through properly on sand shots, your clubface should be pointing toward the sky with the palm of your right hand facing up.

THE 19TH HOLE
"The pin placements weren't too tough, but whoever set them missed ten greens."   —Leonard Thompson

Quiz Answer: Old Tom Morris, who was 46 when he won the tournament in 1867.

M A Y

TODAY'S THOUGHT:

"Ben Hogan would rather have a coral snake rolling in his shirt than hit a hook." —Claude Harmon

ON THIS DATE—

In 1948, Ben Hogan defeated Mike Turnesa in match play to win the PGA Championship. Less than three weeks later, Hogan went on to win the U.S. Open. Born: D.A. Weibring (1953).

CHIP SHOT

At the 1964 PGA Championshiop, Arnold Palmer became the first golfer to shoot four sub-70 rounds in a major. But he still finished second.

TRIVIA QUIZ—

True or false: PGA Tour player Scott Verplank once won the NCAA championship as a member of the Oklahoma State golf team.

TODAY'S TIP—

Playing the ball out on the toe of your putter and using a normal stroke will help you handle downhill putts on fast greens. The deadened impact will let the ball roll slower.

THE 19TH HOLE

"Isn't it fun to go out on the course and lie in the sun?"
—Bob Hope, on cheating

Quiz Answer: True. Verplank won it in 1986.

M A Y

TODAY'S THOUGHT:

"We know a lot about the swing, one college golf coach said to me, but not much about how to help golfers learn it."

—W. Timothy Gallwey, writer

ON THIS DATE—

In 1991, Betsy King scored six birdies and no bogeys in the final round to win the LPGA Corning Classic by six shots. Born: Ronnie Black (1958); Steve Pate (1961).

CHIP SHOT

"Champagne" Tony Lema got his nickname when he told the press he would set them up with champagne instead of beer if he won the 1962 Orange County Open.

TRIVIA QUIZ—

This Japanese golfer made her name on the American golf scene when she was named LPGA Player of the Year in 1987. Do you know her?

TODAY'S TIP—

Most times a ball sitting on top of coarse rough will fly off the clubhead with very little spin and more distance than expected. Use one less club when faced with that situation.

THE 19TH HOLE

"I only hit the ball about 220 off the tee, but I can always find it."   —Bonnie Lauer

Quiz Answer: Ayako Okamoto.

M A Y

TODAY'S THOUGHT:
"Forget your opponents; always play against par."   —Sam Snead

ON THIS DATE—
In 1912, "Slammin'" Sammy Snead was born. The holder of a record 81 victories on the PGA Tour, Snead won seven major championships in his career. He finished runner-up four times at the U.S. Open, the only major to elude him.

CHIP SHOT
At the 1939 U.S. Open, Snead needed a par-five on the last hole to win by one stroke. He thought he needed a birdie, however, and hit into the rough and two bunkers before three putting for an eight. He lost by two strokes to Byron Nelson.

TRIVIA QUIZ—
Roberto DeVicenzo will always be known as the man who signed an incorrect scorecard to lose the 1968 Masters. But he did win a major in his career. Which one?

TODAY'S TIP—
If you find yourself in a slump, head to the driving range with just a pitching wedge. Short shots will allow you to focus on your tempo and making contact with the ball.

THE 19TH HOLE
"The rest of the field."
    —Roger Maltbie, on what he had to shoot to win

Quiz Answer: DeVicenzo won the 1967 British Open.

M A Y

TODAY'S THOUGHT:
"The Masters is Scarborough Fair, the gathering of eagles. Everyone wants to make the trip to Mecca."   —Bobby Jones

ON THIS DATE—
In 1991, Horn Hardin resigned as chairman of the Augusta National Golf Club. The often-controversial Hardin was replaced by Jackson Stephens as head of The Masters. Born: Shelley Hamlin (1949).

CHIP SHOT
Jack Nicklaus is the only six-time winner of The Masters. He's also the only golfer to win the tournament five times.

TRIVIA QUIZ—
The first Curtis Cup was held in 1932. But it wasn't until years later that the American women amateurs lost a match on their home ground. What year did they suffer their first loss?

TODAY'S TIP—
Don't rush your downswing. Start down slowly, building up speed as you approach impact.

THE 19TH HOLE
"I liked the oil business. I didn't have to go to the press room and explain my day."   —Bruce Crampton

Quiz Answer: In 1986 the US lost, 13-5, to the British Isles.

M A Y

TODAY'S THOUGHT:
"I would rather play Hamlet with no rehearsal than play golf on television." —Jack Lemmon

ON THIS DATE—
In 1977, Sue Press made the history books when she became the first woman to hit consecutive holes-in-one. Press aced the 13th and 14th holes at the Chatswood Golf Club in Sydney, Australia. Born: PGA Hall of Famer Bob Hope (1903).

CHIP SHOT
Golf is played in the United States at least once a year by over 20 million people on more than 12,400 courses.

TRIVIA QUIZ—
Which continent has the least golfers and the fewest golf courses in the world? Don't count Antarctica!

TODAY'S TIP—
An iron is not necessarily the weapon of choice if you're stuck in medium rough a long way from the green. A wood can cut through medium rough nicely while still making solid contact for the distance you need.

THE 19TH HOLE
"I'm a nineteen handicap and I think my husband's about a nineteen, but he cheats more than I do."
—Delores Hope, wife of Bob

Quiz Answer: South America.

M A Y

TODAY'S THOUGHT:

"From being a kid it has been my dream to leave a legacy. I want people to say 'Did you see Nick Faldo play?' "   —Nick Faldo

ON THIS DATE—

In 1937, Denny Shute won his second straight PGA Championship when he defeated Harold McSpaden in the final round.

CHIP SHOT

Club pro Craig Thomas' joy at qualifying for the 1993 Buick Open turned to embarrassment when he fired a whopping 92 in the first round. His inflated score, and deflated ego, included quadruple bogies on the 10th and 11th holes.

TRIVIA QUIZ—

She lost the U.S. Women's Open in 1957 because she turned in an incorrect scorecard and was disqualified. Who was it?

TODAY'S TIP—

When practicing your swing, concentrate first on such things as grip, aim, address, and stance before moving on to fundamentals like backswing, downswing, hand position at the top of the swing, and overall tempo.

THE 19TH HOLE

"Sometimes I wish I had no talent and a lousy golf swing. Then I'd win because nobody would expect me to."   —Lori Garbacz

Quiz Answer: Jacqueline Pung.

M A Y

TODAY'S THOUGHT:
"Here we are, making thousands of dollars a year, and we're trying to change our swings."   —Johnny Miller

ON THIS DATE—
In 1942, Sam Snead won the first major title of his career, topping Jim Turnesa in the PGA Championship. Snead won his second PGA title exactly to the day seven years later.

CHIP SHOT
The winner of the AT&T Pebble Beach National Pro-Am is awarded a 58-piece suite of crystal made by Waterford as well as a replica of the tournament trophy.

TRIVIA QUIZ—
You're my caddie as we head into the final back nine of The Masters. I ask you to give me my baffy. What club will you hand me?

TODAY'S TIP—
When hitting a fairway wood from an uphill lie, play the ball toward the middle of your stance for more distance. Many golfers have a tendency to play the ball too far forward in their stance and end up skying the ball.

THE 19TH HOLE
"I paid my dues. That's golfer-talk for hitting a million balls."   —Jim Thorpe
---

Quiz Answer: The 5-wood.

J U N E

TODAY'S THOUGHT:
"Golf combines two favorite American pastimes: taking long walks and hitting things with a stick." —P.J. O'Rourke, writer

ON THIS DATE—
In 1986, Pat Bradley became the first golfer to win all four LPGA majors in her career. Bradley ran away from the field for an 11-stroke victory in the LPGA Championship. Born: John Huston (1961).

CHIP SHOT
In 1990, Rob MacGregor bounced a golf ball on the face of his sand wedge 3,699 times. The old record was held by Mark Mooney, who did it 1,764 times.

TRIVIA QUIZ—
Who were the first two golfers elected to the Woman's Hall of Fame?

TODAY'S TIP—
Playing a ball from under a bush involves a swing using primarily the hands and arms. Kneel down, planting your knees wide and aim to the right to allow for a hook.

THE 19TH HOLE
"Real golfers have two handicaps: one for braggin' and one for bettin'." —Anonymous

Quiz Answer: Patty Berg and Babe Zaharias, who were inducted in 1951.

JUNE

TODAY'S THOUGHT:
"All the golf swing is, is two turns and a swish."   —Mary Bryan

ON THIS DATE—
In 1985, Nancy Lopez won her second LPGA Championship, this time by eight strokes. Lopez never missed a fairway on her way to an 8-stroke win. Born: Craig Stadler (1953).

CHIP SHOT
In a full drive by an average adult male golfer, the clubhead swings through the ball at about 100 mph. In contrast, PGA Tour players range from about 115 to 135 mph.

TRIVIA QUIZ—
Who's the only African-American golfer to have won the Vardon Trophy for scoring average?

TODAY'S TIP—
One way to read the break of a putt is the "plumb bob." Squat behind your ball and suspend the putter in front of you. Line up the shaft with the ball and sight the club with your stronger eye. The ball will break to the side where the hole is.

THE 19TH HOLE
"Nancy Lopez is planning on marrying a sportscaster. I thought she had better taste."
—Dick Schaap, writer

Quiz Answer: Calvin Peete, who won the trophy in 1984.

JUNE

TODAY'S THOUGHT:
"If you work very hard, they call you lucky. When they call you lucky, you know you're good." —Chi Chi Rodriguez

ON THIS DATE—
In 1984, Patty Sheehan successfully defended her LPGA Championship. Sheehan tamed the Jack Nicklaus Golf Club course to fnish 16-under-par and ten strokes ahead of runners-up Beth Danie and Pat Bradley. Born: Hale Irwin (1945); Deb Richard (1963).

CHIP SHOT
Arnold Palmer's first PGA Tour check came at the 1955 Indiana Open. It was a modest $142.

TRIVIA QUIZ—
Name the golfer who won four consecutive PGA Championships.

TODAY'S TIP—
If you have to chip from the putting surface, leave the pin in the hole. It gives you a better chance of success if you keep the fag in.

THE 19TH HOLE
"I'll get up at five in the morning to do only two things: go to the bathroom and play golf."
—Jim McMahon, pro football quarterback

Quiz Answer: Walter Hagen, who won it every year between 1924 and 1927.

J U N E

TODAY'S THOUGHT:
"Golf is like fishing or hunting. What counts is the companionship and fellowship of friends, not what you catch or shoot."
—George Archer

ON THIS DATE—
In 1927, the United States and Great Britain faced off in the first Ryder Cup competition at Worcester Country Club in Massachusetts. The US won, 9½ to 2½. Born: Sandra Haynie (1943).

CHIP SHOT
A pair of brass clubheads recovered in the 1970's from a Dutch ship that had sunk in 1653 were sold at auction in 1989. The price? $14,000 each.

TRIVIA QUIZ—
What Senior PGA Tour player scored eight straight birdies in the 1987 Silver Pages Classic?

TODAY'S TIP—
You can control the distance of your sand shot by swinging the same but hitting further behind the ball. The extra sand will deaden the ball and produce a softer shot.

THE 19TH HOLE
"I've seen better swings in a condemned playground."
—Arnold Palmer, to Bob Hope

Quiz Answer: Chi Chi Rodriguez.

J U N E

TODAY'S THOUGHT:
"My worst day on the golf course still beats my best day in the office." —John Hallisey, writer

ON THIS DATE—
In 1925, Scottish pro Willie Macfarlane upset amateur Bobby Jones by one stroke to win the U.S. Open. The championship wasn't settled until the final hole of a second playoff when Macfarlane shot a four to Jones' five.

CHIP SHOT
Willie Macfarlane was the first U.S. Open champion to win wearing eyeglasses.

TRIVIA QUIZ—
Cary Middlecoff and Lloyd Mangrum battled through the longest sudden-death playoff in history, eleven holes, in the 1949 Motor City Open. Who won the event?

TODAY'S TIP—
Remember that an open stance will produce a left-to-right shot, or fade. Your shoulder, body, and hip rotation is restricted, creating an outside-to-inside swing.

THE 19TH HOLE
"Seve, I wouldn't give my mother two strokes a side."
—Tommy Bolt, to Seve Ballesteros

Quiz Answer: Both were declared co-winners after darkness halted play.

J U N E

TODAY'S THOUGHT:
"Good night, this game teaches you a lot about yourself. You can tell by the way a guy walks how he's doing."   —Ben Crenshaw

ON THIS DATE—
In 1992, Arizona State left-hander Phil Mickelson won his third NCAA golf title. Mickelson joined Ben Crenshaw as the only two golfers to win three national titles.

CHIP SHOT
The trophy of the BellSouth Classic is a bronze replica of the Vardon grip. The model for the cast was Bobby Jones.

TRIVIA QUIZ—
What golfer holds the record for the most consecutive years on the top ten money-winning list?

TODAY'S TIP—
A closed stance will give you a right-to-left shot, or hook. In a closed stance your back foot is set away from the ball, resulting in an inside-to-outside swing.

THE 19TH HOLE
"I didn't need to finish college to know what golf was all about. All you need to know is to hit the ball, find it and hit again until it disappears into the hole in the ground."   —Fuzzy Zoeller

---

Quiz Answer: Jack Nicklaus, who was on the list every year from 1962 to 1978, or 17 times.

J U N E

TODAY'S THOUGHT:

"Good golfing temperament falls between taking it with a grin or shrug and throwing a fit." —Sam Snead

ON THIS DATE—

In 1952, the Britain-Ireland team won the Curtis Cup from the United States. The victory was the team's first since the series started in 1932.

CHIP SHOT

On a hot summer day at the 1986 Anheuser Busch Golf Classic, Bill Kratzert managed to lose three balls during play and had to withdraw from the event because he ran out of balls. His caddie, trying to lighten the golf bag, didn't bring any extra balls!

TRIVIA QUIZ—

Legal or illegal: After being struck, my ball accidentally hits my golf cart.

TODAY'S TIP—

A good cut shot will land the ball on the green, bounce once, and either stop or roll back. Use an open stance, and swing out to in, keeping your hands ahead of the ball.

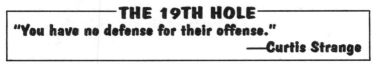

THE 19TH HOLE

"You have no defense for their offense."
—Curtis Strange

Quiz Answer: Illegal. It's a two-stroke penalty and I play the ball where it lies.

J U N E

TODAY'S THOUGHT:
"The wit of man has never invented a pastime equal to golf for its healthful recreation, its pleasurable excitement, and its never-ending source of amusement." —A.J. Balfour, British prime minister

ON THIS DATE—
In 1980, Sally Little won the first major of her career, taking the LPGA Championship. Little was the only golfer to finish under par for the tournament.

CHIP SHOT
Mary Queen of Scots was publicly criticized in 1567 for playing golf so soon after her husband was murdered. The critics said it showed a lack of decency.

TRIVIA QUIZ—
What Senior PGA Tour player holds the record for most consecutive years winning at least one tournament?

TODAY'S TIP—
Don't start the downswing with your hands. Proper hip rotation will allow the hands to follow naturally and will also improve your clubhead speed.

THE 19TH HOLE
"I'll be the better for this tournament. After all, a smooth sea never produced a skillful sailor."
—Mac O'Grady

Quiz Answer: Miller Barber did it nine straight years from 1981-1989.

JUNE

TODAY'S THOUGHT:

"Golf fans have a remarkable sixth sense that tells them what is happening elsewhere on the course, often a mile away. Some sort of telepathic wizardry takes place."   —Dan Hruby, writer

ON THIS DATE—

In 1991, Billy Andrade followed his career-first win at the Kemper Open with a two-stroke victory in the Buick Classic. Andrade took command with a one-under 34 over the back nine.

CHIP SHOT

An Australian tournament sponsor, a funeral director, once offered a prepaid funeral to anyone scoring an ace on a designated hole. Talk about a buried lie!

TRIVIA QUIZ—

True or false: Yale University has won the most NCAA Team Golf Championships.

TODAY'S TIP—

It may seem like a pause at the top of your swing, but it isn't. Your hips are turning to start the downsing. Pausing on purpose will disrupt the rhythm of your swing.

THE 19TH HOLE

"The trouble with golf is you're only as good as your last putt."   —Doug Sanders

Quiz Answer: True. Yale has won it 21 times.

J U N E

TODAY'S THOUGHT:

"Golf is so popular simply because it is the best game in the world at which to be bad." —A.A. Milne, writer

ON THIS DATE—

In 1977, Al Geiberger holed an eight-foot putt on the final hole of the second round of the Memphis Classic to become the first golfer to shoot a round of 59. Geiberger went on to win the tournament.

CHIP SHOT

The only videotape of Geiberger's round was destroyed in a fire at the TV station that had the filmed record.

TRIVIA QUIZ—

How is golfer J.C. Snead related to the great Sam Snead?

TODAY'S TIP—

At the top of your backswing, your right elbow should be pointing to the ground and your left knee should be pointed to the right of the ball. If not, you're hurting yourself by shortening your takeaway.

THE 19TH HOLE

"My caddie and I had a difference of opinion about which way the putt broke. He was wrong, but I'm the one who had to take the score." —Hale Irwin

Quiz Answer: J.C. is Sam's nephew.

JUNE

TODAY'S THOUGHT:
"The night I led the U.S. Open after the first round, I couldn't sleep, couldn't eat. I couldn't wait to get back to the golf course, so I could shoot seventy-three and let somebody else take the lead." —Jim Thorpe

ON THIS DATE—
In 1919, the first postwar U.S. Open was won by Walter Hagen in a playoff with Mike Brady. The Open had not been held in 1917 and '18.

CHIP SHOT
The night before the playoff, Hagen took a date to the theater and, later, they socialized with the star of the show, Al Jolson. Hagen faced Brady with less than three hours of sleep.

TRIVIA QUIZ—
I won the 1973 U. S. Open, the 1976 British Open, and was PGA Player of the Year in 1974. Who am I?

TODAY'S TIP—
Inexperienced golfers will cock their wrists too quickly during the takeaway. Your wrists don't begin to break until after passing the hips.

THE 19TH HOLE
"I never wanted to be a millionaire. I just wanted to live like one." —Walter Hagen

---

Quiz Answer: Johnny Miller.

J U N E

TODAY'S THOUGHT:
"The Open is simply the Kentucky Derby, the Indy 500, and the Rose Bowl of its sport." —Dan Jenkins, writer

ON THIS DATE—
In 1939, Byron Nelson won the only U.S. Open title of his career. The 26-year old Nelson beat Craig Wood in a playoff for the championship.

CHIP SHOT
In 1946, Nelson was in the hunt for his second U.S. Open title when his caddy lost his balance and kicked Nelson's ball. That cost Nelson a penalty stroke which came back to haunt him. He eventually lost the title in a three-way playoff.

TRIVIA QUIZ—
Who holds the PGA record for career holes-in-one?

TODAY'S TIP—
A square stance at address is very important. A stance too wide or narrow has an effect on your balance and can, in fact, restrict power. Keep your feet shoulder-width apart and aligned squarely at the target.

THE 19TH HOLE
"If I'da cleared the trees and drove the green, it woulda been a great tee shot." —Sam Snead

Quiz Answer: Art Wall, Jr. Wall aced 37 holes in his career.

J U N E

TODAY'S THOUGHT:
"The U.S. Open eliminates a lot of players. Some players just weren't made to win the U.S. Open. Quite often, a lot of them know it." —Jack Nicklaus

ON THIS DATE—
In 1953, Ben Hogan won his record-tying fourth U.S. Open. Only Bobby Jones and Willie Anderson had won four Opens to that point.

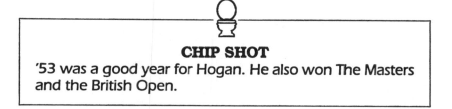

CHIP SHOT
'53 was a good year for Hogan. He also won The Masters and the British Open.

TRIVIA QUIZ—
You know that Ben Hogan, Bobby Jones, and Willie Anderson won four U.S. Opens. A fourth golfer has also done it. Who is it?

TODAY'S TIP—
By gripping the club in mid-air, you don't know if the face of the club is open or closed. To grip it properly, set it on the ground with the club head in a soled position and the club face square to the target.

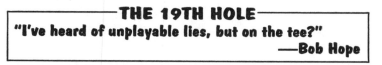

THE 19TH HOLE
"I've heard of unplayable lies, but on the tee?"
—Bob Hope

Quiz Answer: Jack Nicklaus, who won the tournament in 1962, '67, '72, and '80.

JUNE

TODAY'S THOUGHT:

"But when he saw a chance at the bacon hanging over the last green, he could put as much fire and fury into a finishing round of golf as Jack Dempsey could into a fight."
—Bobby Jones, on Gene Sarazen

ON THIS DATE—

In 1922, Gene Sarazen beat Emmet French, 4 & 3, to win the PGA Championship. It was the first of two straight titles for Sarazen. Born: Fred Funk (1956).

CHIP SHOT

The National Association of Left-Handed Golfers has over 1,250 members. It's headquartered in Houston, Texas.

TRIVIA QUIZ—

This golfer won nine tournaments in his rookie year, but is best remembered as the winner of the first Masters. Who is it?

TODAY'S TIP—

If all you see is the top of your ball sticking out of the sand, don't panic. Swing with the clubface closed and bring the club down directly behind the ball. The ball won't fly far, but it will come out running. Allow for plenty of roll.

THE 19TH HOLE

"We have so many small players out here on tour, that's why I look like Big Mama."
—JoAnne "Big Mama" Carner

Quiz Answer: Horton Smith.

J U N E

TODAY'S THOUGHT:
"Trying to catch Jack Nicklaus from eight shots back is like trying to climb Mt. Everest in street shoes." —Tom Kite

ON THIS DATE—
In 1980, Jack Nicklaus tied and broke records on the way to his fourth U.S. Open championship. His total of 272 broke his own record by three strokes. An opening round 63 tied the mark set by Johnny Miller.

CHIP SHOT
The sixth green at the Riviera CC in Los Angeles was designed with a bunker in the middle of it.

TRIVIA QUIZ—
Sam Trahan, Mike McGee, Kenny Knox, and Andy North share the record of 18 for the fewest in a round. Fewest what?

TODAY'S TIP—
Your set-up in the sand is as important as the shot. Dig your feet into the sand so your spikes take hold and you won't slip. Also, your feet will be below the ball. Play the ball off your left heel. Once you're set up, shorten up on the club and place your hands forward.

THE 19TH HOLE
"You drive for show and putt for dough." —Al Balding

Quiz Answer: Putts.

J U N E

TODAY'S THOUGHT:

"You must expect anything in golf. A stranger comes through, he's keen for a game, he seems affable enough, and on the eighth fairway he turns out to be an idiot."

—Alistair Cooke, writer

ON THIS DATE—

In 1968, Lee Trevino topped defending champ Jack Nicklaus by four strokes to win his first U.S. Open. Born: Phil Mickelson (1970).

CHIP SHOT

In that Open, Trevino shot rounds of 69, 68, 69, and 69 to become the first in Open history to play four sub-70 rounds.

TRIVIA QUIZ—

Name the only major championship Byron Nelson didn't win in his career.

TODAY'S TIP—

When you miss a putt, it's important to stay cool. To get the most out of your performance, never get overexcited after making a putt or disappointed after missing one. Instead, focus on your next shot.

THE 19TH HOLE

"At the 1968 U.S. Open, I was trying to get so far ahead I could choke and still win."   —Lee Trevino

Quiz Answer: Nelson never won the British Open.

J U N E

TODAY'S THOUGHT:
"Nobody wins the Open. It wins you."
— Dr. Cary Middlecoff, on the U.S. Open

ON THIS DATE—
In 1973, Johnny Miller shot a final round 63 at the Oakmont CC to come from six strokes back to win the U.S. Open. Twenty-one years later to the day, at the same course, Arnold Palmer announced his retirement from big-time golf, saying he would still play in an occasional tournament.

CHIP SHOT
Palmer, one of four golfers overcome by Miller's record round, was introduced to championship golf at Oakmont in 1942 at the age of 12.

TRIVIA QUIZ—
Why do we call Cary Middlecoff, "Doctor"?

TODAY'S TIP—
To chip from high grass stand closer to the ball. With the toe of the club down and the heel of the club raised, the shaft will be vertical allowing a normal stroke to putt the chip.

THE 19TH HOLE
"Short putts test the character of the golfer. Long putts test the patience of the other golfers in his foursome."
—Anonymous

Quiz Answer: Before turning pro in 1947, Middlecoff was a dentist. He served in the Army Dental Corps during World War II.

JUNE

TODAY'S THOUGHT:
"If you can't outplay them, outwork them."   —Ben Hogan

ON THIS DATE—
In 1960, Arnie's Army got bigger as Arnold Palmer came from seven strokes back to win his first U.S. Open. Twenty-year old U.S. Amateur champion, Jack Nicklaus, finished two strokes back.

CHIP SHOT
Nicklaus' playing partner for that final round was 47-year old Ben Hogan. Hogan finished two strokes behind Nicklaus.

TRIVIA QUIZ—
This woman was the leading money winner on the LPGA Tour a record eight times. Do you know who she is?

TODAY'S TIP—
Always allow the loft of the club to lift your ball. Resist hitting chip shots with a "scoop" action. Rather, you should putt your chips. You don't have to guide the ball into the air, let the club do it for you.

THE 19TH HOLE
"Jack Nicklaus is a real live wire. His idea of fun is to sit home on a Saturday night with a glass of hot cocoa singing Ohio State fight songs."
                                    —Don Rickles, comedian

Quiz Answer: Kathy Whitworth, who earned $1,719,804 in her career.

JUNE

TODAY'S THOUGHT:
"The Lord answers my prayers everywhere except on the golf course." —Reverend Billy Graham

ON THIS DATE—
In 1954, nearly 40,000 people were on hand at Baltusrol to watch Ed Furgol finish one stroke ahead of Gene Littler to win the U.S. Open.

CHIP SHOT
Besides being the first tournament to rope off the fairways, the '54 championship was the first to be televised nationally.

TRIVIA QUIZ—
Only one golfer has been able to win two straight U.S. Opens at Baltusrol GC. Who is it?

TODAY'S TIP—
The idea of a chip shot is to get the ball safely on the green so it can roll. Keep your swing compact with very little follow-through. Overswing, and your ball will go off-line.

THE 19TH HOLE
"Heck, I wish they'd make the gallery ropes out of bounds. We're the only sport that plays in the audience."
—Lee Trevino

Quiz Answer: Jack Nicklaus, who won the championship at Baltusrol in 1967 and the next time it was held there in 1980.

J U N E

TODAY'S THOUGHT:

"Golf is a game of expletives not deleted."
—Irving A. Gladstone, writer

ON THIS DATE—

In 1964, Ken Venturi overcame 100 degree temperatures to win his first major at the U.S. Open. Thirty years later to the day, Ernie Els won the Open for his first victory in a major championship.

CHIP SHOT

Venturi was treated for heat prostration between rounds at the Congressional Club in Washington, D.C. The following year the USGA changed the format of the tournament to one round per day.

TRIVIA QUIZ—

Name the state where Shinnecock Hills GC, host to three U.S. Opens, is located.

TODAY'S TIP—

Overanalyzing your putting stroke will disrupt its natural flow. Instead, just remember one thing: hit the middle of the ball with the middle of the putter's face.

THE 19TH HOLE

"I may not be the prettiest girl in the world, but I'd like to see Bo Derek look like a 10' after playing 18 holes of golf in 100-degree weather."   —Jan Stephenson

Quiz Answer: New York. More precisely, Southampton, NY.

J U N E

TODAY'S THOUGHT:
"I've been out here fourteen years and I've never played in a U.S. Open. Jack Nicklaus points his year toward the major championships. I point away from them." —Gary McCord

ON THIS DATE—
In 1981, David Graham became the first Australian to win the U.S. Open. Graham, with 273, was one stroke shy of Jack Nicklaus' record for the event.

CHIP SHOT
Woodrow Wilson was on the golf course in 1915 when he was informed of the sinking of the *Lusitania*. He immediately returned to the White House.

TRIVIA QUIZ—
True or false: Senior PGA Tour golfer Jay Sigel never played on the regular Tour, but did win two U.S. Amateur titles.

TODAY'S TIP—
Unless you're Davis Love III, it might be a good idea to shorten up a bit on your grip. You'll sacrifice distance for accuracy and control. Go one club lower to regain the distance.

THE 19TH HOLE
"I'm allergic to grass. Hey, it could be worse. I could be allergic to beer." —Greg Norman

Quiz Answer: True. He was top amateur in 1982 and '83.

J U N E

TODAY'S THOUGHT:
"I called my neighbor, who is an avid golfer in the sense that if he had to choose between playing golf and achieving world peace, he'd want to know how many holes."
—Dave Barry, writer

ON THIS DATE—
In 1958, Patty Berg was the winner, once again, at the Western Open. It marked the seventh time that Berg had won the LPGA major.

CHIP SHOT
Real golfers don't cry when they line up their fourth putt.

TRIVIA QUIZ—
Patty Berg was one of four founders of the LPGA. Can you name the other three?

TODAY'S TIP—
When faced with a long putt, don't be too concerned with the hole. Pick a spike mark as your target. A quick look at the hole could cause you to push or pull the ball.

THE 19TH HOLE
"I'm so busy I can only play in one tournament at a time."   —Jack Nicklaus

Quiz Answer: Betty Jameson, Louise Suggs, and Babe Zaharias, along with Berg, formed the LPGA in 1950.

J U N E

TODAY'S THOUGHT:
"I'm not like these young stars. I just throw some junk in the air and hope it stays out of the rough and eventually gets to the green." —Julius Boros

ON THIS DATE—
In 1963, Arnold Palmer lost a playoff at the U.S. Open for the second straight year. Julius Boros beat Palmer and Jacky Cupit over 18 holes to win the championship, his second. Born: Simon Hobday (1940); Colin Montgomerie (1963).

CHIP SHOT
To mark the 50th anniversary of Francis Ouimet's victory over Harry Vardon and Ted Ray, the Open returned to the site of that event, the Brookline CC in Massachusetts.

TRIVIA QUIZ—
Who was the first golfer to successfully defend her title at the U.S. Women's Open?

TODAY'S TIP—
If your ball is stopped against the collar of a green, use your sand wedge to putt the ball. Play the ball back in your stance and shift your weight to the left.

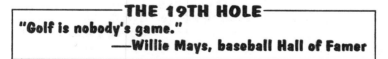

THE 19TH HOLE
"Golf is nobody's game."
——Willie Mays, baseball Hall of Famer

Quiz Answer: Mickey Wright, who won in 1958 and '59.

JUNE

TODAY'S THOUGHT:
"These younger players all think they're so much better. Good grief. Maybe they are." —Shelley Hamlin

ON THIS DATE—
In 1968, Sandra Post became the first rookie to win the LPGA Championship. Born: Billy Casper (1931); Loren Roberts (1955); Juli Inkster (1960).

CHIP SHOT
The original plans for Augusta National included a par-three 19th hole, where the loser of a match could try to recoup his losses in a double-or-nothing bet. It was never built.

TRIVIA QUIZ—
Can you name the famous four courses that are clustered on the Monterey (CA) peninsula?

TODAY'S TIP—
Sometimes courtesy is not the intention when your partner always lifts the flag from the hole. He could be pacing off the distance of his own putt.

—THE 19TH HOLE—
"I can't describe how I feel. It's the greatest thing in the world to win a professional golf tournament especially if you're a professional golfer."
—Dave Eichelberger

Quiz Answer: Cypress Point, Pebble Beach, Monterey Peninsula, and Spyglass Hill.

JUNE

TODAY'S THOUGHT:

"This putting is wicked. It is sinful."
—James Braid, five-time British Open winner

ON THIS DATE—

In 1921, Jock Hutchinson became the first American to win the British Open. Hutchinson, who was St. Andrews born and bred, had moved to Chicago twenty years earlier.

CHIP SHOT

Bobby Jones made his first appearance at the Open that year, but played so poorly that he quit in the middle of the third round.

TRIVIA QUIZ—

Can you name the two golf courses where the most British Opens have been held?.

TODAY'S TIP—

Putting can be tough enough, so don't make it harder for yourself by hitting your putts too hard. A fast-moving putt will only fall into the hole if it hits dead center. Don't make the hole smaller!

THE 19TH HOLE

"There's nothing wrong with the St. Andrews course that a few hundred bulldozers couldn't put right."
—Ed Furgol

Quiz Answer: St. Andrews and the Prestwick Golf Course.

J U N E

TODAY'S THOUGHT:

"Eighteen holes of match play will teach you more about your foe than 19 years of dealing with him across a desk."
—Grantland Rice, writer

ON THIS DATE—

In 1914, Babe Didrikson was born. The Texas native went on to win ten major golf championships.

CHIP SHOT

Didrickson was a versatile athlete. In addition to golf she excelled in track and field, winning gold medals in the 800-meter hurdles and the javelin throw in the 1932 Olympics.

TRIVIA QUIZ—

Besides Jack Nicklaus, what other golfer won two Masters during the 1970's?

TODAY'S TIP—

Looking at the ball position too long after impact can cause your head to be lifted by the body as it unwinds. Swivel your head sideways without lifting so the body swings under it.

━━━THE 19TH HOLE━━━

"Look at him! When I married him, he was a Greek god. Now he's a big fat Greek."   —Babe, on husband, and former pro wrestler, Gorgeous George Zaharias

Quiz Answer: Gary Player won it in 1974 and '78.

J U N E

TODAY'S THOUGHT:

"The founders of the game accepted nature for what it gave, or took away. Wind and rain are great challenges. They separate real golfers." —Tom Watson

ON THIS DATE—

In 1975, Lee Trevino, Jerry Heard, and Bobby Nichols were struck by lightning during the second round of the Western Open. Only Heard was able to return to play, finishing fourth in the tournament.

CHIP SHOT

A golfer blames fate for his bogies, but when he makes a birdie, he's personally responsible.

TRIVIA QUIZ—

What does the phrase "through the green" mean?

TODAY'S TIP—

On a slow green, use a short, wristy stroke so the ball pops off your blade and the grain won't misdirect the ball.

THE 19TH HOLE

"Hold up a one-iron and walk. Even God can't hit a one-iron." —Lee Trevino, on how to deal with lightning

---

Quiz Answer: It means the entire golf course except the teeing ground, the putting green, and all hazards. Out-of-bounds is, of course, not considered to be part of the course.

J U N E

TODAY'S THOUGHT:
"If you're stupid enough to whiff, you should be smart enough to forget it." —Arnold Palmer

ON THIS DATE—
In 1992, Gibby Gilbert won a golf tournament for the first time since 1977. Gilbert went wire-to-wire to take the Southwestern Bell Classic on the Senior PGA Tour.

CHIP SHOT
Players at the Kampala Golf Club in Uganda are cautioned to avoid the water hazards on 10 of the 18 holes because of crocodiles.

TRIVIA QUIZ—
This golfer won the U.S. Amateur in 1974 and, two years later, was the U.S. Open champion. Name him.

TODAY'S TIP—
A sidehill shot with the ball below your feet will fade. Grip the club close to the end, flex your knees, balance on your heels, stay down, and aim left of the hole. Swing compactly.

THE 19TH HOLE
"The Senior Tour is like a class reunion. It's the same as it was thirty years ago. We tell the same dirty jokes only they're funnier now." —Bob Toski

Quiz Answer: Jerry Pate.

JUNE

TODAY'S THOUGHT:

"You win because you are the last one to fall on your face."
—Val Skinner

ON THIS DATE—

In 1957, Jacqueline Pung's worst nightmare came true. Pung was low scorer at the U.S. Women's Open, but signed an incorrect scorecard. Betsy Rawls was declared the winner.

CHIP SHOT

Spectators, feeling sorry for Pung, passed the hat and collected $3,000 for her, $1,200 more than the first prize.

TRIVIA QUIZ—

How frequently are the Ryder Cup matches held?

TODAY'S TIP—

When playing a long-iron keep the ball forward in your stance. You want to be able to sweep the clubhead through instead of hitting down at the ball. Swing at the same tempo you would with a wood.

THE 19TH HOLE

"The only thing worse than missing a cut is missing a cut and staying in the same town. That's torture. That's like staying at the scene of the crime."

—Joey Sindelar

Quiz Answer: Ryder Cup matches are held every other year on a home-and-home basis.

J U N E

TODAY'S THOUGHT:
"There's something haunting about getting up at dawn and walking a golf course, checking pin placements. It's easy to lose track of reality." —Ernest "Creamy" Carolan, caddie

ON THIS DATE—
In 1991, Meg Mallon dropped in a ten-foot birdie putt on the final hole of the LPGA Championship to win her first major title. Born: Roger Maltbie (1951).

CHIP SHOT
R.J. Jackson designed a three-wheel, gas-powered golf cart called the Arthritis Special. The driver's seat was a park bench, and the cart could carry four sets of clubs. However, only three golfers could fit on the seat.

TRIVIA QUIZ—
The lowest scoring average for a season by an LPGA player is 70.73 strokes. Who did it?

TODAY'S TIP—
Moving the ball back in your stance is not the only thing to do if you want to hit a lower shot. Make sure you move your hands back in proportion to the ball placement.

THE 19TH HOLE
"Golf is a game in which you yell *'fore'*, shoot six, and write down five."
——Paul Harvey, commentator and writer

Quiz Answer: Nancy Lopez in 1985.

J U L Y

TODAY'S THOUGHT:

"Anyone who criticizes a golf course is like a person invited to a house for dinner who, on leaving, tells the host that the food was lousy." —Gary Player

ON THIS DATE—

In 1961, Mickey Wright won her third U.S. Women's Open title in four years, beating defending champ Betsy Rawls by six strokes. Wright was the only golfer to finish under par.

CHIP SHOT

The 107 yard, par-3 seventh hole at Pebble Beach GL is the shortest hole on the PGA Tour.

TRIVIA QUIZ—

Only one of the major championships on the PGA Tour is held at the same golf course every year. Which one?

TODAY'S TIP—

If you're just off of the green and decide to putt your ball through the fringe, keep your head still. That way you'll resist the tendency to put any body movement into the shot.

THE 19TH HOLE

"Chris, the boys are hitting the ball longer now because they're getting more distance."
—Byron Nelson, to Chris Schenkel

Quiz Answer: The Masters, which is held every April at Augusta National Golf Club.

J U L Y

TODAY'S THOUGHT:
"Every day I try to tell myself this is going to be fun today. I try to put myself in a great frame of mind before I go out - then I screw it up with the first shot."   —Johnny Miller

ON THIS DATE—
In 1967, Catherine Lacoste of France became the first and only amateur to take the U.S. Women's Open. Lacoste won despite shooting ten-over-par.

CHIP SHOT
The Chicago Golf Course in Wheaton, Illinois was the first 18-hole golf course. It was built in 1894.

TRIVIA QUIZ—
True or false: PGA Tour players Scott Simpson and Craig Stadler both attended the University of Southern California.

TODAY'S TIP—
Remember, the heavier the club, the stronger you have to be to control it. So select your clubs to match your physique. Less powerful swingers can achieve distance and accuracy with lighter clubs because, with more control, they can get the square impact they need for a long, straight drive.

THE 19TH HOLE
"Some players would complain if they were playing on Dolly Parton's bedspread."   —Jimmy Demaret

Quiz Answer: True.

J U L Y

TODAY'S THOUGHT:
"There's an old saying: If a man comes home with sand in his cuffs and cockleburs in his pants, don't ask him what he shot."

—Sam Snead

ON THIS DATE—
In 1951, Sam Snead won the third PGA Championship of his career, beating Walter Burkemo, 7 & 6. Burkemo's turn came two years later when he won the title.

CHIP SHOT
The average PGA Tour caddie is paid $300-$400 a week plus 6 percent of his player's winnings. It can go as high as 10 percent if the player wins the tournament.

TRIVIA QUIZ—
Four players have shot a round of 63 in the PGA Championship. How many can you name?

TODAY'S TIP—
One school of thought believes you should use only one ball when practicing putting. Why? Better concentration than if you were putting one ball after another.

THE 19TH HOLE
"Do you think he can get there?" "Yes. If he can hit it far enough."

——Exchange between two TV announcers

Quiz Answer: Bruce Crampton, 1975; Raymond Floyd, 1982; Gary Player, 1984; and, Vijay Singh, 1993.

JULY

TODAY'S THOUGHT:

"Golf is twenty percent mechanics and technique. The other eighty percent is philosophy, humor, tragedy, romance, melodrama, companionship, camaraderie, cussedness, and conversation."

—Grantland Rice

ON THIS DATE—

In 1965, Carol Mann picked up the only major title of her career, shooting four-under-par to win the U.S. Women's Open.

CHIP SHOT

Golf is a game which separates the men from the poise.

TRIVIA QUIZ—

Two golfers have won the Vare Trophy for low scoring average on the LPGA Tour five times. Who are they?

TODAY'S TIP—

Practice your short game three times more than the long game. Experts will tell you that improving your putting and chipping will knock the strokes right off your game.

THE 19TH HOLE

"What does it matter who Orville Moody is? At least he brought the title back to America."
—Dave Marr, after Moody succeeeded Lee Trevino as U.S. Open champion in 1969

Quiz Answer: Mickey Wright and JoAnne Carner. Kathy Whitworth holds the record of seven times.

JULY

TODAY'S THOUGHT:

"One reward golf has given me, and I shall always be thankful for it, is introducing me to some of the world's most picturesque, tireless, and bald-faced liars." —Rex Lardner, writer

ON THIS DATE—

In 1970, Donna Caponi became only the second golfer to defend her title in the U.S. Women's Open. Caponi edged Sandra Haynie and Sandra Spuzich despite a double-bogey on the last hole.

CHIP SHOT

Hollywood stars presented the golfers to the gallery when Los Angeles hosted the PGA Championship in 1929. Actress Fay Wray introduced Walter Hagen as "the Opium Champion of Great Britain."

TRIVIA QUIZ—

True or false: Byron Nelson won the 1943 U.S. Open.

TODAY'S TIP—

If your lie is on hard sand, the club of choice should be a 9-iron or pitching wedge. Hard sand will cause a sand wedge to bounce, while the others will cut through the sand.

THE 19TH HOLE

"Every time I have the urge to play golf I lie down until the urge passes." —Sam Levenson, humorist

Quiz Answer: False. The 1943 Open was canceled because of World War II.

J U L Y

TODAY'S THOUGHT:
"In other games you get another chance. In baseball you get three cracks at it; in tennis you lose only one point. But in golf the loss of one shot has been responsible for the loss of heart."

—Tommy Armour

ON THIS DATE—
In 1959, two Hall of Famers battled to the end at the LPGA Championship. Betsy Rawls won her first title, beating Patty Berg in the only major Berg never won in her career. Born: Lauri Merten (1960).

CHIP SHOT
Real golfers never question their client's score.

TRIVIA QUIZ—
Legal or illegal: I swing at a ball and top it. When it's in the air my club strikes it a second time.

TODAY'S TIP—
When you need a high shot, set the ball slightly forward in your stance and open the clubface a bit. Uncock your wrists through impact, stay behind the ball, and allow for a fade.

THE 19TH HOLE
"I am going to win so much money this year my caddie will make the top twenty money-winners list."

—Lee Trevino

Quiz Answer: Illegal with a one-stroke penalty. If I was lying three before the first swing, I now lie five.

JULY

TODAY'S THOUGHT:

"The person I fear in the last two rounds is myself." —Tom Watson

ON THIS DATE—

In 1994, PGA Tour veteran Bob Lohr fired a 10-underpar 61 in the opening round of the Anheuser-Busch Golf Classic. The only scores better than the 61 were the 59's of Al Geiberger and Chip Beck and nine rounds of 60.

CHIP SHOT

In 1973, Arthur Thompson shot a round of 103 at the Uplands Golf Course in British Columbia. Not bad for a man who was 103 years old.

TRIVIA QUIZ—

Name the golf club that hosted the first U.S. Open in 1895.

TODAY'S TIP—

Need less than a full swing, but afraid of letting up and missing the shot? Shorten the swing, not the power. Choke down on the club and hit away as hard as usual. Choking down will also give you better feel.

THE 19TH HOLE

"Every driver has its own personality. I am looking for one that matches my own." —Morris Hatalsky

Quiz Answer: The Newport (RI) Golf Club.

JULY

TODAY'S THOUGHT:
"There are no points for style when it comes to putting. It's getting the ball to drop that counts." —Brian Swarbrick, writer

ON THIS DATE—
In 1976, Fuzzy Zoeller was red-hot as he fired off eight consecutive birdies in the first round of the Quad Cities Open. Zoeller shot a 63 for the round.

CHIP SHOT
Only one golfer has shot two holes-in-one in British Open competition. Charles Ward aced the eighth at St. Andrews in 1946 and, two years later, shot a hole-in-one on the 13th at Muirfield.

TRIVIA QUIZ—
In what decade did the Walker Cup matches begin?

TODAY'S TIP—
If you don't start your downswing with the feet and knees, the weight will remain on your right side and your legs will stiffen. As a result, you'll raise your body up as the club swings down, causing a bad shot.

THE 19TH HOLE
"I'd like to see the fairways more narrow. Then everybody would have to play from the rough, not just me."
—Seve Ballesteros

Quiz Answer: The 1920's. The first Walker Cup match was held in 1922.

J U L Y

TODAY'S THOUGHT:
"I enjoyed playing in the last group behind Jack Nicklaus. Only trouble was the tournament director kept taking the pins off the greens once Nicklaus played through." —Lou Graham

ON THIS DATE—
In 1966, Jack Nicklaus conquered Muirfield to win his first British Open. With the win Nicklaus joined an elite club of Gene Sarazen, Ben Hogan, and Gary Player as the only men to win all four majors.

CHIP SHOT
Nicklaus was a member of the 1959 Walker Cup team when he made his only previous visit to Muirfield. He won all his matches.

TRIVIA QUIZ—
Who has won more British Open titles, Jack Nicklaus or Gary Player?

TODAY'S TIP—
For more accuracy on your iron shots, make sure your shoulder comes down under your chin as you start down toward the ball.

THE 19TH HOLE
"If a great swing put you high on the money list, there'd be some of us who would be broke."
—Raymond Floyd

Quiz Answer: Both have won three British Open championships.

JULY

TODAY'S THOUGHT:
"What is it when the forty-footers drop? It's magic. When they stop, that's just the other side of the razor's edge. It's the game. That's why it's so brutal."   —George Archer

ON THIS DATE—
In 1971, Lee Trevino's hot streak continued with a victory in the British Open. In a 19-day stretch Trevino had won the Open, the U.S. Open, and the Canadian Open.

CHIP SHOT
American J.J. McDermott wanted to play in the 1914 British Open, but when he arrived in England, he discovered that he was a week late for qualifying. McDermott showed up at the course the day qualifying rounds were completed.

TRIVIA QUIZ—
I am the only U.S. Junior Amateur champion to go on and win the U.S. Open. These days, the bulk of my work is done behind a microphone instead of behind a putter. Who am I?

TODAY'S TIP—
In wet conditions, your ball will spin less and fly lower and longer. Because the greens will hold better when wet, use one less club than usual.

THE 19TH HOLE
"You can talk to a fade, but a hook won't listen."
—Lee Trevino

Quiz Answer: Johnny Miller.

JULY

TODAY'S THOUGHT:

"You may cry in victory, but don't ever cry in defeat again."
—Mrs. Venturi, Ken's mom

ON THIS DATE—

In 1993, Tom Weiskopf was back in Jack Nicklaus' shadow again. Weiskopf, a two-time runner-up to Nicklaus in The Masters, was one stroke behind as the Golden Bear won the U.S. Senior Open.

CHIP SHOT

Craig Wood won the 1941 U.S. Open, but was unable to defend his title for five years. After America entered WW II, the USGA canceled all championships for the duration of the war.

TRIVIA QUIZ—

Who was the first LPGA golfer to earn over $100,000 in a season?

TODAY'S TIP—

Most pros wear a glove for every shot they hit, except putting. The reason is feel. You'll probably gain more putting feel by putting without a golf glove for that critical extra touch on the green.

THE 19TH HOLE

"If I knew what was going through Jack Nicklaus's head, I would have won this golf tournament."
—Tom Weiskopf, after the 1986 Masters

Quiz Answer: Judy Rankin, who earned $150,734 in 1976.

J U L Y

TODAY'S THOUGHT:

"Don't make it happen, let it happen."
—Bob Rotella, sports psychologist

ON THIS DATE—

In 1930, Bobby Jones became the first golfer to break par in the U.S. Open and, as a result, won his fourth Open title. It was his third major championship on his march to the Grand Slam. Born: Paul Runyan (1908).

CHIP SHOT

Jones was feeling the pressure of the Grand Slam. During that Open, Jones lost 14 pounds.

TRIVIA QUIZ—

What is Paul Runyan's claim to fame, other than winning the PGA Championship two times?

TODAY'S TIP—

When faced with a fairway wood shot out of the rough, minimize the amount of grass between the ball and clubface at impact. Stand a little closer to the ball, pick up the club quicker on the backswing, and hit down sharply on the downswing.

THE 19TH HOLE

It's always hard to sleep when you've got a big early lead. You just lay there and smile at the ceiling all night." —Dave Stockton

Quiz Answer: Runyan was the PGA Tour's first official leading money-winner. He took in $6,767 in 1934.

J U L Y

TODAY'S THOUGHT:
"After taking the stance, it is too late to worry. The only thing to do then is to hit the ball."   —Bobby Jones

ON THIS DATE—
In 1980, Amy Alcott fought off 100-degree temperatures in Nashville to win the U.S. Women's Open. Alcott finished nine strokes ahead of the field.

CHIP SHOT
The only time a son succeeded a father as champion of a major was when Old Tom Morris won the 1867 British Open and Young Tom Morris won the title in 1868.

TRIVIA QUIZ—
True or false: Byron Nelson won the first Byron Nelson Golf Classic.

TODAY'S TIP—
If your ball is in a hardpan lie, play it back, open your stance, and keep the left hand firm through impact.

THE 19TH HOLE
"I've thrown or broken a few clubs in my day. In fact, I guess at one time or another I probably held distance records for every club in the bag."   —Tommy Bolt

Quiz Answer: False. Miller Barber won it in 1968. The event was known as the Dallas Classic before the name change in '68. Nelson won the first Dallas Classic in 1944.

JULY

TODAY'S THOUGHT:

"I never had a good bounce. All I ever had were bad ones."
—Arnold Palmer

ON THIS DATE—

In 1991, two weeks after winning the LPGA Championship, Meg Mallon fired three birdies on the back nine on her way to winning the U.S. Women's Open. Born: Brett Ogle (1964).

CHIP SHOT

If your dream is to see The Masters in person, wake up. The waiting list for tickets was closed in 1978.

TRIVIA QUIZ—

You're my caddie as I play the back nine of the British Open. I ask for my "jigger." What club do you hand me?

TODAY'S TIP—

Try this drill if you're struggling with your swing. Tee up 10 balls in a line. Using a 5-iron, address the first ball and swing through. Take two small steps forward, swing back to the top and hit the second ball. Continue until you've hit all 10 balls. The idea is to focus on rhythm and tempo.

THE 19TH HOLE
"I played so bad, I got a get-well card from the IRS."
—Johnny Miller, on his 1977 season

Quiz Answer: The 4-iron.

J U L Y

TODAY'S THOUGHT:

"Advice is seldom welcome. Those who need it the most always like it the least."   —The Earl of Chesterfield

ON THIS DATE—

In 1923, Bobby Jones finally put his name on the list of major tournament winners with a victory in the U.S. Open. The 21-year old amateur edged Bobby Cruikshank by two strokes in a playoff for the first major championship of his career.

CHIP SHOT

Jones was a grizzled veteran of major tournaments despite his young age. He had been trying for a major since the age of 14.

TRIVIA QUIZ—

Was Nick Faldo the first golfer to use a female caddie while playing in The Masters?

TODAY'S TIP—

Common sense will help prevent extra strokes on the green. Check the line of your putt to see if there are any pebbles, ball marks, or twigs that could throw the ball off line.

THE 19TH HOLE

"I deny allegations by Bob Hope that during my last game I hit an eagle, a birdie, an elk, and a moose."
—Gerald Ford

Quiz Answer: No. George Archer's daughter caddied for him in the 1983 tournament.

J U L Y

TODAY'S THOUGHT:
"Golf is a nonviolent game played violently from within."
—Bob Toski

ON THIS DATE—
In 1993, Nick Faldo shattered the course record at Royal St. George's in the second round of the British Open. Faldo's 63 was three strokes better than anyone else could manage on the course in that tournament.

CHIP SHOT
A golf cart is started and stopped an average of 150 times during a round of golf.

TRIVIA QUIZ—
Of the four major championships, what is the only one Walter Hagen didn't win in his career?

TODAY'S TIP—
If the sand is firm, the lie is clean, and the lip is low, you may want to chip, rather than explode, out of a greenside bunker. Set up a wide stance with the ball back slightly. With your hands ahead of the ball, hit the ball crisply using little wrist action, making sure to hit the ball before the sand.

THE 19TH HOLE
"Never bet with anyone you meet on the first tee who has a deep suntan, a one-iron in his bag, and squinty eyes."   —Dave Marr

Quiz Answer: Hagen never won The Masters.

J U L Y

TODAY'S THOUGHT:

"The terrible thing about a missed shot in golf is that the thing is done, irrevocably, irretrievably. Perhaps that is why golf is so great a game; it is so much like the game of life. We don't have the shots over in either."   —O.B. Keeler, writer

ON THIS DATE—

In 1955, Beverly Hanson won the first LPGA Championship. Louise Suggs was three strokes behind in second place.

CHIP SHOT

My golf game has been so bad, I'm just gonna buy a bucket of balls and practice my drop.

TRIVIA QUIZ—

What's a stymie?

TODAY'S TIP—

Practice wedge shots by bringing the club back no farther than waist high. Cock your wrists so the club is pointing straight up and start the downswing, accelerating through the ball.

THE 19TH HOLE

"You know the economy is bad when you have to wait one hour to tee off because 100 people are grazing on the greens."   —Johnny Carson

Quiz Answer: An intentional putt between an opponent's ball and the hole without marking the ball. Thus, the opponent is forced to putt around the ball. The shot was outlawed in 1951.

J U L Y

TODAY'S THOUGHT:
"It's a silly game where nobody wins."
—Thomas Fuller, writer, on golf

ON THIS DATE—
In 1993, Greg Norman, playing the best golf of his life, captured his second British Open title. Norman's four-round score of 267 was the lowest score in the championship's 122 years. Born: Calvin Peete (1943); Bruce Lietzke (1951).

CHIP SHOT
Until Norman's victory, only one other winner had broken par in twelve Opens held at Royal St. George's. Spectators also saw Nick Faldo and Payne Stewart shoot record rounds of 63.

TRIVIA QUIZ—
Name the two golfers Fuzzy Zoeller beat in a playoff to win the 1979 Masters.

TODAY'S TIP—
Losing your hold on the club with your right hand at the top of the swing forces you to regrip on the way down. Place a blade of grass between the right thumb pad and the base of the left thumb. Practice full shots, making sure to keep the right hand firm to keep the blade of grass from falling out.

THE 19TH HOLE
"I owe a lot to my parents, especially my mother and father."   —Greg Norman

Quiz Answer: Ed Sneed and Tom Watson.

J U L Y

TODAY'S THOUGHT:
"I thank the press from the heart of my, well, bottom."
—Nick Faldo, after the 1992 British Open

ON THIS DATE—
In 1992, Nick Faldo squandered a four-stroke lead, but came back to win his third British Open. Faldo survived despite shooting a final round two-over-par 73.

CHIP SHOT
The golf clubs of Presidents Warren Harding, William Howard Taft, Franklin D. Roosevelt, and Woodrow Wilson are on display at the Burning Tree Club in Bethesda, MD.

TRIVIA QUIZ—
In the 1980's, two Englishmen won their home Open. Name them.

TODAY'S TIP—
Slowing down at impact with a long iron produces slices. It's important that you make sure your hands accelerate through the impact area.

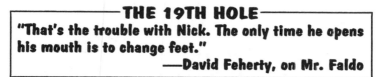

THE 19TH HOLE
"That's the trouble with Nick. The only time he opens his mouth is to change feet."
—David Feherty, on Mr. Faldo

Quiz Answer: Sandy Lyle, who won in 1985, and Nick Faldo, who took home the title in 1987.

J U L Y

TODAY'S THOUGHT:

"Golf is just the old-fashioned pool hall moved outdoors, but with no chairs around the walls." —Will Rogers

ON THIS DATE—

In 1958, Dow Finsterwald won the first PGA Championship conducted as a stroke play event. For 39 years, the tournament called for match play.

CHIP SHOT

Only one golfer has won the PGA Championship more than two times since it moved to stroke play. Jack Nicklaus has done it five times.

TRIVIA QUIZ—

Name the other golfer who, like Nicklaus, won the PGA Championship five times.

TODAY'S TIP—

A good takeaway is important to getting the clubhead on a good backswing path. For a good takeaway, pick out a spot about a foot directly behind the ball. Concentrate on swinging the club back directly over that spot, and let the arms take their natural course into the backswing.

THE 19TH HOLE

"Any game where a man 60 can beat a man 30 ain't no game." —Burt Shotten, baseball manager

---

Quiz Answer: Walter Hagen.

JULY

TODAY'S THOUGHT:
"Golf's like life with the volume turned up."   —Mike Reid

ON THIS DATE—
In 1991, Ian Baker-Finch left nothing to chance in winning his first British Open. The 31-year old Australian birdied five of the first seven holes on his way to the title. Born: Gene Littler (1930).

CHIP SHOT
Richard Boxall was only three strokes behind the leaders when he stepped to the ninth tee in the third round. Boxall broke his leg while swinging and had to withdraw. His final tee shot, ironically, was right down the middle.

TRIVIA QUIZ—
In the 1983 British Open, this American missed a three-inch putt and eventually lost the championship by one stroke. Who was it?

TODAY'S TIP—
Don't let your head and eyes drift backward as you take the club back. Make sure you focus on the back of the ball during the entire swing.

THE 19TH HOLE
"I wish my name was Tom Kite."
             —Ian Baker-Finch, on signing autographs

Quiz Answer: Hale Irwin. He tried to tap the ball in with a backhand stroke...and missed it.

J U L Y

TODAY'S THOUGHT:
"Indeed, the highest pleasure of golf may be that on the fairways and far from all the pressures of commerce and rationality, we can feel immortal for a few hours."   —Coleman McCarthy, writer

ON THIS DATE—
In 1984, Kathy Whitworth earned her 85th career win at the Rochester Open. The victory pushed her past Sam Snead as golf's winningest player.

CHIP SHOT
Between 1958 and 1978, Arnold Palmer, Jack Nicklaus, and Gary Player won 38 percent of the 84 major championships played.

TRIVIA QUIZ—
This golfer won a Purple Heart for his efforts during the Battle of the Bulge and, after World War II, came home and won the 1946 U.S. Open. Do you know his name?

TODAY'S TIP—
When faced with a green that slopes away from you, it's not necessary to land on the green with your approach shot. Hit your shot so that it lands in front and bounces onto the green.

THE 19TH HOLE
"If you could get the digging rights to Sam's backyard, you'd never have to work again in your life."
   —Doug Sanders, on Snead's legendary thriftiness

Quiz Answer: Lloyd Mangrum.

J U L Y

TODAY'S THOUGHT:

"In tennis, you're too busy running around to get shaky. But in golf, that little white ball just sits there. A man can beat himself before he ever swings at it." —Ellsworth Vines, tennis champ turned golfer

ON THIS DATE—

In 1960, Betsy Rawls won her record-setting fourth U.S. Women's Open. Eighteen years later to the day, Hollis Stacy won her second straight Open. Born: Ken Green (1958).

CHIP SHOT

Jo Ann Washam is the only golfer to ace two holes in the same LPGA tournament. Washam did it in the second and final rounds of the 1979 Women's Kemper Open.

TRIVIA QUIZ—

Name the last golfer to successfully defend her U.S. Women's Open title.

TODAY'S TIP—

To hit a high pitch shot that stops quickly, grip the club lightly with soft hands. Allow the club to swing back and through while keeping that grip. The clubface will remain open and the shot will fly high and land softly.

THE 19TH HOLE

"Hollis Stacy, shirttail hanging out, hair blowing in the wind, dragging on a cigarette. That's sex appeal."
—Arnold Palmer

Quiz Answer: Betsy King, who won in 1989 and '90.

J U L Y

TODAY'S THOUGHT:

"I dropped off the tour and went home and started working with my Dad doing taxes. After two months of that, I decided golf looked pretty good." —John Fought

ON THIS DATE—

In 1966, "Champagne" Tony Lema lost his life in a plane crash near Lansing, Michigan. Lema was on his way to Chicago after playing in the PGA Championship that day in Akron, Ohio.

CHIP SHOT

The plane in which the 1964 British Open winner was riding came down on the seventh green of a golf course before sliding into a lake.

TRIVIA QUIZ—

Since 1950, only one PGA golfer has been able to win more than ten tournaments in a year. Who was it?

TODAY'S TIP—

Sometimes the clubhead will get ahead of the hands and twist to the left at impact, producing a closed face and a bad hook. That means you're swinging the clubhead and not your hands. Think hands first.

THE 19TH HOLE

"Golf is easier than catching, but there's nothing easy about finding my ball."
—Johnny Bench, Baseball Hall of Fame catcher

Quiz Answer: Sam Snead, who won 11 events in 1950.

J U L Y

TODAY'S THOUGHT:
"My philosophy is: Never do anything stupid."   —Ben Crenshaw

ON THIS DATE—
In 1993, Lauri Merten ended a nine-year victory drought with a win in the most prestigious event in women's golf. Merten birdied two of the last three holes to win the U.S. Women's Open by one stroke.

CHIP SHOT
W.F. Davis of the Royal Montreal GC is acknowledged as North America's first greenkeeper. Hired as club pro in 1888, Davis was also expected to perform the duties of greenkeeper. Thinking that part of the job demeaning, Davis soon quit.

TRIVIA QUIZ—
This Hall of Fame golfer was named captain of the United States Ryder Cup 6 times, more than anyone else. Who is it?

TODAY'S TIP—
Club selection becomes critical when the ground slopes. The more it slopes, the greater the effect on the flight of the ball. The ball will fly higher and shorter from an uphill lie, lower and farther from a downhill lie.

THE 19TH HOLE
"I should have played that hole in an ambulance."
—Arnold Palmer, on the Road Hole at St. Andrews

Quiz Answer: Walter Hagen.

JULY

TODAY'S THOUGHT:

"Golf is not a game you can rush. For every stroke you try to force out of her, she is going to extract two strokes in return."

—Dave Hill

ON THIS DATE—

In 1981, Pat Bradley added another major title to her resume with a win in the U.S. Women's Open. Born: Wayne Grady (1957).

CHIP SHOT

Sam Snead didn't carry a putter in his bag until he went on the PGA Tour in 1937. His first set of clubs, purchased in the 1920's, cost him $9.50.

TRIVIA QUIZ—

Under USGA rules, how long can you look for a lost ball:
          a) 10 minutes   b) 5 minutes   c) 7 minutes?

TODAY'S TIP—

If you consistently slice your approach shots, don't aim directly at the flagstick. Aim left of the hole and your shot will finish near the hole. And even if you actually shoot it straight, you'll still be putting on the green.

THE 19TH HOLE

"Now here's Jack Lemmon, about to play the all important eighth shot." —Jim McKay

Quiz Answer: B.

J U L Y

TODAY'S THOUGHT:

"If the following foursome is pressing you, wave them through and then speed up."   —Deane Beman

ON THIS DATE—

In 1992, Patty Sheehan forced a playoff in the U.S. Women's Open by making two straight birdies on the final holes. Her third straight, on the first playoff hole, gave her the title over Julie Inkster.

CHIP SHOT

Grantland Rice suggested that the first Masters, in 1934, be held in late March so baseball writers returning north from spring training could cover the tournament.

TRIVIA QUIZ—

What's the term for a slice that starts left and then faces?

TODAY'S TIP—

There are times when your ball will find itself in very deep or thick rough. Those are the times when your goal is to simply put the ball back onto the fairway and not swing for the green. Using a sand wedge, take the same swing you would use to explode the ball from sand.

THE 19TH HOLE
"I believe my future is ahead of me."
        —Chip Beck, after his first PGA Tour win

Quiz Answer: You've just hit a "banana ball."

JULY

TODAY'S THOUGHT:
"I try to have peace of mind. If you have that, you are a mental millionaire. It doesn't cost anything." —Chi Chi Rodriguez

ON THIS DATE—
In 1987, the longest U.S. Women's Open came to an end with Laura Davies winning in a playoff. The event lasted six days because of the playoff and the cancellation of one day's play because of heavy thunderstorms.

CHIP SHOT
After winning the 1949 LA Open, Lloyd Mangrum dropped his pants before the media to show why he won: lucky pajama bottoms, which he wore under his golf pants.

TRIVIA QUIZ—
Two Americans each won back-to-back British Opens in the 1920's. Who were they?

TODAY'S TIP—
Work on the tempo of your swing by using a full body turn to get the club back, and strong leg drive to get it started down, then bring the hands and wrists into play. Don't overdo hand and wrist action at the expense of your back and legs.

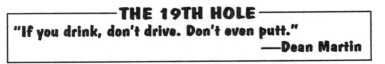

THE 19TH HOLE
"If you drink, don't drive. Don't even putt."
—Dean Martin

QUIZ ANSWER Bobby Jones won it in 1926 and '27, then Walter Hagen won the championship in 1928 and '29.

J U L Y

TODAY'S THOUGHT:

"The average golfer doesn't play golf. He attacks it."

—Jackie Burke, Jr.

ON THIS DATE—

In 1991, Jack Nicklaus became the only man to win major USGA titles in five decades with a playoff victory over Chi Chi Rodriguez in the U.S. Senior Open. Born: Brian Claar (1959).

CHIP SHOT

Nicklaus and Arnold Palmer are the only men to win the U.S. Amateur, the U.S. Open, and the U.S. Senior Open.

TRIVIA QUIZ—

This golfer posted the lowest score ever shot by an amateur at the U.S. Open when he shot a 282 in 1960. Do you know who it was?

TODAY'S TIP—

Here's a drill to help you develop better touch, or feel, on the green. Hit some 20-foot putts. Don't look up to follow the ball. Instead, with head and eyes down, call out where you think the ball stopped. It will help you develop the feel for a straight, solid stroke.

THE 19TH HOLE

"Arnold Palmer is the biggest crowd pleaser since the invention of the portable sanitary facility."

—Bob Hope

Quiz Answer: Jack Nicklaus.

JULY

TODAY'S THOUGHT:
"There are two things in life which Ben Hogan especially dislikes. One is losing a golf match. The other is teaching golf."
—Jimmy Demaret

ON THIS DATE—
In 1961, Jerry Barber survived a playoff with Don January to win the PGA Championship for the only major title of his career.

CHIP SHOT
Barber, trailing by four strokes with three holes to play, forced the playoff when he holed birdie putts of 22, 44, and 58 feet.

TRIVIA QUIZ—
What's the name of the trophy, donated by the son of a department store magnate, which is given to the winner of the PGA Championship?

TODAY'S TIP—
A way to get the feel of a good weight transfer is to warm up by swinging your wedge with your left arm only. You won't swing it smoothly without a smooth weight transfer.

THE 19TH HOLE
"I want a ruling. I want to know which club to hit this guy with."
—Hubert Green, after someone drove over his ball

Quiz Answer: The Wanamaker Trophy.

JULY

TODAY'S THOUGHT:

"Those who cannot drive suppose themselves to be good putters."
—Sir Walter Simpson

ON THIS DATE—

In 1983, Australian Jan Stephenson's victory in the U.S. Women's Open left her one short of a career grand slam. The Nabisco Dinah Shore is the only major to elude Stephenson.

CHIP SHOT

After leading through 54 holes of the 1967 U.S. Open, amateur Marty Fleckman decided to turn pro. He won the Cajun Classic in his pro debut, but never won again on the Tour.

TRIVIA QUIZ—

Name the native country of 1963 British Open winner Bob Charles.

TODAY'S TIP—

A lot of one and two-foot putts are missed because you're tapping the ball. Pick a spot about six inches on your line. Stroke the ball firmly over that spot while the clubhead continues straight at the hole.

THE 19TH HOLE

"Sometimes I think that the only way the Spanish people will recognize me is if I win the Grand Slam and then drop dead on the 18th green."
—Seve Ballesteros

Quiz Answer: New Zealand.

AUGUST

TODAY'S THOUGHT:

"Even when times were good, I realized that my earning power as a golf professional depended on too many ifs and putts."
—Gene Sarazen

ON THIS DATE—

In 1993, Nick Price won his fourth tournament of the year with a three-stroke victory in the Federal Express-St. Jude Classic. Born: Brad Faxon (1961).

CHIP SHOT

Through an 11-month stretch in 1991 and '92, Fred Couples won $2.5 million. As a result, his caddie, Joe LaCava, earned $200,000.

TRIVIA QUIZ—

I won the U.S. Open twice. Each time I won, a different brother of mine finished second. Who am I?

TODAY'S TIP—

To get yourself used to firing your right side through the ball, hit some 5-iron shots using only your right arm. You'll find yourself pulling your shots less and less.

THE 19TH HOLE

"Peter Jacobsen is in a position where a birdie will help him more than a bogey."
—Steve Melnyk, announcer, at the 1983 Colonial

Quiz Answer: Alex Smith. His brother, Willie, was runner-up in 1906, while Macdonald Smith finished second in 1910.

A U G U S T

TODAY'S THOUGHT:

"Golf is the hardest game in the world to play and the easiest to cheat at."   —Dave Hill

ON THIS DATE—

In 1959, Bob Rosburg overcame a six-stroke deficit by firing a final-round 66 to win the PGA Championship. Rosburg had finished second in the U.S. Open earlier in the year.

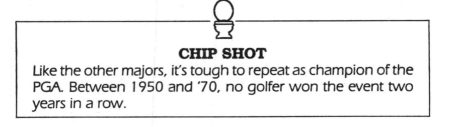

CHIP SHOT

Like the other majors, it's tough to repeat as champion of the PGA. Between 1950 and '70, no golfer won the event two years in a row.

TRIVIA QUIZ—

Name the only golfer to win consecutive British Open titles in the 1980's.

TODAY'S TIP—

To pop a high pitch out of a divot, open the clubface of your wedge, grip the club firmly, and play the ball forward. Use an outside-in swing, and make sure the clubhead keeps facing the target.

THE 19TH HOLE

"If you can't break 80, you have no business playing golf. If you can break 80, you have no business."
—old British saying

Quiz Answer: Tom Watson, who won the championship in 1982 and 1983.

AUGUST

TODAY'S THOUGHT:
"The man who hates golfers is what they call me. They couldn't be more wrong. I design holes that are fun to play."
—Robert Trent Jones, golf course designer

ON THIS DATE—
In 1975, three players tied for second as Susie Berning won the Lady Keystone Classic.

CHIP SHOT
Ray Ainsley shot a 19 on the 16th hole at Cherry Hills CC in the 1938 U.S. Open, a record that still stands. Ainsley hit his ball into a creek and, as the current carried the ball along, he kept swinging away.

TRIVIA QUIZ—
The lowest score for 72 holes in an LPGA tournament is 268. Who is the golfer who set this record in 1985?

TODAY'S TIP—
When hitting to a green with a strong wind at your back, aim the ball just short of the pin. The wind will cause the ball to spin less, so expect a bounce and roll. Remember, too, that wind will make the green harder.

THE 19TH HOLE
"Saw a course you'd really like, Trent. On the first tee, you drop the ball over your shoulder."
—Jimmy Demaret, to Robert Trent Jones

Quiz Answer: Nancy Lopez. Lopez fired four sub-70 rounds at the Henredon Classic, finishing 20-under-par.

AUGUST

TODAY'S THOUGHT:

"It's like eating. You don't think to feed yourself. All my concentration was on the scoring, not the swing, so I'll never know what caused it." —Byron Nelson, on his winning streak

ON THIS DATE—

In 1945, Byron Nelson won the Canadian Open for his 11th straight tour victory, a record that still stands.

CHIP SHOT

During a three year span, Nelson played in 75 tournaments, winning 35 of them.

TRIVIA QUIZ—

Two golfers were honored by *Sports Illustrated* with the magazine's Sportsman of the Year award in the 1970's. Can you name them?

TODAY'S TIP—

Modern golf technology has given us clubs that are very forgiving, both on bad swings and on the body when you hit the ground. But if your game is fine and your older clubs are holding up, then stick with them and enjoy the game.

THE 19TH HOLE

"I envy that man. Because he makes a hundred thousand dollars a year like I do, but nobody knows him." —Mickey Mantle, on Miller Barber

Quiz Answer: Lee Trevino and Jack Nicklaus. Trevino was honored in 1971. Nicklaus won the award in 1978.

AUGUST

TODAY'S THOUGHT:

"Playing with your spouse on the golf course runs almost as great a marital risk as getting caught with someone else's anywhere else."
—Peter Andrews, writer

ON THIS DATE—

In 1979, Nancy Lopez continued her domination of the LPGA, finishing 14-under-par to win the Colgate European Open. It was the seventh of eight wins for Lopez that year.

CHIP SHOT

Laura Davies once won a long-driving competition by out-hitting 40 men with a drive of 312 yards.

TRIVIA QUIZ—

In 1987, South African David Frost won over a half million dollars and had the best scoring average on the PGA Tour, yet didn't win the Vardon Trophy. Why not?

TODAY'S TIP—

To keep your tee shot from shooting to a high peak early in flight, start the clubhead back by holding your wrists firm until the club is waist high.

THE 19TH HOLE

"The best diet I know is pride in yourself. If I gain an inch on my waist, I have to send 200 pairs of slacks out for alteration."   —Doug Sanders

Quiz Answer: Frost was not a member of the PGA.

AUGUST

TODAY'S THOUGHT:
"Patience. Patience and memory."
—Art Wall, on what it takes to be a great golfer

ON THIS DATE—
In 1978, John Mahaffey put matters to rest when he dropped in a birdie putt on the second hole of sudden-death to win the PGA Championship. Mahaffey was tied with Tom Watson and Jerry Pate. Born: Harry Cooper (1904); Billy Mayfair (1966).

CHIP SHOT
Byron Nelson chose the PGA Championship to make his final appearance. Nelson played in the 1946 PGA, bidding farewell to the PGA Tour.

TRIVIA QUIZ—
Who won the first PGA Championship in 1916?

TODAY'S TIP—
When it comes to bounces and rolls, high-lofted wedge shots can be unpredictable. So if you're trying to pitch over a bunker to the green, use an 8- or 9-iron. Pitch the ball and let it roll to the hole.

THE 19TH HOLE
"He hits it into the woods so often he should get an orange hunting jacket."
—Tom Weiskopf, on then-rookie Ben Crenshaw

Quiz Answer: Jim Barnes. Barnes also won the second championship when the tournament resumed in 1919. The event wasn't held for two years because of World War I.

AUGUST

TODAY'S THOUGHT:
"It seems like everywhere we go this year, the galleries increase in size, and decrease in sanity."   —Pat Summerall, announcer

ON THIS DATE—
In 1983, second-year pro Hal Sutton held off Jack Nicklaus by one stroke to win the PGA Championship. Sutton finished the year as the tour's leading money-winner.

CHIP SHOT
When Julius Boros won the 1968 PGA Championship, he became the oldest man to triumph in the event. Boros was 48.

TRIVIA QUIZ—
Legal or illegal: My ball is in the fairway and a loose twig is touching it. I pick up the twig and, in the process, my ball moves.

TODAY'S TIP—
Practicing putting on your living room carpet is not the same as putting under the pressure of competition, so play games with yourself. Practice putting one foot from the cup, then three feet, and so on. Make yourself sink five straight putts. If you miss, start all over again.

THE 19TH HOLE
"He married the first girl who'd shag balls for him."
—George Low, on Arnold Palmer

Quiz Answer: Illegal. I am assessed a one-stroke penalty.

A U G U S T

TODAY'S THOUGHT:

"Golf is a fickle game and must be wooed to be won."
—Willie Park, Jr., British Open champion

ON THIS DATE—

In 1982, Ray Floyd couldn't be stopped as he took home the PGA Championship. Floyd, who shot an opening round 63, led the event from start to finish.

CHIP SHOT

The largest collection of golf books in the world belongs to the USGA Museum and Library. The library has a collection of golf magazines dating to 1880.

TRIVIA QUIZ—

True or false: Gary Player never won the PGA's Player of the Year award in his career.

TODAY'S TIP—

To get the ball up quickly from a greenside bunker, hover your wedge a few inches above the ball and slightly behind it. You'll be in a position that will force an upright takeaway and cause you to hit the sand with a steep, descending blow.

THE 19TH HOLE

"I couldn't even smile because my mouth was so dry my lips were stuck to my teeth."
—JoAnne Carner, after the win that put her into the LPGA Hall of Fame

Quiz Answer: True.

AUGUST

TODAY'S THOUGHT:
"Golfers find it a very trying matter to turn at the waist, more particularly if they have a lot of waist to turn." —Harry Vardon

ON THIS DATE—
In 1981, Larry Nelson's four-stroke lead held up for the final round as Nelson won his first major, the PGA Championship. Nelson's cushion was fluffed by two rounds of 66.

CHIP SHOT
Nelson's victory in the PGA earned him a berth on the Ryder Cup team, replacing the unfortunate Howard Twitty, who had already been measured for his Cup outfit.

TRIVIA QUIZ—
This golfer was the first to win a PGA Tour event with a colored ball. Who was it?

TODAY'S TIP—
Here's a different way to help you get the feel of proper hand action. First, take a seat. Hit some practice shots with a 7-iron from a folding chair. It'll make you cock your wrists, release, and re-cock your wrists on the follow-through.

THE 19TH HOLE
"If this was an airport, it would have been closed."
—Larry Nelson, after a windy tournament

Quiz Answer: Wayne Levi won the 1982 Hawaiian Open using a yellow ball.

AUGUST

TODAY'S THOUGHT:

"I've never played a perfect 18 holes. There's no such thing."
—Walter Hagen

ON THIS DATE—

In 1980, Jack Nicklaus joined Walter Hagen as the only five-time winners of the PGA Championship. Nicklaus had won his fourth title exactly five years earlier to the day.

CHIP SHOT

One year the famous azaleas at Augusta National were blooming too early for the tournament. Workers were ordered to pack ice around the plants to slow the process down.

TRIVIA QUIZ—

What's a "featherie?"

TODAY'S TIP—

Always keep your set-up to the ball as relaxed as possible. The more contorted you make it, the harder it is to reproduce on every swing.

THE 19TH HOLE

"When Jack Nicklaus plays well, he wins. When he plays badly, he finishes second. When he plays terribly, he finishes third."   —Johnny Miller

Quiz Answer: A golf ball used until about 1850, the featherie was a leather sack filled with wet goose feathers. When the feathers dried, they expanded and made the ball hard.

AUGUST

TODAY'S THOUGHT:

"Nothing goes down slower than a golf handicap."

—Bobby Nichols

ON THIS DATE—

In 1991, long-hitting and longshot rookie John Daly surprised everyone by winning the PGA Championship. Daly was the ninth alternate on the qualifying list for the tournament.

CHIP SHOT

Daly gained entry into the tournament when five players backed out, three alternates didn't make the trip, and Nick Price withdrew when his wife was about to give birth. Price won the next year.

TRIVIA QUIZ—

I won the U.S. Open in 1986. However, I competed in 22 Opens before finally winning, the most of any Open champion. Who am I?

TODAY'S TIP—

If your downhill putts go charging past the hole, just shorten your putting stroke. All you want to do is get the ball rolling. Focus on a spot just to the front of the hole and try to get the ball to die there.

THE 19TH HOLE

"I hit two fairways - well, maybe four, but only two I was aiming at."

—John Daly

Quiz Answer: Raymond Floyd.

A U G U S T

TODAY'S THOUGHT:

"It calls for a doughty, resourceful competitor, the sort of fellow who is not ruffled by his opponent's fireworks and is able to set off a few of his own when it counts."

—Herbert Warren Wind, on match play

ON THIS DATE—

In 1973, Jack Nicklaus' win in the PGA Championship gave him 14 major victories in his career, breaking the record held by Bobby Jones.

CHIP SHOT

When rain washed out the first two rounds of the 1983 Hong Kong Open, Greg Norman practiced by driving golf balls out the open window of his hotel room into the harbor. He won the tourney.

TRIVIA QUIZ—

Orville Moody won only one major tournament in his PGA career. Which one?

TODAY'S TIP—

Another way to promote a smoother takeaway and backswing is to press forward with your hands. Pressing your hands slightly forward just before beginning the takeaway puts them in the proper position in front of the ball.

THE 19TH HOLE

"He has won more titles at more weights than Sugar Ray Leonard."
—John Brodie, on the waistline of Billy Casper

Quiz Answer: Moody won the 1969 U.S. Open.

AUGUST

TODAY'S THOUGHT:

"If I miss one day's practice I know it; if I miss two days the spectators know it; and if I miss three days the world knows it."　—Ben Hogan

ON THIS DATE—

In 1912, William Benjamin Hogan was born. Hogan, voted in 1973 as one of America's five greatest golfers, won nine majors in his career. Also born: Charles Coody (1937); Betsy King (1955).

CHIP SHOT

When Hogan won the British Open at Carnoustie in 1953, the green fee was 49 cents.

TRIVIA QUIZ—

The first five British Opens played in England were played at two courses. Name them.

TODAY'S TIP—

If you put too much pressure on yourself to hole out when putting, relax yourself by realizing that missing is not the end of the world. It will improve the flow of your putting.

THE 19TH HOLE

"Golf Pro: An optimistic doctor who has a cure for dying."
—Jim Bishop, writer

Quiz Answer:　The host clubs were the Royal Liverpool GC in Hoylake and the Royal St. George's GC in Sandwich.

AUGUST

TODAY'S THOUGHT:
"Never give up. If we give up in this game, we'll give up on life. If you give up that first time, it's easier to give up the second, third, and fourth times." —Tom Watson

ON THIS DATE—
In 1977, the PGA Championship became the first major tournament to be decided in a sudden-death playoff. Lanny Wadkins beat Gene Littler on the third hole of the playoff.

CHIP SHOT
Bob Charles is known as the first left-hander to win a major tournament. He did it by beating Phil Rodgers in a 36-hole playoff in the 1963 British Open.

TRIVIA QUIZ—
Who was the first foreign-born player to win a million dollars in her career on the LPGA Tour?

TODAY'S TIP—
Consistent problems with slicing the ball are usually caused by poor foot alignment. Instead of compensating by opening your stance, use a square alignment and swing from the inside out.

THE 19TH HOLE
"You've just one problem. You stand too close to the ball - after you've hit it." —Sam Snead, to a pupil

Quiz Answer: Australian Jan Stephenson, who cracked the barrier in 1985 with a win at the GNA Classic.

AUGUST

TODAY'S THOUGHT:
"You don't know what pressure is until you play for five bucks with only two in your pocket."   —Lee Trevino

ON THIS DATE—
In 1948, Babe Zaharias burst from the field to win the U.S. Women's Open by eight strokes. It was the first of three Open wins for Zaharias.

CHIP SHOT
After shooting a 77 in the first round of the 1974 U.S. Open, Homero Blancas was asked if he had had any uphill putts. Blancas replied, "Yeah, after each of my downhill putts."

TRIVIA QUIZ—
I'm heading into Amen Corner at The Masters when I ask you, my caddie, to give me my trusty "spoon." What club do I want?

TODAY'S TIP—
When faced with slow greens, don't read too much break into your putts. Putts 10 feet or less should be played with a firm stroke.

THE 19TH HOLE
"Honey, I don't care if you send it out and get it dry-cleaned."   —Babe Zaharias, to a player asking for relief from casual water

Quiz Answer: The 3-wood.

AUGUST

TODAY'S THOUGHT:
"Real golfers go to work to relax." —Anonymous

ON THIS DATE—
In 1992, Nick Price picked up the first major title of his career with a three-stroke victory in the PGA Championship, while Sherri Steinhauer captured the duMaurier Classic, the last major of the season on the LPGA Tour.

CHIP SHOT
Defending PGA champ, John Daly, finished 20-over-par, 26 strokes behind Price.

TRIVIA QUIZ—
A number of players have won two majors in the same year. Name the two golfers who did it in the 1980's.

TODAY'S TIP—
To make a stiff swing less restrictive, grip the club tightly with the little finger of your top hand. Your wrists will release naturally on the back and downswings.

THE 19TH HOLE
"I didn't say he was the biggest moron in the booth. I said he was the biggest Mormon. Somebody dropped the 'm'."
—Paul Azinger, on Johnny Miller's TV commentary

Quiz Answer: Jack Nicklaus won the U.S. Open and the PGA Championship in 1980. Tom Watson won the U.S. and British Opens in 1982.

AUGUST

TODAY'S THOUGHT:
"Great golf courses should have at least one silly hole."
—Frank Hannigan

ON THIS DATE—
In 1969, Raymond Floyd held off Gary Player by one stroke to win the PGA Championship, the first major win of his career. Born: Dottie Mochrie (1965).

CHIP SHOT
For every doctor advising a patient to play golf, there's an instructor advising him to quit.

TRIVIA QUIZ—
This Swedish golfer's first victory on the LPGA Tour was at the 1988 U.S. Women's Open. That year she was named the Tour's Rookie of the Year. What's her name?

TODAY'S TIP—
One way to check your alignment is to put a club on the ground pointing to your target. Then set up and put another club in front of your toes. If those two clubs are not parallel, then your alignment is off. Chances are that that poor alignment would result in a slice.

THE 19TH HOLE
"It's a marriage. If I had to choose between my wife and my putter, well, I'd miss her." —Gary Player

Quiz Answer: Liselotte Neumann.

AUGUST

TODAY'S THOUGHT:
"If there is any larceny in a man, golf will bring it out."
—Paul Gallico, writer

ON THIS DATE—
In 1957, Nick Faldo was born. Faldo, hooked on golf as a kid by television, gave TV viewers many memorable moments between 1987 and 1992 when he won three British Open titles and back-to-back Masters tournaments.

CHIP SHOT
Faldo won those two Masters in sudden-death playoffs. In 1989 he beat Scott Hoch and, in 1990, Raymond Floyd was the victim. The wins came on the 11th hole, the second of the playoff.

TRIVIA QUIZ—
Name the golfer from Fiji who was named PGA Tour Rookie of the Year in 1993.

TODAY'S TIP—
Rolling your left hand too far to the right will cause you to hit the ball with a closed clubface at impact. To prevent rolling your hands into the ball, move your left hand back so you can only see one or two knuckles.

THE 19TH HOLE
"Let's see, I think right now, I'm third in money-winning and first in money-spending."   —Tony Lema

Quiz Answer: Vijay Singh.

AUGUST

TODAY'S THOUGHT:
"Gentlemen, this beats rifle shooting for distance and accuracy. It is a game I think would go in our country."
—H.K. Vanderbilt, on golf

ON THIS DATE—
In 1984, 44-year old Lee Trevino won his first major in ten years, and sixth overall, taking the PGA Championship. Trevino played all four rounds under 70 to finish 15-under-par.

CHIP SHOT
King Hassan of Morocco had a nine-hole course built within the palace walls. Having trouble with the sand shot, the king ordered workers to fill in the 40 plus bunkers with sod.

TRIVIA QUIZ—
How many Vardon Trophies have Jack Nicklaus, Johnny Miller, and Raymond Floyd won between them?

TODAY'S TIP—
On putts in the 3 to 5-foot range, stroke the ball and keep the back of your left hand facing the hole. It matches the putter's clubface and will keep it square to the hole.

THE 19TH HOLE
"I'd just as soon pull a rattlesnake out of my bag as a two-iron."   —Lee Trevino

Quiz Answer: One. Raymond Floyd won it in 1983. Nicklaus and Miller never won the award for low scoring average for the year.

A U G U S T

TODAY'S THOUGHT:

"Only when he stands at the altar on his wedding day does a man experience the same sensation of impending doom as he feels each week on the first tee on a Sunday morning."

—Norman Mailer, writer

ON THIS DATE—

In 1944, a relative unknown from Indiana named Robert Hamilton upset Byron Nelson in the finals to win the PGA Championship. Born: Duffy Waldorf (1962).

CHIP SHOT

At that time, most of the top pros were fighting the war in Europe. Nelson was rejected by the Army because he was a hemophiliac.

TRIVIA QUIZ—

Name the only two brothers who have each won more than $1.5 million in their careers on the PGA Tour.

TODAY'S TIP—

If you want to work out to improve your golf game, don't try to bulk up with heavy weights. Your workout should be geared to increasing strength and flexibility. Do hand, forearm, and leg exercises with a light weight and many repetitions.

THE 19TH HOLE

"I think most of the rules of golf stink. They were written by the guys who can't even break a hundred."

—Chi Chi Rodriguez

Quiz Answer: Bobby and Lanny Wadkins.

AUGUST

TODAY'S THOUGHT:
"It has no rough, in the accepted sense of the term, and no semi-rough. Your ball is either on the fairway, in which case it sits invitingly on a flawless carpet of turf, or it is not."
—Henry Longhurst, on Pine Valley

ON THIS DATE—
In 1971, 16-year old Laura Baugh became the youngest golfer to win the U.S. Women's Amateur title when she beat Beth Barry in the final round.

CHIP SHOT
Real golfers don't cry when they line up for their fourth putt.

TRIVIA QUIZ—
Jack Nicklaus has won The Masters six times. Who's next on the list with four green jackets?

TODAY'S TIP—
Your ball is better off low than high when you're playing around the green. In other words, if you can putt, putt. If not, chip. Your last resort is the pitch and run.

THE 19TH HOLE
"Now, I don't dare throw a club."
—JoAnne Carner, after winning the Bob Jones Award for sportsmanship in 1981

Quiz Answer: Arnold Palmer. Palmer won the tournament in 1958, '60, '62, and '64.

A U G U S T

TODAY'S THOUGHT:

"When you start driving your ball down the middle, you meet a different class of people." —Phil Harris, comedian

ON THIS DATE—

In 1993, Phil Mickelson won his second tournament of the year with an easy victory in The International. Born: Gene Sauers (1962).

CHIP SHOT

The International uses a modified Stableford scoring system. Medal scores don't count. Instead, points are awarded for a player's performance on each hole (5 for eagle, 2 for birdie, etc.).

TRIVIA QUIZ—

Who was the youngest winner of the British Open?

TODAY'S TIP—

Anxious to get your kids out on the course? Most pros agree that five or six years old is too young because a child's attention span is too short. Get them started at the age of nine or ten with serious lessons waiting until the age of 14.

THE 19TH HOLE

"My goal this year is basically to find the fairways."
—Lauri Peterson

Quiz Answer: Young Tom Morris. Morris was 17 years old when he succeeded his father as Open champion in 1868.

AUGUST

TODAY'S THOUGHT:
"Even the best swing doesn't work all the time. You have to be able to post a good number on those days when you can't even write your own damn name." —Gardner Dickinson

ON THIS DATE—
In 1955, Hall of Famer Betty Jameson won the last LPGA title of her career, shooting 3-under-par to win the White Mountain Open. Born: Peter Thomson (1929).

CHIP SHOT
The BBC carried the British Open live for the first time in 1955, the year Peter Thomson won the second of five championships.

TRIVIA QUIZ—
What American city had the first muni, or, municipal golf course?

TODAY'S TIP—
An explosion shot should be hit with an open stance and an open clubface. Align your feet slightly left of target and swing along your body line. Remember, the ball rides the sand.

THE 19TH HOLE
"We took a mulligan."
—Cheryl Kratzert, on her divorce and subsequent remarriage to husband, Bill

Quiz Answer: New York City. Van Cortlandt GC was founded in the Bronx in 1895, and is still in operation.

AUGUST

TODAY'S THOUGHT:

"You show me a player who swings out of his shoes and I'll show you a player who isn't going to win enough to keep himself in a decent pair of shoes for very long."   —Sam Snead

ON THIS DATE—

In 1984, Pat Bradley set an LPGA record for nine holes, firing a 28 at the Columbia Savings Classic. Bradley finished the round at 65, five-under-par.

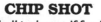

CHIP SHOT

Bradley had the record all to herself for less than a week. Mary Beth Zimmerman shot a 28 at the Tour's next event, the Rail Charity Golf Classic.

TRIVIA QUIZ—

Who was the first foreign-born player to win The Masters?

TODAY'S TIP—

The slightest move of your head can turn a pitch shot into a poor pitch shot. Here's a way to keep your head steady. Don't look up until you hear the ball land on the green. Resist that temptation and you will be rewarded.

—THE 19TH HOLE—

"Golf got complicated when I had to wear shoes and begin thinking about what I was doing."

—Sam Snead

Quiz Answer: South African Gary Player won it in 1961.

AUGUST

TODAY'S THOUGHT:

"The only bruises in golf are to the spirit. The only bones that break are those in the skeleton of the personality."

—Thomas Boswell, writer

ON THIS DATE—

In 1991, Mitch Voges made Manny Zerman a runner-up for the second straight year with a 7 & 6 victory in the title match of the U.S. Amateur Golf Championship.

CHIP SHOT

After Ben Crenshaw sent his ball into a palm tree at Palm Springs, his caddie climbed a ladder and shook the tree. More than two dozen balls fell out, none of them belonging to Crenshaw.

TRIVIA QUIZ—

Name the Senior PGA Tour golfer who never played on the PGA Tour, but won back-to-back U.S. Amateur Golf Championships.

TODAY'S TIP—

Don't just visualize the distance to the hole on an approach shot. Keep in mind the trajectory in club selection and address. How the shot should properly fly can vary widely.

THE 19TH HOLE

"Any self-respecting tournament wants to be won by Tom Watson." —Jim Murray, writer

Quiz Answer: Jay Sigel. Sigel won the U.S. Amateur in 1982 and '83.

AUGUST

TODAY'S THOUGHT:
"In Japan, player who scores hole-in-one while leading tournament always lose. It's proven jinx." —Ayako Okamoto

ON THIS DATE—
In 1962, Mickey Wright won her third consecutive event, taking the Salt Lake City Open. Wright won a fourth tournament before her streak was stopped.

CHIP SHOT
Sam Snead was playing in a tournament on the day of the 1948 presidential election. As early returns started to come in, someone mentioned to Snead that Dewey was leading. "What'd he go out in?" Snead asked.

TRIVIA QUIZ—
Only one man has won the U.S. Open in three different decades. Name him.

TODAY'S TIP—
Yes, practice is important to enjoying golf. But don't practice when you lose interest. That's when bad habits start creeping in.

THE 19TH HOLE
"The divorce is from my old putter. I think it's final - at least we're due for a long separation."
—Shelley Hamlin

Quiz Answer: Jack Nicklaus. Nicklaus won the Open twice in the '60's and one each in the '70's and '80's.

AUGUST

TODAY'S THOUGHT:
"If you ever get a tee time in hell, there will be two certainties: 1) You will be playing behind Bernhard Langer, and 2) The course will include Hazeltine's 16th." —Rick Reilly, writer

ON THIS DATE—
In 1957, Bernhard Langer was born. Langer, known for his slow play, won the 1985 and 1993 Masters, but is remembered for the four-foot putt he missed that gave the 1991 Ryder Cup to the United States.

CHIP SHOT
As a boy, Seve Ballesteros practiced all his shots with a 3-iron. He had no choice - it was his only club.

TRIVIA QUIZ—
What's the only major championship Tom Watson hasn't won in his career?

TODAY'S TIP—
The winding of your torso in the backswing creates energy for the downswing. A transfer of weight to the inside of the rear foot goes along with that. Most beginners don't, however, reducing energy and creating an incorrect swing arc and weak slice.

THE 19TH HOLE
"Seve Ballesteros drives the ball into territory Daniel Boone couldn't find." —Fuzzy Zoeller

Quiz Answer: Watson has never won the PGA Championship.

AUGUST

TODAY'S THOUGHT:

"An amateur golfer is one who plays for honor– in my mind, that's tougher than playing for money."

—Willie Turnesa, 1938 U.S. Amateur champion

ON THIS DATE—

In 1922, the United States defeated Great Britain and Ireland in the first official Walker Cup match, 8-4. Born: Rick Fehr (1962); Lee Janzen (1964).

CHIP SHOT

British writer Bernard Darwin, who came to America to cover the match, became the team's captain and a player, too. Darwin replaced Robert Harris, who fell ill, and won the only match he played. Talk about getting the inside scoop.

TRIVIA QUIZ—

The USGA celebrated the 100th anniversary of the U.S. Open in 1995 when it was played at Shinnecock Hills GC. How many other Opens had the course hosted before that landmark year?

TODAY'S TIP—

Think of your pitching wedge as a precise instrument. Don't make it your goal to simply get the ball on the green. Aim right at the pin to give yourself more one-putt opportunities.

THE 19TH HOLE

"I never did see the sense in keeping my head down. The only reason I play golf at all is to see where the ball goes." ——Charles Price, writer

Quiz Answer: Two, in 1896 and 1986.

AUGUST

TODAY'S THOUGHT:
"The players themselves can be classified roughly into two groups - the attractions and the entry fees."
—Jimmy Demaret, on the PGA Tour

ON THIS DATE—
In 1993, Brandie Burton made a birdie putt on the first playoff hole to win the rain-drenched duMaurier Classic. Burton led Betsy King by two on the 18th tee, but double-bogeyed to force the playoff.

CHIP SHOT
The first African-American to tee it up at The Masters was Lee Elder, who missed the cut in 1975.

TRIVIA QUIZ—
Five Americans have won the British Open in consecutive years. Name two of them.

TODAY'S TIP—
If you find yourself shanking the ball, rotate your arms from right to left earlier in your downswing.

THE 19TH HOLE
"You mustn't blow your nose when your partner is addressing the ball - otherwise the book of rules is mostly nonsense." ——Henry Longhurst, writer

Quiz Answer: Bobby Jones (1926 & '27); Walter Hagen (1928 & '29); Arnold Palmer (1961 & '62); Lee Trevino (1971 & '72); Tom Watson (1982 & '83).

AUGUST

TODAY'S THOUGHT:

"Like one's own children, golf has an uncanny way of endearing itself to us while at the same time evoking every weakness of mind and character, no matter how well hidden."

—W. Timothy Gallwey, writer

ON THIS DATE—

In 1992, Dottie Mochrie and Judy Dickinson battled for six playoff holes at the LPGA Challenge before Mochrie two-putted for par to win the tournament.

CHIP SHOT

The LPGA's low stroke average award is named after Glenna Collett Vare. In her debut, at the 1918 Rhode Island Championship, the 15-year old Vare finished dead last with a *round* of 132.

TRIVIA QUIZ—

Who is second on the list of golfers with the most LPGA tournament wins?

TODAY'S TIP—

Feet spinning in place will more likely, than not, send your ball to the right. It means you're standing too flatfooted. Make an effort to set up with your weight on the balls of your feet, and finish with all of your weight on the left foot.

THE 19TH HOLE

"Women who seek equality with men lack ambition."
—bumper sticker on the back of Patty Sheenan's car

Quiz Answer: Mickey Wright, who won 82 tournaments in her career.

AUGUST

TODAY'S THOUGHT:

"All I know is that Nicklaus watches Hogan practice, and I never heard of Hogan watching Nicklaus practice."   —Tommy Bolt

ON THIS DATE—

In 1992, Justin Leonard won the U.S. Amateur Golf Championship, beating Thomas Sherrer, 8 & 7, at the Muirfield Village Golf Club. Leonard never trailed in the finals. Born: Isao Aoki (1942).

CHIP SHOT

Leonard's victory made him the third native Texan to win the title. The others were Billy Maxwell in 1951 and Scott Verplank in 1984.

TRIVIA QUIZ—

Quick! Name the PGA Hall of Famer and 1954 U.S. Amateur champion who was born in Latrobe, Pennsylvania.

TODAY'S TIP—

As you well know, golf is as much a mental game as a physical one. Always take the positive approach. You're a better golfer than you think. Tell yourself, "If I can play one good nine, I can play two."

THE 19TH HOLE

"Anytime a golfer hits a ball perfectly straight with a big club it is, in my view, a fluke."   —Jack Nicklaus

Quiz Answer: Arnold Palmer.

SEPTEMBER

TODAY'S THOUGHT:
"The good chip is like the good sandtrap shot, it's your secret weapon. It allows you to whistle while you walk in the dark alleys of golf." —Tommy Bolt

ON THIS DATE—
In 1946, Patty Berg won the first U.S. Women's Open ever played. Berg defeated Betty Jameson, 5 & 4, in the finals of the match play event.

CHIP SHOT
LPGA players Betsy King, Beth Daniel, and Dottie Mochrie all attended Furman College in Greenville, SC.

TRIVIA QUIZ—
In what decade did the entire PGA Tour prize money for a year reach a million dollars?

TODAY'S TIP—
Cure yourself of hitting behind the ball by practicing 8-iron shots. Hit low and through the ball, taking divots in front of the ball. Gradually return to a normal shot.

THE 19TH HOLE
"Johnny Carson plays fantastic golf on television when he stands in front of the camera with his funny little swing. On the golf course, the man has trouble walking against the wind." —Don Rickles

Quiz Answer: The 1950's. Prize money reached the one million dollar mark in 1958.

SEPTEMBER

TODAY'S THOUGHT:
"The only shots you can be dead sure of are those you've had already." —Byron Nelson

ON THIS DATE—
In 1940, Byron Nelson added another major to his list of victories, defeating Sam Snead in the finals of the PGA Championship. Nelson had already won The Masters and the U.S. Open in his career.

CHIP SHOT
Nelson played in three consecutive finals at the PGA between 1939 and '41, but could win only one.

TRIVIA QUIZ—
In the 1980's, two golfers became U.S. Open champions by winning playoffs. Who were they, and, who did they beat?

TODAY'S TIP—
If your ball is on the green but against the fringe, use your pitching wedge as a putter. Be careful to stroke it in the middle of the ball.

THE 19TH HOLE
"At the start, Sam Snead was a simple lad who couldn't tell the time in a clock factory."
—Herb Graffis, writer

Quiz Answer: Fuzzy Zoeller and Curtis Strange. Zoeller beat Greg Norman in 1984 for his Open victory. Strange won the other playoff of the decade in 1988, topping Nick Faldo.

SEPTEMBER  **3**

TODAY'S THOUGHT:

"I would much rather be hitting the driver and a nine-iron out of the rough than hitting a driver and a four-iron out of the fairway."
—Jack Nicklaus

ON THIS DATE—

In 1967, Kathy Whitworth won the LPGA Tour's richest event, edging Carol Mann at the Ladies' World Series of Golf. Whitworth took home $10,000 of the $32,000 purse.

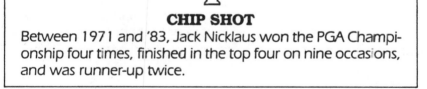

CHIP SHOT

Between 1971 and '83, Jack Nicklaus won the PGA Championship four times, finished in the top four on nine occasions, and was runner-up twice.

TRIVIA QUIZ—

Name the only foreign-born player to win the Vardon Trophy twice.

TODAY'S TIP—

Try to play with golfers who are better than you as often as possible. Watch how they swing and manage the course, using the day as a playing lesson.

─THE 19TH HOLE─

"Cypress Point is so exclusive that it had a membership drive and drove out forty members."   —Bob Hope

Quiz Answer: Australian Bruce Crampton won the award in 1973 and '75.

SEPTEMBER

TODAY'S THOUGHT:
"A man who can putt is a match for anyone."   —Willie Park, Sr.

ON THIS DATE—
In 1932, Spaniard Olin Dutra won the PGA Championship for the first major of his career. Dutra went on to win the U.S. Open two years later. Born: Raymond Floyd (1942); Tom Watson (1949).

CHIP SHOT
The first time Dr. Frank Stableford's scoring system was used was in 1932. Awarding points for performance against par was employed in a tournament near Liverpool, England.

TRIVIA QUIZ—
Tom Watson's 1977 British Open record of 268 was broken in 1993. Who did it, and, what was his score?

TODAY'S TIP—
To hit a low draw that will roll, aim slightly right of the target and play the ball back in your stance. A flat swing will shoot the ball out low and hard.

THE 19TH HOLE
"The eight hundred members of Los Angeles Country Club comprise the elite of California and legend has it that when one member proposed a movie star for membership once, they not only turned the star down, they threw out the guy who proposed him."   —Jim Murray, writer

Quiz Answer: Greg Norman shot a 13-under-par 267.

S E P T E M B E R

TODAY'S THOUGHT:

"What a shame to waste those great shots on the practice tee. I'd be afraid to stand out there and work on my game like that. I'd be afraid of finding out what I was doing wrong."   —Walter Hagen

ON THIS DATE—

In 1993, Billy Mayfair celebrated his first PGA Tour victory. Mayfair, who had lost two playoffs earlier in his career, won in sudden-death at the Greater Milwaukee Open.

CHIP SHOT

PGA Tour player Lon Hinkle is a fifth cousin, once removed, of Abraham Lincoln.

TRIVIA QUIZ—

Pebble Beach is one of three public courses to host the PGA Championship. Can you name the other two?

TODAY'S TIP—

If you've lost concentration, regain it by fixing your eyes on the back of the ball when you hit it.

THE 19TH HOLE

"If you moved Pebble Beach fifty miles inland, no one would have heard of it."   —Jimmy Demaret

Quiz Answer: North Carolina's Tanglewood GC hosted the tourney in 1974. In 1989, the championship was played at Kemper Lakes GC in Illinois.

6 SEPTEMBER

TODAY'S THOUGHT:

"A good player who is a great putter is a match for any golfer. A great hitter who cannot putt is a match for no one."

—Ben Sayers, writer

ON THIS DATE—

In 1916, Ed Oliver was born. Known as "Porky" because of his generous girth, Oliver was never the bride at the majors but was a disappointed bridesmaid many times.

CHIP SHOT

Oliver and five other golfers were disqualified from the 1940 U.S. Open for starting the fourth round before their scheduled tee time. Oliver would have been in a three-way playoff for the title if he had not been disqualified.

TRIVIA QUIZ—

Name the Hall-of-Famer who holds the record for appearing in the most Masters.

TODAY'S TIP—

Can't decide on what club to use? If there's trouble over the green, take the lesser club. If there's no difference, take a longer club and swing smoothly.

THE 19TH HOLE

"My handicap? Arthritis." —Bobby Jones

Quiz Answer: Sam Snead played in 44 Masters tournaments in his career.

SEPTEMBER 7

TODAY'S THOUGHT:

"A noted psychiatrist's wife asked him why he never let her play golf with him. My dear, he admonished her, there are three things a man must do alone: testify, die, and putt."

—Bennett Cerf, humorist

ON THIS DATE—

In 1923, Louise Suggs was born. A founder and charter member of the LPGA, Suggs was the first woman elected to the Hall of Fame in 1951. Also born: Mark McCumber (1951).

CHIP SHOT

The shortest hole on the British Open rota is the eighth at Royal Troon, Scotland. It's 126 yards long.

TRIVIA QUIZ—

This golfer's only victory in the 1950's was a memorable one. He beat Ben Hogan in a playoff to win the 1955 U.S. Open. Who was it?

TODAY'S TIP—

If faced with a blind pin on an elevated green, walk up to the green and stand on line between your ball and the pin. Pick an object behind the pin to use as your target.

THE 19TH HOLE

"It's a lot easier hitting a quarterback than a little white ball."

——Bubba Smith, actor and former football player

Quiz Answer: Jack Fleck.

SEPTEMBER

TODAY'S THOUGHT:
"I used to think pressure was standing over a four-foot putt knowing I had to make it. I learned that real pressure was sixty-five people waiting for their food with only thirty minutes left on their lunch-hour break."   —Amy Alcott, on the pressure of waitressing

ON THIS DATE—
In 1974, JoAnne Carner captured the Dallas Civitan Open for her fifth win of the year. Carner led the LPGA Tour in victories that year with six.

CHIP SHOT
The greater the bet, the longer the short putts become.

TRIVIA QUIZ—
When Mike Souchak won the 1955 Texas Open, he set a record for the lowest 72-hole score. What did Souchak shoot?

TODAY'S TIP—
When you have a real early tee time, prepare by waking up an hour earlier than usual. Your body will be more alert, and you'll feel a lot looser.

THE 19TH HOLE
"After winning the U.S. Open, all of a sudden I'm an expert on everything. Interviewers want your opinion of golf, foreign policy, and even the price of peanuts."
—Hubert Green, 1977 winner

Quiz Answer: Souchak had rounds of 60, 68, 64, and 65 for a 27-under-par 257.

SEPTEMBER

TODAY'S THOUGHT:

"Golf, especially championship golf, isn't supposed to be any fun, was never meant to be fair, and never will make any sense."
—Charles Price, writer

ON THIS DATE—

In 1990, Patty Sheehan won the first of two straight tournaments when she took the Ping-Cellular One Golf Championship. Sheehan finished second on the money-winning list.

CHIP SHOT

After a pro-am at Doral in 1970, Raymond Floyd wrote his front-side score of 36 in the space reserved for the ninth hole. He signed the card and ended up with a round of 110.

TRIVIA QUIZ—

Name the golfer with exactly four letters in his last name who won the 1986 PGA Championship.

TODAY'S TIP—

For better contact, mark practice balls with a small dot. Place the ball so that the dot is where the club will make impact. Focus on the dot with your left eye and make sure you hold that focus through impact. More focus, better contact.

THE 19TH HOLE

"My game is impossible to help. Ben Hogan said every time he gave me a lesson it added two shots to his game." —Phil Harris, comedian

Quiz Answer: Bob Tway.

SEPTEMBER

TODAY'S THOUGHT:
"Under a new USGA rule, anyone using the word charisma in writing about Palmer will be subject to a two-stroke penalty and loss of down." —Herbert Warren Wind, writer

ON THIS DATE—
In 1924, the commander-in-chief of Arnie's Army was born. Arnold Palmer's aggressive style of play would help him become the first golfer to win four Masters.

CHIP SHOT
The golfer who leads the PGA Tour in prize money for the season is awarded the Palmer Trophy.

TRIVIA QUIZ—
Legal or illegal: A candy wrapper is lying on my ball in the fairway. As I pick the wrapper up, my ball moves.

TODAY'S TIP—
Prevent your ball position from changing on every shot by starting your set-up with your feet together. Then set the ball on the tee according to where your left foot is. Then move your right foot into place.

——THE 19TH HOLE——
"His follow-through resembled a duck hunter tracking a teal." —Al Barkow, writer, on Arnold Palmer

Quiz Answer: There is no penalty. A candy wrapper is not a natural object.

S E P T E M B E R

TODAY'S THOUGHT:
"Golf is the 'only-est' sport." —Hale Irwin

ON THIS DATE—
In 1992, Raymond Floyd made his debut on the Senior PGA Tour. Floyd turned in a 1-under-par 71 in the first round of the Bank One Senior Golf Classic, four strokes behind the leader. Born: Jeff Sluman (1957); David Frost (1959); Robert Wrenn (1959).

CHIP SHOT
Skip Kendall's week at the 1995 Nissan Open was a memorable one. On Monday, he crashed a tournament sponsor's courtesy car and escaped unscathed. That night, he awoke in pain from a toothache that needed root canal work. And, finally, Kendall shot a 283 to finish 46th in the tournament.

TRIVIA QUIZ—
True or false: No Asian has ever won a major championship.

TODAY'S TIP—
One way to increase your accuracy on pitches and chips is to set up with your right arm farther away from your body than usual. It'll give you a straight back and through motion.

THE 19TH HOLE
"I sometimes wonder if Ben Crenshaw shouldn't stop reading so much about golf history and start making some." —Dave Marr

Quiz Answer: True.

SEPTEMBER

TODAY'S THOUGHT:
"Professional golf has become a game with too much character and not enough characters." —Thomas Boswell, writer

ON THIS DATE—
In 1993, David Frost birdied the final hole for a one-stroke victory in the Canadian Open. Frost was aided by the back-nine collapse of Brad Bryant, who had a 3-stroke lead. Born: Chip Beck (1956); Cindy Rarick (1959).

CHIP SHOT
Joe Lucius is the golfer who scored 13 aces on the 15th hole at the Mohawk GC in Ohio. Lucius was nearly as successful on the 10th hole, which he aced 10 times.

TRIVIA QUIZ—
The "Augusta National Invitation Tournament" was the original name of what tournament?

TODAY'S TIP—
When you're down in a match, avoid low percentage shots, and wait for your opponent to make a mistake.

THE 19TH HOLE
"I know I haven't won a lot of tournaments, but my banker doesn't know the difference."
—**Payne Stewart**

Quiz Answer: Bobby Jones thought the name "Masters" was presumptuous. But when the press referred to the tournament as The Masters, the name became official the following year.

SEPTEMBER

TODAY'S THOUGHT:

"The fun you get from golf is in direct ratio to the effort you don't put into it." —Bob Allen

ON THIS DATE—

In 1949, the Ladies Professional Golf Association was founded. Babe Zaharias, Louise Suggs, Patty Berg, and Betty Jameson were the leading forces behind the formation of the LPGA. Born: Mark Wiebe (1957).

CHIP SHOT

Clayton Heafner was known as a fiery competitor by his fellow pros. Just before Heafner was about to tee off at the 1941 Oakland (CA) Open, the marshal mispronounced his name. Insulted, Heafner withdrew from the tournament.

TRIVIA QUIZ—

I'm making my charge at the PGA Championship when I ask you, my caddie, to hand me my "lofter." What club do you hand me?

TODAY'S TIP—

If your hip action is getting ahead of your hand and wrist action, you'll slice shots. Slow down your hip unwind or speed up your clubhead release.

THE 19TH HOLE

"Some hotel rugs are impossible to putt."
—Tom Watson

Quiz Answer: My 8-iron.

 SEPTEMBER

TODAY'S THOUGHT:
"You don't go home and talk about the great tennis courts that you played, but you do talk about the golf courses you played."
—Hank Ketcham, cartoonist

ON THIS DATE—
In 1927, Gardner Dickinson was born. Dickinson was a member of US Ryder Cup teams in 1967 and 1971. His wife, Judy, makes her living on the LPGA Tour.

CHIP SHOT
Winless in 18 years on the PGA Tour, Gary McCord had "NO WINS" on his vanity license plate. When he won on the Hogan Tour in 1991, McCord added an asterisk to the plate.

TRIVIA QUIZ—
Oakmont CC was the course where Johnny Miller fired a final round of 63 to win the 1973 U.S. Open. Where is it located?

TODAY'S TIP—
Releasing the club before you have sufficient hip clearance will produce a hook. Either speed up your hip action or hold back a little on your clubhead release.

THE 19TH HOLE
"Jerry Pate withdrew citing a shoulder injury, and Jack Renner withdrew citing his score."
—John Morris, USGA official

Quiz Answer: Oakmont, Pennsylvania.

SEPTEMBER

TODAY'S THOUGHT:
"Show me someone who gets angry once in a while, and I'll show you a guy with a killer instinct. Show me a guy walking down the fairway smiling and I'll show you a loser." —Lee Trevino

ON THIS DATE—
In 1899, Willie Smith won the fifth U.S. Open. Smith and his brothers, Alex and Macdonald, combined to finish in the top 3 at the Open 13 times. Born: Fulton Allem (1957).

CHIP SHOT
In 1899, golfers at the Atlantic City (NJ) CC came up with the word "birdie" when George Crump put his second shot inches from the hole on a par four after his ball hit a bird in flight.

TRIVIA QUIZ—
Tommy Armour won three of the four major championships in his career. What's the only tournament he didn't win?

TODAY'S TIP—
As long as you start down with your lower body and keep it ahead of your upper half, you can't hit too early with your hands and wrists. Get the legs going and let the clubhead fly.

THE 19TH HOLE
"Hell, I don't need to know where the green is. Where is the golf course?"
—Babe Ruth, playing Pine Valley

Quiz Answer: The Masters.

SEPTEMBER

TODAY'S THOUGHT:

"Most golfers prepare for disaster. A good golfer prepares for success." —Bob Toski

ON THIS DATE—

In 1961, 21-year old Jack Nicklaus won his second U.S. Amateur Championship. The Ohio State senior had already won the NCAA individual title earlier in the year. Born: Tom Wargo (1942).

CHIP SHOT

Because the golf course in Tientsin, China is laid out in a cemetery, greens are situated between grave mounds. Local rule: A ball which rolls into an open grave may be lifted without penalty.

TRIVIA QUIZ—

Name the native country of 1967 British Open champion Roberto de Vicenzo.

TODAY'S TIP—

To achieve strong leg action, keep both knees flexed through impact. Stiffening your front leg will cause your shoulders to spin over the ball.

THE 19TH HOLE

"Jack Nicklaus has become a legend in his spare time."
—Chi Chi Rodriguez

Quiz Answer: Argentina.

S E P T E M B E R

TODAY'S THOUGHT:
"What other people may find in poetry or art museums, I find in the flight of a good drive."   —Arnold Palmer

ON THIS DATE—
In 1897, English pro Joe Lloyd became champion of the U.S. Open as foreign-born players continued to dominate. The Open was played for the first time at Chicago GC. Born: Scott Simpson (1955).

CHIP SHOT
The silver claret jug presented to the winner of the British Open is not kept by the champion, but is returned to the Royal & Ancient GC where it is displayed in the club's trophy case.

TRIVIA QUIZ—
When was the last time a golfer won the U.S. Open in his first attempt?

TODAY'S TIP—
Never hurry your shoulders in the downswing. Try to keep the upward movement of your left shoulder as slow as possible. The slower it is, the more time your legs have to move towards the target before your shoulders unwind.

THE 19TH HOLE
"The toughest hole is the nineteenth. I just can't get through it. It takes the longest time to play."
—Craig Stadler

Quiz Answer: 1913, when Francis Ouimet won the championship.

 **SEPTEMBER**

TODAY'S THOUGHT:

"Golf is, I should say offhand, the most useless outdoor game ever devised to waste the time and try the spirit of man." —Westbrook Pegler, writer

ON THIS DATE—

In 1994, the United States beat the International team, 20-12, to win the inaugural Presidents Cup. Fred Couples' birdie putt in his match with Nick Price gave the Americans the victory.

CHIP SHOT

PGA Tour member Bruce Lietzke is actress Kirstie Alley's first cousin.

TRIVIA QUIZ—

What's the last name of the LPGA player known by the first name "Muffin?"

TODAY'S TIP—

Going into your backswing, the lower body works in response to the coiling of your upper body. Coming into your downswing, exactly the reverse must happen, your upper body responding to the uncoiling of your lower body.

THE 19TH HOLE

"My car absolutely will not run unless my golf clubs are in the trunk." —Bruce Berlet, writer

Quiz Answer: Spencer-Devlin.

SEPTEMBER

TODAY'S THOUGHT:

"The player may experiment about his swing, his grip, his stance. It is only when he begins asking his caddie's advice that he is getting on dangerous ground."   —Sir Walter Simpson, writer

ON THIS DATE—

In 1993, South African David Frost won his second straight tournament, defending his title at the Hardee's Golf Classic. Frost was the first golfer in 18 years to win in consecutive weeks while repeating as a tournament winner.

CHIP SHOT

Golf's richest first prize is at the Million Dollar Challenge in Sun City, South Africa. Low score gets $1 million.

TRIVIA QUIZ—

Name the only two golfers to successfully defend their Masters titles.

TODAY'S TIP—

Stop your high iron shots from landing short of the target by setting up with a little extra weight on your front foot. Start down with your legs, hitting down and through the ball.

——THE 19TH HOLE——

"The pay is great, and the only way you can get hurt playing golf is by getting struck by lightning."
—Ted Williams, baseball Hall-of-Famer

Quiz Answer: Jack Nicklaus, who did it in 1965, and Nick Faldo, who was the winner in 1990.

SEPTEMBER

TODAY'S THOUGHT:

"Naturally, it was my hope to win out. I simply tried my best to keep this cup from going to our friends across the water."
                              —Francis Ouiment, after the 1913 U.S. Open

ON THIS DATE—

In 1913, 20-year old Francis Ouimet stunned British greats Harry Vardon and Ted Ray in a playoff to win the U.S. Open. Ouimet was the first amateur to win the title.

CHIP SHOT

Ouimet's caddie for the biggest win of his life was Eddie Lowery, who was ten years old. Also making his Open debut was 20-year old Walter Hagen. He finished three strokes back.

TRIVIA QUIZ—

Who was the only foreign-born player to win the U.S. Open in the 1960's?

TODAY'S TIP—

When faced with a downhill putt on a fast green, grip the club lightly and strike the ball on a slight upswing. That way you won't pop or jab the putt.

THE 19TH HOLE

"The first time Bob Gibson ever let himself get talked into a celebrity golf tournament, he shot a score of 115. It was his own fault. He counted all his strokes."
                    —Bob Uecker, actor and baseball announcer

---

Quiz Answer: Gary Player, who won in 1965.

SEPTEMBER

TODAY'S THOUGHT:

"It matters not the sacrifice which makes the duffer's wife so sore. I am the captive of my slice. I am the servant of my score."
—Grantland Rice

ON THIS DATE—

In 1969, Donna Caponi won her second tournament of the year, edging Kathy Whitworth at the Lincoln-Mercury Open. Caponi's first win that year came at the U.S. Women's Open.

CHIP SHOT

In 1969, Kathy Whitworth was a winner 7 times and finished second 7 times. She also tied the record for consecutive wins with 4.

TRIVIA QUIZ—

Name the first American golf club to have an 18-hole course.

TODAY'S TIP—

Gripping your long-iron too much in the palm of your right hand inhibits full release of the clubhead through the ball and distance on your shot. Grip it more towards your fingers for the slinging action needed on impact to give you distance.

THE 19TH HOLE

"The sand was heavier than I thought, and it only took me four swings to figure it out." —Johnny Miller

Quiz Answer: The Chicago Golf Club, which opened in 1894.

SEPTEMBER

TODAY'S THOUGHT:
"We always considered it quite a feat to get down our six-to-eight footers, but now if a fellow misses from forty feet he grimaces and agonizes like a cowboy struck in the heart by an Indian's arrow." —Ben Hogan

ON THIS DATE—
In 1905, Willie Anderson, the first dominant golfer in America this century, won his third straight U.S. Open. It was his fourth title in 5 years. Born: Missie Berteotti (1963).

CHIP SHOT
Costantino Rocca became the first Italian to play in the Ryder Cup when he played for Europe in 1993.

TRIVIA QUIZ—
This former PGA Championship winner was up to his knickers in money in 1993, winning over $900,000. Yet he didn't win a single tournament that year. Who was it?

TODAY'S TIP—
Don't force the big shot. Use your basic swing, but get your arms higher at the top. Don't start down until you've felt your hands reach above your shoulders.

THE 19TH HOLE
"My putter will not be flying first-class home with me."
—Nick Faldo

Quiz Answer: Payne Stewart, who won $982,875 that year.

SEPTEMBER  23

TODAY'S THOUGHT:

"Great players win with their minds. They see nothing but positives out there."   —Chi Chi Rodriguez

ON THIS DATE—

In 1958, Larry Mize was born. Mize will be forever known as the man who won the 1987 Masters with a 100-foot chip shot on the second hole of a playoff with Greg Norman. The Augusta native birdied the final hole to get into that playoff.

CHIP SHOT

In 1981, Australian TV tycoon Kerry Parker hired PGA Tour pro Phil Rodgers for two weeks of private lessons. The fee, in addition to Rodgers' airfare, was $50,000.

TRIVIA QUIZ—

Only three golfers have ever competed in over 30 consecutive U.S. Opens. Who are they?

TODAY'S TIP—

Losing distance as you get older or heavier? Try a fuller hip turn, letting your hips rotate a little more in response to your arm swing and shoulder wind-up.

—THE 19TH HOLE—

"Things were a lot better when I had only one check-book."   —Patty Sheehan

Quiz Answer: Gene Sarazen, Arnold Palmer, and Jack Nicklaus can claim that honor.

 **SEPTEMBER**

TODAY'S THOUGHT:

"St. Andrews . . . crotchety and eccentric, but also elegant."

—Tony Lema

ON THIS DATE—

In 1895, Tommy Armour was born. The "Silver Scot" won the U.S. and British Opens despite having lost an eye in a mustard gas attack during World War I. Armour had a long, lucrative career as a writer of best-selling instructional books.

CHIP SHOT

Armour's 1931 British Open win came at Carnoustie, the first Open to be played in his homeland, Scotland.

TRIVIA QUIZ—

Bobby Jones won his native state's amateur title at the age of 14. Name the state.

TODAY'S TIP—

Mishits on the green are caused when you have the toe or heel of the putter off the ground. Have someone check your putter as it lies behind the ball. Set the club behind the ball so it just touches the ground, but is flat to the turf.

THE 19TH HOLE

"Gary Player solicits far too much advice on the practice tee. I've seen him taking a lesson at the U.S. Open from a hot dog vendor."   —Dave Hill

---

Quiz Answer: Georgia.

SEPTEMBER

TODAY'S THOUGHT:
"He is the reason we're playing for all this money today."
—Ken Still, on Arnold Palmer

ON THIS DATE—
In 1949, Louise Suggs won the U.S. Women's Open decisively, beating Babe Zaharias by 14 strokes. Suggs carded an opening round of 69 and finished with a record 291. Born: Gil Morgan (1946).

CHIP SHOT
Jack Nicklaus holds the record for the longest time between victories at The Masters. Nicklaus first won the tournament in 1963 and then again in 1986, a span of 23 years.

TRIVIA QUIZ—
From 1897 until 1933, the NCAA golf team champions came from the same conference. Which one?

TODAY'S TIP—
Believe it or not, but a new putter can help you get out of a putting slump. Get one that is completely different than the one you normally use. Because it's different, you'll be forced to focus a little more when putting. Try it.

THE 19TH HOLE
"How did I take a twelve? I had a long putt for an eleven." ——Clayton Heafner

Quiz Answer: The Ivy League, which was dominated by Yale.

 **S E P T E M B E R**

TODAY'S THOUGHT:

"It's funny. You need a fantastic memory in this game to remember the great shots, and a very short memory to forget the bad ones." —Gary McCord

ON THIS DATE—

In 1925, Walter Hagen defended his PGA Championship title at the expense of Bill Mehlhorn, 6 & 5. It was Hagen's third title overall.

CHIP SHOT

Mehlhorn knew he was in for a rough day when Hagen aced the first hole of the match.

TRIVIA QUIZ—

The record for a round during the British Open at St. Andrews is 65. But the course record is 62, shot by this American during a match in the 1987 Dunhill Cup. Who was it?

TODAY'S TIP—

Don't make a bad situation worse. If your ball is in a particularly bad area, consider taking an unplayable lie. Don't think of hitting the miracle shot. Take the small penalty to get your ball to a safe place instead of a high score.

THE 19TH HOLE

"Call every woman 'Sugar' and you can't go wrong."
—Walter Hagen

Quiz Answer: Curtis Strange, who set the standard playing in a match against Greg Norman.

S E P T E M B E R

TODAY'S THOUGHT:

"I have never felt so lonely as on a golf course in the midst of a championship with thousands of people around, especially when things began to go wrong and the crowd started wandering away." —Bobby Jones

ON THIS DATE—

In 1930, Bobby Jones secured his place among golf's greats by winning the U.S. Amateur and completing the Grand Slam. Less than two months later, Jones announced his retirement from golf at the age of 28. Born: Kathy Whitworth (1939).

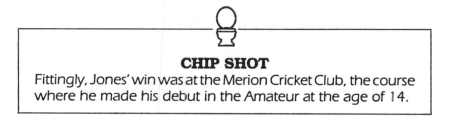

CHIP SHOT

Fittingly, Jones' win was at the Merion Cricket Club, the course where he made his debut in the Amateur at the age of 14.

TRIVIA QUIZ—

Name the native country of PGA Tour player T.C. Chen.

TODAY'S TIP—

Try practicing sand shots without a ball to get the proper feel. Use a smooth swing to get the sand to fly high and splash on the green. Remember, if the sand flies that way, your ball will also.

THE 19TH HOLE

"I'm not concerned about getting in the record books. A good obituary doesn't exactly excite me."
—JoAnne Carner

Quiz Answer: Taiwan.

SEPTEMBER

TODAY'S THOUGHT:
"One of the most fascinating things about golf is how it reflects the cycle of life. No matter what you shoot, the next day you have to go back to the first tee and begin all over again to make yourself into something." —Peter Jacobsen

ON THIS DATE—
In 1921, Walter Hagen won the first of his five PGA Championships. Hagen beat Jim Barnes, that year's U.S. Open champ, 3 & 2.

CHIP SHOT
Raymond Floyd was the first golfer to win on both the PGA Tour and the PGA Senior Tour in the same year. He did it in 1992.

TRIVIA QUIZ—
When this golfer won the 1982 LPGA Championship, she became the first Australian to win an LPGA major. Who was it?

TODAY'S TIP—
For a short lob onto the green, open your stance and the blade of your wedge. Taking the club back slightly to the outside, come down sharply and follow through.

THE 19TH HOLE
"Hell, this is only Wednesday. Nobody ever made money on Wednesday."
        —Jimmy Demaret, after a bad practice round

Quiz Answer: Jan Stephenson.

SEPTEMBER

TODAY'S THOUGHT:
"An amateur golfer truly moves heaven and earth." —Anonymous

ON THIS DATE—
In 1991, the US ended Europe's six-year Ryder Cup reign when Bernhard Langer missed a 5-foot putt on the final hole. And, Pat Bradley came up a winner at the MBS LPGA Classic, her 30th career victory which qualified her for the LPGA Hall of Fame.

CHIP SHOT
Two-time NCAA champion and 1987 U.S. Open winner, Scott Simpson, failed the PGA qualifying school twice before making it through on the third try. His second attempt included a 12 on one hole.

TRIVIA QUIZ—
Who was the first American to win a PGA Championship?

TODAY'S TIP—
Don't jab at an uphill putt with a short stroke. Take a longer backswing and follow-through, sweeping the ball up the hill.

THE 19TH HOLE
"I didn't realize how windy it was yesterday until I got a look at Tom Watson. The wind had blown 14 freckles off his face."
—Jerry McGee, at the 1979 San Diego Open

Quiz Answer: Walter Hagen, who won his first of five PGA titles in 1921.

 **SEPTEMBER**

TODAY'S THOUGHT:

"Looking up is the biggest alibi ever invented to explain a terrible shot. By the time you look up, you've already made the mistake that caused the bad shot."   —Harvey Penick

ON THIS DATE—

In 1973, Sam Adams finished 16-under-par at the Quad Cities Open for his first victory on the PGA Tour. That tournament record held up for 15 years.

CHIP SHOT

Don't you hate playing golf with a player so good, he doesn't have to cheat?

TRIVIA QUIZ—

The youngest golfer to ever win The Masters won it four days after his 23rd birthday. Name him.

TODAY'S TIP—

A good swing won't do you any good if it's not aimed properly. Either have a friend check your alignment periodically, or do it yourself by checking your stance against a club laying on the ground parallel to the target line.

——THE 19TH HOLE——

"I've never been to heaven and, thinkin' back on my life, I probably won't get a chance to go. I guess The Masters is as close as I'm going to get."

—**Fuzzy Zoeller**

Quiz Answer: Seve Ballesteros in 1980.

O C T O B E R

TODAY'S THOUGHT:
"The most advanced medical brains in the universe have yet to discover a way for a man to relax himself, and looking at a golf ball is not the cure."   —Milton Gross, writer

ON THIS DATE—
In 1939, George Archer was born. Serious wrist and back problems short-circuited Archer's PGA Tour career, but the 1969 Masters winner has gone on to become one of the more dominant golfers on the Senior PGA Tour.

CHIP SHOT
The lowest round in U.S. Women's Open history was a 65 by Sally Little, but it's the only major Little has never won.

TRIVIA QUIZ—
Name the last golfer to successfully defend his U.S. Open title.

TODAY'S TIP—
Let the club do the work when you want a high, soft lob shot. Use a lofted wedge and take a long upright swing. Make a high follow-through using only your upper body.

THE 19TH HOLE
"Sam is so loose, that if you cut his wrist, 3-in-1 Oil would come out."
—Gardner Dickinson, on Sam Snead

Quiz Answer: Curtis Strange, who won the U.S. Open championship in 1988 and '89.

OCTOBER

TODAY'S THOUGHT:

"Let's face it, 95 percent of this game is mental. A guy plays lousy golf, he doesn't need a pro, he needs a shrink." —Tom Murphy

ON THIS DATE—

In 1994, Larry Gilbert outdueled Raymond Floyd to win the Senior PGA Tour's Vantage Championship by one stroke. The former club pro shot three rounds of 66. Born: John Cook (1957).

CHIP SHOT

Chick Evans, Jr. played in 50 consecutive U.S. Amateur Golf Championships. He won the title twice.

TRIVIA QUIZ—

Since 1950, three players with exactly four letters in their last names have won the British Open. Who were they?

TODAY'S TIP—

Not satisfied with your wedge shots? Open your stance slightly and align your shoulders and clubface at the target. This will allow you to clear your hips out of the way.

THE 19TH HOLE

"I played nine holes with the new short distance ball. Playing a match with it is like two boxers fighting with pillows." —Sam Snead

Quiz Answer: Tony Lema in 1964, Sandy Lyle in 1985, and John Daly in 1995.

O C T O B E R

TODAY'S THOUGHT:
"We really have to play with 15 clubs. We have 14 in our bag and the 15th in our head." —Greg Twiggs, on the PGA Tour

ON THIS DATE—
In 1993, John Inman prevailed in a five-way playoff to win the Southern Open. For Inman, it was his first victory on the PGA Tour in six years. Born: Harold Henning (1934); Fred Couples (1959).

CHIP SHOT
Seve Ballesteros, when asked if he and Lee Trevino speak Spanish when they see each other, replied, "No, Trevino speaks Mexican."

TRIVIA QUIZ—
What Hall of Fame LPGA golfer is married to a baseball World Series MVP winner?

TODAY'S TIP—
Don't try to correct a slice (there's that word, again) by aiming farther left of the target. Aim a little to the right to make a straighter swing.

THE 19TH HOLE
"That hasn't been Johnny Miller out there. That's been somebody else with somebody else's swing."
—Johnny Miller, in a slump

Quiz Answer: Nancy Lopez. She is married to Ray Knight, who won the award with the New York Mets in 1986.

OCTOBER

TODAY'S THOUGHT:

"When a player flies one into the weeds, the world wants to see him start hacking. We want to see beads of sweat around his corporate visor and hear his muffled curses about cows and corn fields."
—E.M. Swift, writer, on the U.S. Open

ON THIS DATE—

In 1895, ten professionals and an amateur competed in the first U.S. Open at the Newport (RI) GC. 19-year old English pro Horace Rawlins beat Willie Dunn by two strokes after four rounds of Newport's nine-hole layout.

CHIP SHOT

The inaugural Open had been postponed from September so it wouldn't clash with the America's Cup yacht races, which were held in Newport.

TRIVIA QUIZ—

Who is the only man to lose two playoffs and never win the U.S. Open?

TODAY'S TIP—

From wet rough, use a well-lofted wood for distance. Play out safely from bad lies with a wedge.

THE 19TH HOLE

"It's like playing in a straitjacket. They just lay you up on the rack and twist on both ends."
—Ben Crenshaw, on U.S. Open pressure

Quiz Answer: Mike Brady lost playoffs in 1911 and '19.

O C T O B E R

TODAY'S THOUGHT:
"In my opinion, you're a long time dead, so you might as well have fun while you can."   —Laura Davies

ON THIS DATE—
In 1900, Harry Vardon became the first foreign-based professional to win the U.S. Open. Vardon beat that year's British Open champ, J.H. Taylor, by two strokes at the Chicago GC. Born: Laura Davies (1963).

CHIP SHOT
Vardon was in the midst of an American tour when he played the Open. His itinerary covered 20,000 miles and was only interrupted when he returned home to defend his British Open title. He finished second.

TRIVIA QUIZ—
Can you name the amateur golfer who has won the most British Open championships?

TODAY'S TIP—
If your ball is buried in wet sand, play your normal explosion shot with the pitching wedge.

——THE 19TH HOLE——
"Moderation is essential in all things, Madam, but never in my life have I failed to beat a teetotaler."
—Harry Vardon, when asked to join the temperance movement

Quiz Answer: Bobby Jones won in 1926, '27, and '30.

OCTOBER 6

TODAY'S THOUGHT:

"To succeed at anything, you must have a huge ego. I'm not talking about confidence. Confidence is self-assurance for a reason. Ego is self-assurance for no good reason."   —Frank Beard

ON THIS DATE—

In 1928, Leo Diegel topped Al Espinosa, 6 & 5, to win the PGA Championship. Earlier in the tournament, Diegel ended Walter Hagen's unbeaten streak at 22 matches.

CHIP SHOT

Exactly 41 years later to the day, Hagen, the winner of 5 PGA titles, died from throat cancer at the age of 76.

TRIVIA QUIZ—

Byron Nelson holds the record for most victories in one year with 18 wins in 1945. Who's second?

TODAY'S TIP—

To practice a breaking putt, place a coin outside of the hole as a target. Stroke the ball at the coin. On the course, use an imaginary coin to set the break.

THE 19TH HOLE

"One good thing about shooting the way I've been shooting. You get to play early while the greens are still smooth."   —Arnold Palmer

Quiz Answer: The following year, 1946, Ben Hogan won 13 tournaments on the PGA Tour, another number never matched.

O C T O B E R

TODAY'S THOUGHT:

"Too many people carry the last shot with them. It is a heavy and useless burden." —Johnny Miller

ON THIS DATE—

In 1965, Robert Mitura shot the ace of all aces with his 440-yard hole-in-one at the 10th hole of the aptly-named Miracle Hills GC in Omaha, Nebraska. Mitura was aided by a 50 mph wind and a 290-yard drop-off.

CHIP SHOT

Gary Hallberg's hole-in-one in the third round of the 1995 U.S. Open was the 27th known ace in an Open. It was the first in Open competition at Shinnecock Hills GC.

TRIVIA QUIZ—

What golfer was called "Mr. X" by his fellow players during his PGA Tour career?

TODAY'S TIP—

Most of the time a lousy tee shot is caused by rushing at the top of your swing. Start the downswing slowly and let your hands release naturally as you enter the impact area.

THE 19TH HOLE

"I don't say my golf game is bad; but if I grew tomatoes, they'd come up sliced." —Miller Barber

Quiz Answer: Miller Barber. Barber was dubbed "Mr. X" because of his fondness for solitude.

OCTOBER 8

TODAY'S THOUGHT:

"To get an elementary grasp of the game of golf, a human must learn, by endless practice, a continuous and subtle series of highly unnatural movements, involving about 64 muscles, that result in a seemingly natural swing, taking all of two seconds to begin and end." —Alistair Cooke, writer

ON THIS DATE—

In 1973, Jack Nicklaus won the $25,000 first prize at the Ohio-Kings Island Open. The Golden Bear promptly donated the money to charity.

CHIP SHOT

To train Tommy Nakajima to play in the rain, his father used to squirt him in the face with a hose while the future pro hit golf balls.

TRIVIA QUIZ—

A three-time Masters champ, I appeared on the cover of *Golf* magazine's first issue in April, 1959. Who am I?

TODAY'S TIP—

Lining up square is aligning your feet, knees, hips, and shoulders to the target. Set up along the lines of a linoleum floor. If it feels awkward, you've probably been lining up wrong.

THE 19TH HOLE

"Now I can see I can't make anything."
—Jack Nicklaus, on his new contact lenses

Quiz Answer: Jimmy Demaret.

O C T O B E R

TODAY'S THOUGHT:
"The kids on the Tour today are too good at losing. Show me a good loser and I'll show you a seldom winner."   —Sam Snead

ON THIS DATE—
In 1994, Rick Fehr joined the list of single-tournament winners when he captured the Walt Disney World Golf Classic. Only four golfers were able to win more than one event that year on the PGA Tour.

CHIP SHOT
According to the National Golf Foundation, the average 18-hole golf course covers 133 acres, more than half of which is rough. As if you didn't know!

TRIVIA QUIZ—
Name the English golfer who was the only foreign-born player to win the U.S. Open in the 1970's.

TODAY'S TIP—
A backhand shot comes in handy if your ball is against a tree. Turn around so that your back faces the target. Grip the club in your right hand only and remain still while swinging the club at the ball with just your right arm.

THE 19TH HOLE
"If I had known it was going in the water, I wouldn't have hit it there."   —Mike Reid

Quiz Answer: Tony Jacklin, who won in 1970.

 O C T O B E R

TODAY'S THOUGHT:
"My game is not for display right now. I do, however, get great pleasure from playing and replaying holes in my mind."
—Ben Hogan, on retirement

ON THIS DATE—
In 1962, Joseph Boydstone scored three holes-in-one on the front nine of his round. Boydstone aced the 3rd, 4th, and 9th holes of the Bakersfield(CA) GC course.

CHIP SHOT
At the 1992 Players Championship, John Daly, playing with Mark Calcavecchia, dashed around the course in 1 hour, 49 minutes, carded an 80, and received a reprimand from the PGA Tour.

TRIVIA QUIZ—
What's the name of the country club which hosted the first PGA Championship in 1916?

TODAY'S TIP—
Here's something to try if your putts are pulling up short. Place the head of the club two inches behind the ball at address. Focus on the back of the ball and make a short backswing.

THE 19TH HOLE
"Every time it's come to stand up and be counted, I've sat down."
—Hubert Green, before he won the U.S. Open

Quiz Answer: The first PGA Championship was held at Siwanoy CC in Bronxville, NY.

O C T O B E R

TODAY'S THOUGHT:

"Many shots are spoiled at the last instant by efforts to add a few more yards." —Bobby Jones

ON THIS DATE—

In 1991, Chip Beck tied pro golf's all-time low score, shooting a 13-under-par 59 in the third round of the Las Vegas Invitational. Beck matched Al Geiberger's record-score with 13 birdies and 5 pars.

CHIP SHOT

By breaking 60, Beck received a $1 million bonus, half to Beck and half to charity.

TRIVIA QUIZ—

Legal or illegal: My ball is overhanging the lip of the cup and I wait two minutes. At that point, the ball falls into the cup.

TODAY'S TIP—

The mental aspect of golf cannot be emphasized enough. The most important shot is the next one. Don't pout about the putt you just missed. Stay in the present.

—THE 19TH HOLE—

"Belly dancers would make great golfers. They never move their heads." —— Phil Rodgers

Quiz Answer: Illegal. I am assessed with a one-stroke penalty. If it was my fourth shot, I get a five for the hole.

 **OCTOBER**

TODAY'S THOUGHT:

"Sometimes you win tournaments playing just awesome, and I just happened to win a tournament not playing so awesome. Every once in a while you get lucky."
— Patty Sheehan, after the 1995 Rochester International

ON THIS DATE—

In 1991, Chip Beck followed up his record-matching 59 with a 68 in the fourth of five rounds in the Las Vegas Invitational. Andrew Magee went on to win the tournament.

CHIP SHOT

Even though the USGA allowed steel-shafted clubs since 1924, Bobby Jones used hickory-shafted clubs through 1930.

TRIVIA QUIZ—

What golf club is considered to be the oldest American golf club in continuous operation?

TODAY'S TIP—

Don't freeze up on a tough hole. Grip the club lightly, breathe deep, and let the swing flow. Make an extra effort to stay balanced.

—THE 19TH HOLE—

"When Bob Hope sings `Thanks for the Memory' he is recollecting the last time he broke 90 on a miniature golf course." —Gerald Ford

Quiz Answer: St. Andrews of Hastings-on-Hudson, NY. Originally based in Yonkers, NY, the club was founded on November 14, 1888.

O C T O B E R

TODAY'S THOUGHT:
"When I first came on Tour, it terrified me to hit the first drive. I was lucky if I kept it in play. That feeling has disappeared for the most part, but I still feel it once in a while."   —Lon Hinkle

ON THIS DATE—
In 1963, Mickey Wright won the LPGA Championship for the fourth time in six years. Her four wins in that tournament is still an LPGA record.

CHIP SHOT
Arnold Palmer started the 1993 Masters with birdies on the first three holes, a first for the four-time champ. But he bogeyed five of the next six holes, finishing at 2-over 74.

TRIVIA QUIZ—
You remember Gene Sarazen's famous double-eagle on the par-5, 15th hole in the 1935 Masters. But do you remember who his playing partner was that day?

TODAY'S TIP—
Use a less-lofted club on an approach shot in windy conditions. Play the ball back in your stance and keep your follow-through low to the ground for a low and straight shot.

THE 19TH HOLE
"I don't make mistakes. I make disasters."
—Bob Goalby

Quiz Answer: Sarazen was paired with Walter Hagen.

OCTOBER

TODAY'S THOUGHT:
"You come to the 18th hole, someone wins or loses, you don't see them stalk off. They extend their hand, in genuine appreciation of what the other guy's done. No other sport can say that."
—Deane Beman, on professional golf

ON THIS DATE—
In 1984, Bernhard Langer birdied 10 of the first 15 holes at the Spanish Open on his way to a 10-under-par 62. Born: Rocky Thompson (1939); J.C. Snead (1940); Beth Daniel (1956).

CHIP SHOT
Golf is a lot like taxes. You drive hard to get to the green and then wind up in the hole.

TRIVIA QUIZ—
True or false: Kathy Whitworth, the career leader in wins on any tour with 88, never won the U.S. Women's Open.

TODAY'S TIP—
In match play, let your opponent risk going at the pin. If you're hitting to the green first, go for the middle of the green. Remember, pars win holes.

——THE 19TH HOLE——
"I want to win every week. I go to the driving range and bop 'til I drop." —Rocky Thompson

Quiz Answer: True. Whitworth won 6 majors in her career, but the Open wasn't one of them.

O C T O B E R

TODAY'S THOUGHT:

"I know it's difficult to make it, but you've got to try it if you love golf and love the history of golf."

—Gary Hallberg, on qualifying for the British Open

ON THIS DATE—

In 1961, Mickey Wright finished ahead of Louise Suggs to win her second straight LPGA Championship. It was Wright's 10th win of the year, tops on the LPGA Tour.

CHIP SHOT

Wright and Suggs combined for 16 victories and 10 second-place finishes in the 25 tournaments on the LPGA Tour that year.

TRIVIA QUIZ—

The PGA Championship record score for 72 holes is 269. Name the golfer who did it in 1994.

TODAY'S TIP—

For a good chip shot keep your weight on your left side and keep it there. You'll want the club to brush the grass in a straight-back, straight-through motion.

THE 19TH HOLE

"I'm very even-tempered on the golf course. I stay mad all the time." —Bob Murphy

Quiz Answer: Nick Price. Price finished 11-under-par at Southern Hills CC in Tulsa, Oklahoma.

 **OCTOBER**

TODAY'S THOUGHT:

"Hitting a golf ball correctly is the most sophisticated and compli-cated maneuver in all of sport, with the possible exception of eating a hot dog at a ball game without getting mustard on your shirt."
—Ray Fitzgerald, writer

ON THIS DATE—

In 1983, Lanny Wadkins hit an 80-yard wedge shot to within three feet of the pin, then tapped in as the United States won the Ryder Cup, 14½ to 13½. It was the 21st victory for the United States.

CHIP SHOT
Golf is nature's way of making everyone a comedian.

TRIVIA QUIZ—
Who's the oldest golfer to win a PGA Tour event?

TODAY'S TIP—
In heavy rough, you want to eliminate the grass behind the ball. Pick the club up steeply on your backswing and hit the ball with a downswing that strikes the ball first.

THE 19TH HOLE
"Playing in the U.S. Open is like tippy-toeing through hell." —Jerry McGee

Quiz Answer: Sam Snead was 52 years old when he won the 1965 Greater Greensboro Open.

O C T O B E R

TODAY'S THOUGHT:

"The Clubhouse at Lytham is an ominous gabled structure of brick and wood, undoubtedly the former residence of Count Dracula. But you don't get really frightened until you see the golf course. The rough will hide golf balls, bags, and small caddies."

—Art Spander, writer

ON THIS DATE—

In 1860, eight golfers gathered at Prestwick GC to compete in the first British Open. Willie Park shot a 174 over three rounds of Prestwick's 12 holes.

CHIP SHOT

First prize was a belt made of red morocco leather adorned with silver plates. It was to become the permanent property of any player winning the title three times in a row.

TRIVIA QUIZ—

On what course did Greg Norman win his first British Open in 1986?

TODAY'S TIP—

Powdery sand is less resistant to your sand wedge. Hit down slightly farther behind the ball than usual.

THE 19TH HOLE

"You can play a damned good shot there and find the ball in a damned bad place."
—George Duncan, British Open champ, on St. Andrews

Quiz Answer: Turnberry, in Scotland.

 O C T O B E R

TODAY'S THOUGHT:

"Golf is a game whose aim is to hit a very small ball into an even smaller hole with weapons singularly ill-designed for the purpose." —Sir Winston Churchill

ON THIS DATE—

In 1992, England, playing without Nick Faldo, rode the momentum of an upset semi-final victory over the US to beat Scotland and claim the Dunhill Cup International golf championship.

CHIP SHOT

When South African golfer Bobby Locke came to America in 1947, he won six of the 13 tournaments he entered.

TRIVIA QUIZ—

During a match, you putt your ball and it hits my caddie. What's the rule?

TODAY'S TIP—

Don't slam the club into the sand behind the ball on an uphill lie in a bunker. Follow the contour of the sand, swinging the clubhead so it slices through the sand.

THE 19TH HOLE

"My IQ must be two points lower than a plant's."
—Tom Watson, explaining his disqualification for illegally changing putters

Quiz Answer: There is no penalty. You may accept the stroke and let the ball lie where it is, or cancel the stroke, return the ball to its original position, and retake the shot.

O C T O B E R

TODAY'S THOUGHT:
"The yips are that ghastly time when, with the first movement of the putter, the golfer blacks out, loses sight of the ball, and hasn't the remotest idea of what to do with the putter or, occasionally, that he is holding a putter at all." —Tommy Armour

ON THIS DATE—
In 1960, LPGA Tour player Dawn Coe-Jones was born. A native of British Columbia, Coe-Jones was the 1983 Canadian Amateur champion and winner of the 1992 Women's Kemper Open.

CHIP SHOT
When Hale Irwin travels, he takes along his regular set of clubs plus an extra driver, sand wedge, and putter.

TRIVIA QUIZ—
It's the first round of The Players Championship. My ball lies in the fairway of the first hole. I ask you, my trusty caddie, to hand me my "mid mashie." What club do you hand me?

TODAY'S TIP—
An effective club grip must do three things: deliver the clubface square at impact; take the shock of impact without the hands slipping on the club; and, allow the wrists to hinge efficiently.

THE 19TH HOLE
"At my age, I don't even buy green bananas."
—Lee Trevino, 47, at the 1987 British Open

Quiz Answer: My 3-iron.

 **OCTOBER**

TODAY'S THOUGHT:

"People tune in to see the aura of this place, and watch everybody throw up on the back nine. If Jack or Arnold are there, they're going to love it. If it's anybody else, they just like to tune in and watch." —Gary McCord, on the televising of The Masters

ON THIS DATE—

In 1991, Seve Ballesteros equaled Gary Player's record of five World Match Play titles with a 3 & 2 victory over Nick Price. Ballesteros' performance included 10 birdies.

CHIP SHOT

The PGA Tour record for fewest putts in a round is 18, held by Andy North, Kenny Knox, Mike McGee, and Sam Trahan.

TRIVIA QUIZ—

How many holes were played in the shortest U.S. Open and in the longest?

TODAY'S TIP—

For most golfers, the more the alignment of the hands matches the clubface alignment, the straighter your shot will be. If you're hooking, align your hands more to the left.

THE 19TH HOLE

"What's nice about our tour is you can't remember your bad shots." —Bobby Brue, on the Senior PGA Tour

Quiz Answer: The first three Opens were played at 36 holes. The 1931 Open took 144 holes because of two 36-hole playoffs.

O C T O B E R

TODAY'S THOUGHT:

"Everybody has two swings: the one he uses during the last three holes of a tournament and the one he uses the rest of the time."
—Toney Penna, pro golfer

ON THIS DATE—

In 1926, Bob Rosburg was born. Before turning to TV analysis, Rosburg followed up a second-place finish in the 1959 U.S. Open with a win in the PGA Championship.

CHIP SHOT

1959 was Rosburg's year. Besides the PGA title, Rosburg needed only 19 putts in the second round of the Pensacola Open.

TRIVIA QUIZ—

Quick! Who's the oldest golfer to win The Masters?

TODAY'S TIP—

One thing to remember at address is to avoid exaggeration. Anything forced at address will immediately come apart during your swing.

THE 19TH HOLE

"I learn English from American professionals, especially Jim Turnesa, that's why I speak so bad. I call it PGA English."   —Roberto de Vicenzo

---

Quiz Answer: Jack Nicklaus was 46 years old when he won the tournament in 1986.

OCTOBER

TODAY'S THOUGHT:

"Probably the worst hole on the course. Then again, being the worst hole at Pebble is like being the ugliest Miss America."
—Rick Reilly, on the 11th hole at Pebble Beach

ON THIS DATE—

In 1961, Louise Suggs closed out the LPGA season with a win over Kathy Whitworth in the San Antonio Civitan. Suggs won 6 tournaments that year, second only to Mickey Wright's 10 victories.

CHIP SHOT

Dallas amateur Doris Gray made 9 holes-in-one in one year at the Oak Cliff CC. She aced 3 different holes 3 times each in 1982.

TRIVIA QUIZ—

In what state is the Olympic Club, host to three U.S. Opens, located?

TODAY'S TIP—

An upright swing will prevent your club from moving away from the target line. The less that clubhead moves away from the line, the better its chances of being on line at impact.

THE 19TH HOLE

"I can beat any two players in this tournament by myself. If I need any help, I'll let you know."
—Babe Zaharias, to her four-ball partner

Quiz Answer: California.

O C T O B E R

TODAY'S THOUGHT:

"Most people go on vacation twice a year to do what I do all the time. And they pay. I *get* paid." —Chi Chi Rodriguez

ON THIS DATE—

In 1935, one of golf's leading ambassadors was born. Juan "Chi Chi" Rodriguez won 8 events on the PGA Tour before becoming the leading money-winner in the history of the Senior PGA Tour and a Hall-of-Famer.

CHIP SHOT

In 1988, the directors of the Castle Pines GC removed an oil portrait of Jack Nicklaus after Nicklaus told a reporter that he would have skipped The International tournament if it weren't for the fact that he designed the course.

TRIVIA QUIZ—

Name the only major won by Don January in his PGA Tour career.

TODAY'S TIP—

Just off the green but in thick grass is a good shot to practice. Using your putter, top the ball so it spins out of the grass and onto the green.

THE 19TH HOLE

"Like a lot of fellows around here, I have a furniture problem. My chest has fallen into my drawers."
—Billy Casper, on the Senior PGA Tour

Quiz Answer: January won the 1967 PGA Championship.

 **O C T O B E R**

TODAY'S THOUGHT:
"Of all sports, golf least favors an excitable disposition."
—John Updike, writer

ON THIS DATE—
In 1993, Corey Pavin became the first American in 14 years to win the World Match Play Championship in England. Pavin rolled in a 5-foot par putt to cap a scrappy battle with Nick Faldo. Born: Ian Baker-Finch (1960).

CHIP SHOT
Pavin's victory struck another blow for American golf after US wins in the Ryder Cup and Dunhill Cup, both also on British soil.

TRIVIA QUIZ—
Two golfers have shot a record 271 to win The Masters. Who are they?

TODAY'S TIP—
When playing a course for the first time, practice hitting pitches and chips on the practice green. You'll get an idea on how the ball reacts to your shots.

—THE 19TH HOLE—
"When I was younger, I was 'an angry player.' Now all of a sudden I'm a ˜ fiery competitor.' I like the change in vocabulary." ——Corey Pavin

Quiz Answer: Jack Nicklaus in 1965 and Raymond Floyd in 1976.

O C T O B E R

TODAY'S THOUGHT:
"He took a swing like a man with a wasp under his shirt and his pants on fire, trying to impale a butterfly on the end of a scythe."
—Paul Gallico, writer, on his playing partner

ON THIS DATE—
In 1992, Nick Price became the fourth $1 million winner of the season when Steve Elkington missed a 3-foot putt in a playoff at the Texas Open. The win was the second of the year for the PGA champion.

CHIP SHOT
North Carolinian Lang Martin once balanced seven golf balls vertically without any adhesive. Who held the old record of six? Martin!

TRIVIA QUIZ—
Name the native country of five-time British Open winner, Peter Thomson.

TODAY'S TIP—
Afraid to use your driver? Play a round using only your 3-wood or long-irons off the tee and watch how little your score is affected.

THE 19TH HOLE
"I couldn't read the break in the green from the tee."
—Gary Player, after just missing a hole-in-one

Quiz Answer: Thomson was from Australia.

 **O C T O B E R**

TODAY'S THOUGHT:
"PGA West is what I call a one-time course. You play it to say you did and never play it again." —Fuzzy Zoeller

ON THIS DATE—
In 1969, Carol Mann won her 8th tournament of the year despite shooting two-over-par at the Corpus Christi Civitan Open. Mann led the LPGA in earnings that year.

CHIP SHOT
Kathy Whitworth was the top money-winner for 4 straight years before Mann. Whitworth then won the title 4 consecutive years after Mann.

TRIVIA QUIZ—
Five golf clubs were charter members of the USGA when it was founded in 1894. How many can you name?

TODAY'S TIP—
Don't even think about starting a round without stretching your back muscles. Turn gently at first and then extend until you feel relaxed.

—THE 19TH HOLE—
"Hubert Green's swing looks like a drunk trying to find a keyhole in the dark." —Jim Murray, writer

Quiz Answer: The charter members were St. Andrews Golf Club, The Country Club, Shinnecock Hills Golf Club, Newport Golf Club, and Chicago Golf Club.

O C T O B E R

TODAY'S THOUGHT:

"Everyone in Ireland is studying golf technique like mad. Every young lad now aspires to be another Palmer or Nicklaus. We may go centuries before we produce another playwright."
— Joe Carr, 1947 Ryder Cup competitor

ON THIS DATE—

In 1991, former NFL quarterback John Brodie scored his first victory on the Senior PGA Tour, beating Chi Chi Rodriguez and George Archer in a playoff at the Security Pacific Senior Classic. Brodie's winless drought covered 7 years and 157 events. Born: Patty Sheehan (1956).

CHIP SHOT

No golfer named Joe has ever won a major championship in this century.

TRIVIA QUIZ—

Name the only golfer named Andy to win the U.S. Open.

TODAY'S TIP—

Focus on the hole to read the distance of a putt. Taking this tact on the green will let your mind focus on the hole instead of the mechanics of your swing.

THE 19TH HOLE

"You have to put your putter out to pasture every so often, let it eat and get fat so it can get more birdies."
— Greg Norman

Quiz Answer: Andy North won it in 1978 and '85.

 **O C T O B E R**

TODAY'S THOUGHT:

"Remember, they were friends. For years they had shared each other's sorrows, joys, and golf balls, and sliced into the same bunkers." —P.G. Wodehouse, *A Woman Is Only A Woman*

ON THIS DATE—

In 1972, JoAnn Prentice, Sandra Palmer, and Kathy Whitworth probably thought the day would never end. Prentice was the winner after ten holes of sudden death in the Corpus Christi Civitan Open, an LPGA playoff record.

CHIP SHOT

Golf is for backward executives: they talk nothing but golf in the office, and nothing but business on the links.

TRIVIA QUIZ—

Ben Hogan is renowned for winning all the majors except the PGA Championship in 1953. Why did Hogan have no chance to win the PGA?

TODAY'S TIP—

On long putts, don't try to be perfect. Lag the ball into an imaginary two-foot area around the hole. Anything else will just create tension.

THE 19TH HOLE

"Bad sausage and five bogeys will give you a stomach ache every time."   —Miller Barber

Quiz Answer: It was held the same week as the British Open.

O C T O B E R

TODAY'S THOUGHT:

"It's ridiculous the way they are building courses these days, nothing but ponds and lakes, island greens, rivers running beside fairways that are as narrow as a gun barrel. Sometimes I think the architects are ghouls or sadists, they take delight in watching balls sail in the water."   —Gene Sarazen

ON THIS DATE—

In 1929, Gene Sarazen sank a hole-in-one in the first demonstration of night golf. A 400-million candlepower spotlight illuminated the course at the Briarcliff Manor GC in New York.

CHIP SHOT

The famous Old course at St. Andrews is actually a public golf course owned by the City of St. Andrews, Scotland.

TRIVIA QUIZ—

Four golfers topped the annual money-winning list throughout the 1970's. Who were they?

TODAY'S TIP—

Remember, if hitting downwind, the ball flies straighter. Try to favor running shots over pitches.

THE 19TH HOLE

"Another weekend with nothing to do."
          —Arnold Palmer, after missing a cut

Quiz Answer: Johnny Miller (1), Jack Nicklaus (5), Lee Trevino (1), and Tom Watson (3).

 **O C T O B E R**

TODAY'S THOUGHT:

"John Wayne gave up golf. How could a guy who won the West, recaptured Bataan and won the battle of Iwo Jima, let himself be defeated by a little hole in the ground?"

—James Edward Grant, screenwriter

ON THIS DATE—

In 1994, Mark McCumber dropped a 45-foot birdie put on the first playoff hole to beat Fuzzy Zoeller in the season-ending Tour Championship.

CHIP SHOT

Zoeller had five runner-up finishes that year, but it marked the first time he earned more than $1 million in a season. He finished with $1,016,804.

TRIVIA QUIZ—

Do you know what college Fuzzy Zoeller attended?

TODAY'S TIP—

To avoid hitting the ball in the middle, let the club swing past your head before you straighten up. Your front foot should brace your weight as you swing through the ball. Don't straighten up until your right shoulder comes under your chin.

——THE 19TH HOLE——

"I had some bad gravity out there. It's gravity that makes the ball drop in the hole, right? Well, I was hitting the putts beautiful but the ball wasn't dropping."
—Harry Toscano, after a bad round at the Tuscon Open

Quiz Answer: Zoeller went to school at the University of Houston.

O C T O B E R

TODAY'S THOUGHT:

"Don't change the arc of your swing unless you are fairly sure you blundered in some way earlier."   —Rex Lardner, writer

ON THIS DATE—

In 1991, the new, $2 million Tour Championship got underway on the No. 2 course at Pinehurst. John Daly birdied all the par-5 holes en route to a 3-under-par 68.

CHIP SHOT

When Poppy Hills replaced Cypress Point in the course rotation for the AT&T Pebble Beach National Pro-Am, Johnny Miller was heard to say, "It's like replacing Bo Derek with Roseanne Barr."

TRIVIA QUIZ—

Glenn Ford had the title role in a 1950's movie about Ben Hogan. What was the name of the movie?

TODAY'S TIP—

To find out your strengths and weaknesses, keep a chart on fairway hits, greens in regulation, sand saves, and putts for ten rounds. Spend most of your practice time on your weakest area and concentrate on it when playing on the course.

THE 19TH HOLE

"If you want to beat somebody on the golf course, just get him mad."   —Dave Williams

Quiz Answer: *Follow the Sun.*

 **N O V E M B E R**

TODAY'S THOUGHT:
"Were he to land in hell . . . he would probably immediately start talking about what a wonderful place it is."
　　　　—Dan Gleason, writer, on Gary Player's positive thinking

ON THIS DATE—
In 1935, Gary Player was born. The Hall-of-Famer is one of four players to have won all four major championships, and, is the last golfer to win three consecutive PGA Tour events.

CHIP SHOT
When Player won the 1965 U.S. Open, he handed $25,000 of his $26,000 prize back to the USGA. $20,000 was to promote junior golf, $5,000 to fund cancer research.

TRIVIA QUIZ—
Craig Stadler has one major championship on his victory list. Which one was it?

TODAY'S TIP—
Keep your right knee slightly flexed inward at address. Maintain the flexed position as you go into the backswing, allowing the leg to accept the weight transfer but not stiffening to do it.

THE 19TH HOLE
"When you are shooting 80 and standing over a one-foot putt, you aren't thinking." —Tom Kite

Quiz Answer: Stadler won The Masters in 1982.

N O V E M B E R

TODAY'S THOUGHT:

"Golf is like bicycle shorts. It reveals a lot about people."

—Rick Reilly, writer

ON THIS DATE—

In 1941, Senior PGA Tour player Dave Stockton was born. Stockton was a two-time winner of the PGA Championship and captain of the 1991 Ryder Cup team which won the cup back from the Europeans.

CHIP SHOT

Stockton is a direct descendant of Richard Stockton, one of the signers of the Declaration of Independence.

TRIVIA QUIZ—

A live bug is crawling on your ball on the green. You mark your ball, pick it up, blow the bug off, and replace the ball. Is there any penalty?

TODAY'S TIP—

Use some practice time to learn to draw and fade the ball. Learning those shots will enable you to avoid trouble, place your ball in strategic spots and, in the end, score better.

—THE 19TH HOLE—

"I've been a test pilot for Foot-Joy forever. I test their alligator shoes to see if standing in them for long periods of time in a bar brings them any serious damage.
—George Low, former Tour professional

Quiz Answer: No.

3 NOVEMBER

TODAY'S THOUGHT:

"Golf is in the interest of good health and good manners. It promotes self-restraint and affords a chance to play the man and act the gentleman."   —President William Howard Taft

ON THIS DATE—

In 1976, Donna Caponi won the Mizuno Japan Classic for her third straight LPGA victory. The win boosted Caponi's earnings for the year over the $100,000 mark, a career first.

CHIP SHOT

At the 1984 Memorial, Jack Nicklaus hit a tee shot that landed on the front porch of a nearby home. He hit a three-wood back to the fairway and finished with a bogey for the hole. Yes, he did win the tournament.

TRIVIA QUIZ—

This golfer easily out-distanced the field when he won the 1965 Masters by nine strokes. Who was it?

TODAY'S TIP—

If your ball lies just off the green and you've decided to putt it through the fringe, remember to keep the putterhead moving toward the target at impact.

THE 19TH HOLE

"If I swung the gavel the way I swung that golf club, the nation would be in a helluva mess."
—Eugene "Tip" O'Neill, Speaker of the House

Quiz Answer: Jack Nicklaus.

N O V E M B E R

TODAY'S THOUGHT:
"Golf puts a man's character on the anvil and his richest qualities - patience, poise, restraint - to the flame."   —Billy Casper

ON THIS DATE—
In 1973, Ben Crenshaw, playing in his first event as a PGA Tour member, won the San Antonio-Texas Open. Earlier in the year, Crenshaw was the winner in the Western Amateur.

CHIP SHOT
The winner's trophy for The Masters is a silver replica of the clubhouse, with the champions' names inscribed on the base. A smaller version is awarded to the winner every year.

TRIVIA QUIZ—
Can you name the first player on the LPGA Tour to hail from South Africa?

TODAY'S TIP—
Keep the grips of your clubs soft and tacky by washing them once a week with a pine-based cleaning solution. You'll be able to hold the club with a soft, but controlled grip.

THE 19TH HOLE
"The reason the Road Hole at St. Andrews is the most difficult par-4 in the world is that it was designed as a par-6."   —Ben Crenshaw

Quiz Answer: Sally Little. Little has won every major title except the U.S. Open in her career.

 **NOVEMBER**

TODAY'S THOUGHT:
"No one remembers who came second."   —Walter Hagen

ON THIS DATE—
In 1927, Walter Hagen won the PGA Championship for an unmatched fourth time in a row and a fifth overall. Hagen's victim in the final match, in case you forgot, was Joe Turnesa.

CHIP SHOT
Hagen defeated reigning U.S. Open champ, Tommy Armour, in a quarterfinal match. It was his first head-to-head win against Armour.

TRIVIA QUIZ—
What was unique about the winners of the four majors in 1994?

TODAY'S TIP—
Practice putting in a spot where the shadow of your head is over the ball. Make sure that your head stays still until the ball has left the shadow area.

THE 19TH HOLE
"These greens are so fast, I have to hold my putter over the ball and hit it with the shadow."   —Sam Snead

Quiz Answer: For the first time ever, none of the winners was an American. Jose Maria Olazabal of Spain won The Masters, Ernie Els of South Africa took the U.S. Open, and, South African Nick Price won the British Open and the PGA Championship.

N O V E M B E R

TODAY'S THOUGHT:

"We tournament golfers are much overrated. We get paid too much."   —Tom Watson

ON THIS DATE—

In 1994, Ernie Els made up a five-stroke deficit in six holes to win the inaugural Sarazen World Open Championship. Els beat Fred Funk by 3 strokes to earn $200,000.

CHIP SHOT

Fred Daly remains the only Irishman to win a major championship. Daly sank a 30-foot putt on the last green to win the 1947 British Open by one stroke.

TRIVIA QUIZ—

Of the following match play events, which is the oldest? Is it: a) the Solheim Cup b) the Walker Cup c) the Curtis Cup d) the Ryder Cup?

TODAY'S TIP—

Having trouble with one hole in particular? At the range, imagine yourself on the tee of that hole. Hit shot after shot until you feel comfortable with that image, and bring that confidence to the golf course.

THE 19TH HOLE

"I had a reputation for being tough. You had to be when you were Italian."   —Gene Sarazen

Quiz Answer: B. The first Walker Cup was held in 1922.

NOVEMBER

TODAY'S THOUGHT:
"Golf has drawbacks. It is possible, by too much of it, to destroy the mind." —Sir Walter Simpson, writer

ON THIS DATE—
In 1991, five-time British Open champion, Tom Watson, was selected as captain of the US team in its 1993 Ryder Cup matches against Europe. The US did win, 15-13.

CHIP SHOT
In the 1950's, about 1,000 golf cars were in use. By the mid-60's, they numbered about 120,000. Today, there are more than 1,000,000.

TRIVIA QUIZ—
Who was the amateur from Arizona State who, in 1991, won the PGA's Northern Telecom Tuscon Open?

TODAY'S TIP—
Keep the back of your left hand in line with your forearm through the backswing. This will keep the wrists firm, enabling them to cock at the correct angle in response to the weight of the clubhead.

THE 19TH HOLE
"My luck is so bad that if I bought a cemetery, people would stop dying."
—Ed Furgol, 1954 U.S. Open champion

Quiz Answer: Phil Mickelson. Mickelson, the reigning NCAA champ, was given a sponsor's exemption to the tournament.

NOVEMBER

TODAY'S THOUGHT:
"The game required a certain cold toughness of mind, and absorption of will. There was not an athlete I talked to from other sports who did not hold the professional golfer in awe . . . "
—George Plimpton, writer

ON THIS DATE—
In 1964, Mickey Wright fired a record-setting 62 to win the Tall City Open in Midland, Texas. Wright came back from a ten-stroke deficit to beat Sherry Wheeler.

CHIP SHOT
The longest par-3 hole on the PGA Tour is the 246-yard 13th at Dorall CC's Blue Course in Miami.

TRIVIA QUIZ—
The only major title to elude Tom Watson is the PGA Championship. In 1978, he came close, losing in a playoff. Who beat him?

TODAY'S TIP—
Better arm extension can help prevent spraying shots all over the course. Firm wrists will keep the clubface on the ball as long as possible after impact.

THE 19TH HOLE
"I don't care to join any club that's prepared to have me as a member."   —Groucho Marx

Quiz Answer: John Mahaffey.

 NOVEMBER

TODAY'S THOUGHT:
"The better you putt, the bolder you play." —Don January

ON THIS DATE—
In 1895, Mrs. Charles B. Brown won the first U.S. Women's Amateur Golf Championship. Brown shot *132* over 18 holes to win the title. Born: Tom Weiskopf (1942).

CHIP SHOT
Thirteen competitors played nine holes before lunch and nine holes after the meal. Brown shot a 69 for the first nine, and 63 for the second.

TRIVIA QUIZ—
Three of the four golfers to defeat Greg Norman in major championship playoffs had the letter "z" in their last name. How many do you know?

TODAY'S TIP—
When playing wet fairways, play the ball a bit forward, and use a sweeping action with your club.

THE 19TH HOLE
"Be funny on a golf course? Do I kid my best friend's mother about her heart condition?"
—Phil Silvers, comedian

Quiz Answer: Fuzzy Zoeller beat Norman in the 1984 U.S. Open. At the 1987 Masters, Larry Mize was the winner. Paul Azinger won in a playoff at the 1993 PGA Championship. There was no "z" in Calcavecchia at the 1989 British Open, just a win.

N O V E M B E R

TODAY'S THOUGHT:

"Golf: a game in which you claim the privileges of age, and retain the playthings of childhood."   —Samuel Johnson, writer

ON THIS DATE—

In 1991, last-minute substitute Liselotte Neumann shot a 3-under-par 69 to win the LPGA's Mazda Japan Classic by two shots. Caroline Keggi and Dottie Mochrie tied for second.

CHIP SHOT

Englishman John Ball won 8 British Amateur titles between 1888 and 1912, a time when it was considered a major championship. It's the most victories in any major by one person.

TRIVIA QUIZ—

I won only three tournaments in my first 20 years on the PGA Tour. But two of them were at the U.S. Open. Who am I?

TODAY'S TIP—

Your swing should remain the same with every club in your bag. The shorter the club, the closer you'll stand to the ball. But don't make any changes in your swing on normal shots.

THE 19TH HOLE

"He dresses like a gardener and usually plays like one."   —Henry Cotton, on 1935
British Open winner, Alf Perry

Quiz Answer: Andy North, who won the Open in 1978 and '85. He also won the Westchester Classic in 1977.

NOVEMBER

TODAY'S THOUGHT:
"I love the game. It's all I am."   —Dave Marr, TV analyst, on golf

ON THIS DATE—
In 1962, the United States won the Canada Cup for the third straight year. The US team, led by Arnold Palmer and Sam Snead, averaged just under 70 for their eight rounds of golf. Born: Fuzzy Zoeller (1951).

CHIP SHOT
Alcohol was prohibited in the US from 1920 until 1933. Oddly, Americans won 12 of the 14 British Opens played during those years. After 1933, however, American golfers won only twice in the next 21 years.

TRIVIA QUIZ—
Name the golfer who holds the record for playing on more United States Ryder Cup teams than anyone else.

TODAY'S TIP—
Some changes in your equipment might help your game as you get older. Lighter clubs with wider soles and thicker club grips can improve your score in your senior years.

THE 19TH HOLE
"If this was any other tournament but The Masters, I'd have shot 66. But I was choking out there. That green coat plays castanets with your knees."
—Chi Chi Rodriguez

Quiz Answer: Billy Casper, who played in 8 Ryder Cup competitions.

NOVEMBER

TODAY'S THOUGHT:

"Any player can win a U.S. Open, but it takes a helluva player to win two."   —Walter Hagen

ON THIS DATE—

In 1912, Ralph Guldahl was born. Guldahl became the fifth golfer to successfully defend his U.S. Open title when he won in 1938. Guldahl topped off his career with a win in the 1939 Masters.

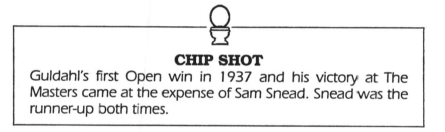

CHIP SHOT

Guldahl's first Open win in 1937 and his victory at The Masters came at the expense of Sam Snead. Snead was the runner-up both times.

TRIVIA QUIZ—

Between 1954 and 1958, Peter Thomson won 4 British Opens. In 1957, Thomson was runner-up. Who was the winner?

TODAY'S TIP—

Keep the thumb of your bottom hand in contact with the grip throughout your swing. Place it slightly to the left of center of your grip, and don't move it during the swing.

THE 19TH HOLE

"The golf swing is like sex in this respect. You can't be thinking about the mechanics of the act while you're performing."   —Dave Hill

Quiz Answer: Bobby Locke of South Africa.

NOVEMBER

TODAY'S THOUGHT:

"Golf is a better game played downhill." —Jack Nicklaus

ON THIS DATE—

In 1994, the team of Fred Couples and Davis Love III set a tournament record by winning the World Cup of Golf for the third straight time. Their victory broke a mark set twice in the 1960's by Jack Nicklaus and Arnold Palmer.

CHIP SHOT

21 years after coming back from 7 strokes down to win the 1960 U.S. Open, Arnold Palmer came from 6 back after 36 holes to win the U.S. Senior Open.

TRIVIA QUIZ—

What's the only major tournament that Lee Trevino has never won in his career?

TODAY'S TIP—

When driving the ball, you want as little backspin as possible. Teeing the ball higher will let you catch it right at the bottom of your swing, giving you minimum backspin and plenty of distance.

THE 19TH HOLE

"Arnold Palmer was aggressive. He might be leading by one or two shots, but he wouldn't be cautious. He'd go for the flag from the middle of an alligator's back."
—Lee Trevino

Quiz Answer: Trevino has never won The Masters.

N O V E M B E R

TODAY'S THOUGHT:

"The best perks of this office are who you get to play golf with. I've played with Jack Nicklaus, Arnold Palmer, Raymond Floyd, Amy Alcott."   —President Bill Clinton

ON THIS DATE—

In 1888, Scotsman John G. Reid became the founder of St. Andrews GC in Yonkers, NY. Reid converted a cow pasture into a 3-hole course.

CHIP SHOT

Why is it that the golfer who tells his opponent it's only a game is the one who's winning?

TRIVIA QUIZ—

Oak Hill CC was the site of Curtis Strange's 1989 U.S. Open victory. Where is the club located?

TODAY'S TIP—

Don't ruin a good day by trying to steer your shots as you head to the home hole. Think only of the shot you are about to play and trust the swing that got you there.

——THE 19TH HOLE——

"When Jack Nicklaus or Tom Watson shoots a low score, it's great golf. But when Paul Azinger or Bob Tway shoots 65, it's attributed to square grooves, titanium shafts and the golf ball going too far."
                    —Tom Sieckmann, PGA Tour player

Quiz Answer: Rochester, NY.

NOVEMBER

TODAY'S THOUGHT:

"It is impossible to imagine Goethe or Beethoven being good at billiards or golf."   —H.L. Mencken, writer

ON THIS DATE—

In 1992, Davis Love III eagled the par-5, 18th hole to break a tie with Mike Hulbert and win the Kapalua International by one stroke.

CHIP SHOT

Love had finished second in the event three times, including the previous year when Hulbert beat him in a playoff.

TRIVIA QUIZ—

We're playing at Turnberry during the British Open when I ask you, my caddie, for my "brassie." What club do you give me?

TODAY'S TIP—

It generally takes less than two seconds to complete a golf swing. So, don't paralyze yourself by trying to think of all the things you have to do for a good swing. Keep your focus on no more than two thoughts. Start with taking the club straight back from the ball, and, keeping your head steady.

THE 19TH HOLE

"I want to win, but if I started turning down all those second-place checks, my banker would kill me."
—Payne Stewart

Quiz Answer: My 2-wood.

N O V E M B E R

TODAY'S THOUGHT:
"The PGA Tour has lots of sheep, but Pavin is one of the wolves."
—Johnny Miller, on Corey Pavin

ON THIS DATE—
In 1959, Corey Pavin was born. Pavin shed the label of Best Player Never to Have Won a Major when he won the centennial U.S. Open in 1995 at Shinnecock Hills GC.

CHIP SHOT
Conditions were so tough at Shinnecock Hills that 13 golfers, with 36 major titles between them, didn't make the cut. Pavin won the tournament with an even-par 280.

TRIVIA QUIZ—
If Roberto DeVicenzo's scorecard at the 1968 Masters had shown a lower score for the 17th hole instead of the higher one that cost him the title, what would the ruling have been?

TODAY'S TIP—
To promote a solid stroke when putting, visualize your follow-through before you putt.

THE 19TH HOLE
"Man, I go rabbit hunting in that stuff. You don't go in there; you send your beagle in there to get something out."
—Fuzzy Zoeller, on the rough at Shinnecock Hills

Quiz Answer: If you write a score higher than what you shot, you are credited with that score. Writing a lower score means disqualification from the tournament.

NOVEMBER

TODAY'S THOUGHT:

"Winners are a different breed of cat. They have an inner drive and are willing to give of themselves whatever it takes to win."

—Byron Nelson

ON THIS DATE—

In 1930, 28-year old Bobby Jones announced his retirement from competitive golf. Jones capped his career less than two months earlier by winning golf's Grand Slam.

CHIP SHOT

Jones would only come out of retirement to play in the Masters. He finished tied for 13th in the first tournament.

TRIVIA QUIZ—

Sam Snead is the oldest player to win a PGA tournament. Who is the oldest golfer to win a LPGA event? Give yourself extra credit if you know her age at the time.

TODAY'S TIP—

Some backspin is needed to make the ball rise in the air. That's why you hit iron shots slightly downward. A drive with topspin, however, will give you a short ground ball.

THE 19TH HOLE

"When I ask you what kind of club to use, look the other way and don't answer."

—Sam Snead, to his caddie

Quiz Answer: JoAnne Carner was 46 years old when she won the Safeco Classic in 1985.

NOVEMBER

TODAY'S THOUGHT:

"It's just as hard to put yourself in there with a chance to win as it is to win." —Greg Norman, on trying to win a major

ON THIS DATE—

In 1901, Craig Wood was born. Wood ended years of frustration and second-place finishes when he won the 1941 Masters and U.S. Open. Wood was also a member of the US Ryder Cup team.

CHIP SHOT

Wood is one of two golfers to lose all four majors in playoffs. Wood lost the 1933 British Open; the 1934 PGA Championship; the 1935 Masters; and, the 1939 U.S. Open.

TRIVIA QUIZ—

The first time total prize money at a U.S. Open exceeded $1,000 was in: a) 1909 b) 1916 c) 1922 d) 1931.

TODAY'S TIP—

Here's another method to try when practicing putting. Stick a tee into the ground on the practice green and putt 5-footers to the tee. You'll find when you get on the course that the hole will look like a manhole cover.

THE 19TH HOLE

"I can't figure out where the crowds all came from - even Thursday and Friday. I thought people worked during the week."

—Carol Rissel, tournament executive

Quiz Answer: B. 1916.

 **N O V E M B E R**

TODAY'S THOUGHT:

"The mark of a champion is the ability to make the most of good luck and the best of bad."   —Anonymous

ON THIS DATE—

In 1942, Larry Gilbert was born. Gilbert joined the Senior PGA Tour in 1993 after years of success as a club pro. Tour life agreed with Gilbert as he won over $500,000 in his rookie year.

CHIP SHOT

Tommy Armour III needed an 8 on the par-4 final hole during the qualifying round of the 1983 Tournament Players Championship to make the cut. Armour hit three straight drives into the lake and ended play with a 9.

TRIVIA QUIZ—

In 1945, three golfers won 29 of the 35 events on the PGA Tour. Who were they?

TODAY'S TIP—

To make sure you and your putter are square to the target line, align your putter first. Square it to the line and then take your stance according to where the putter is aligned.

——————THE 19TH HOLE——————
"I may go for it or I may not. It all depends on what I elect to do on my backswing."   —Billy Joe Patton

---

Quiz Answer: Byron Nelson, Ben Hogan, and Sam Snead.

N O V E M B E R

TODAY'S THOUGHT:

"For when the One Great Scorer comes to write against your name, He marks - not that you won or lost - but how you played the game." —Grantland Rice

ON THIS DATE—

In 1993, 28-year old Heather Farr lost her four-year battle with cancer. Farr was the youngest player ever to qualify for the LPGA Tour at age 20 in 1986.

CHIP SHOT

O.B. Keeler, a reporter for the *Atlanta Journal*, made the first trans-Atlantic broadcast of a sporting event in 1930. He reported on the British Open via radio.

TRIVIA QUIZ—

Betsy King's win at the 1995 ShopRite LPGA Classic made her the third golfer to enter the LPGA Hall of Fame in the 1990's. Who were the other two players?

TODAY'S TIP—

Great golfers don't become great without practicing. If you don't have the time to practice every day, at least put five minutes a day aside to swing a club.

THE 19TH HOLE

"Golf seems to me an arduous way to go for a walk. I prefer to take the dogs out."
—Princess Anne of England

Quiz Answer: Pat Bradley in 1991 and Patsy Sheehan in 1993.

 **NOVEMBER**

TODAY'S THOUGHT:

"Money was never a goal for me because of my amateur training. I was taught to win, and that was it."   —JoAnne Carner

ON THIS DATE—

In 1993, Raymond Floyd and Steve Elkington teamed up to win the $1.1 million Shark Shootout. Floyd's share of the purse lifted him into first place on the tournament's all-time money list.

CHIP SHOT

In 1982, a radio station incorrectly reported that actor Victor Mature had died. Afterward, Mature said, "I'm the first dead man to make six double bogeys on the back nine on the day of his funeral."

TRIVIA QUIZ—

Hal Sutton has won one major tournament in his career. Which one?

TODAY'S TIP—

High handicappers run into problems with long irons because they swing too hard, disrupting the swing plane. Long irons will provide distance if struck solidly with a smooth swing.

THE 19TH HOLE

"You all know Jerry Ford - the most dangerous driver since Ben Hur."   —Bob Hope

---

Quiz Answer: The 1983 PGA Championship.

NOVEMBER

TODAY'S THOUGHT:

"The major championships always comes down to the ast nine holes. It takes character to win a major championship."

—Nick Price

ON THIS DATE—

In 1936, Englishman Densmore Shute defeated Jimmy Thomson, 3 & 2, to win the first of two straight PGA Championships. Shute's other major win was in the 1933 British Open.

CHIP SHOT

British great Harry Vardon was the first athlete to sign an endorsement contract. Vardon toured America promoting his ball, the Vardon Flyer, which was made by Spalding.

TRIVIA QUIZ—

Gene Sarazen's famous double eagle at the 15th hole in the final round of the 1935 Masters traveled about 220 yards. What club did Sarazen use for the shot?

TODAY'S TIP—

Changing your swing to compensate for wind can be self-defeating. Swing slower in the wind rather than speeding up. Tee the ball slightly lower than normal and concentrate on good contact.

——THE 19TH HOLE——

"She is so small, she might get lost in an unreplaced divot."   —Bob Toski, on LPGA player, Judy Rankin

Quiz Answer: Sarazen used a 4-wood on the par-5, 485-yard hole.

NOVEMBER

TODAY'S THOUGHT:

"Years ago we discovered the exact point, the dead center of middle age. It occurs when you are too young to take up golf and too old to rush up to the net." —Franklin P. Adams, writer

ON THIS DATE—

In 1985, 50-year old rookie, Gary Player, won the Quadel Classic for his first victory on the Senior PGA Tour. It was Player's only win on the Tour that year.

CHIP SHOT

Because of the wartime rubber shortage, golf balls were in scarce supply in 1945. Sam Snead, who said he was paying $100 a dozen for balls, won the Los Angeles Open playing the entire tournament with one ball. It was given to him by Bing Crosby.

TRIVIA QUIZ—

I joined the PGA Tour in 1987 and had at least one win in each of my first seven years. I also won my first major at the PGA. Who am I?

TODAY'S TIP—

The most common cause of a stubbed chip shot is being too wristy. Keep a firm left wrist and use a pendulum-type swing with your arms. Let the loft of the club do the work.

THE 19TH HOLE

"Here, Eddie, hold the flag while I putt out."
—Walter Hagen, to Edward, Prince of Wales

Quiz Answer: Paul Azinger, who won the PGA in 1993.

N O V E M B E R

TODAY'S THOUGHT:
"I couldn't wait for the sun to come up the next morning so that I could get out on the course again." —Ben Hogan

ON THIS DATE—
In 1991, Wayne Grady shot a final round 69 for a three-stroke victory in the Australian PGA Championship. Born: Scott Hoch (1955).

CHIP SHOT
Grady's previous win to the Australian victory was in the 1990 US PGA Championship.

TRIVIA QUIZ—
In 1990, the first match play competition between the professional female golfers of the United States and Europe was held. The event, begun as a counterpart to the Ryder Cup, was the brain-child of the inventor of Ping golf clubs. What's the name of the tournament and its namesake?

TODAY'S TIP—
Use those striped balls that you find on the driving range to your advantage. Practice putting. Putt a striped ball so that if rolled properly, the stripe will remain sold.

THE 19TH HOLE
"Never saw one that was worth a damn."
—Harry Vardon, on left-handed golfers

Quiz Answer: The tournament is the Solheim Cup, named after Karsten Solheim.

 **N O V E M B E R**

TODAY'S THOUGHT:

"A good golf course is like good music. It does not necessarily appeal the first time one plays it."

—Alister MacKenzie, golf course architect

ON THIS DATE—

In 1991, Pat Bradley was named LPGA Player of the Year for the second time in her career. Bradley had gained entry into the LPGA Hall of Fame earlier in the year. Born: Nolan Henke (1964).

CHIP SHOT

When Shelley Hamlin won the 1992 Phar-Mor, she ended a record 14-year victory drought. The previous win recorded by Hamlin was at the 1978 Patty Berg Classic.

TRIVIA QUIZ—

True or false: Pat Bradley has won every major on the LPGA Tour at least once in her career.

TODAY'S TIP—

Distance is only good to you if it's in a forward direction. Ease back on power in order to achieve more solid contact through control of your club. Swing control will let you hit the ball squarely more than strength.

THE 19TH HOLE

"I don't trust doctors. They are like golfers. Every one has a different answer to your problems."

—Seve Ballesteros

Quiz Answer: True.

NOVEMBER

TODAY'S THOUGHT:
"No power on earth will deter men from using a ball that will add to the length of their drive." —*Golf Illustrated*, 1902

ON THIS DATE—
In 1962, PGA Tour player, John Inman, was born. Inman turned pro in 1985 after a spectacular college career at North Carolina. In 1984, Inman won the NCAA individual title and was named College Player of the Year.

CHIP SHOT
When Ben Hogan returned home after winning the 1953 British Open, he was given a ticker-tape parade up Broadway. It was the first for an American golfer since Bobby Jones in 1930.

TRIVIA QUIZ—
This tournament has grown in status to the point that it's sometime called the "fifth major." What is it?

TODAY'S TIP—
Don't waste shots in a waste bunker. Try not to sweep the dirt away behind the ball on your backswing. You *can* remove impediments and ground your club in a waste bunker.

THE 19TH HOLE
"If someone dropped an atom bomb on the sixth hole, the press would wait for a golfer to come in and tell them about it." —Ben Hogan

Quiz Answer: The Tournament Players Championship.

 **N O V E M B E R**

TODAY'S THOUGHT:
"I'm aware that golf is probably some kind of mental disorder like gambling or women or politics." —Dan Jenkins, writer

ON THIS DATE—
In 1994, Tom Watson topped a four-man field in the Skins Game with $210,000 in winnings. For Watson, it was his first American triumph since the 1987 Nabisco Championships. Born: Danielle Ammaccapana (1965).

CHIP SHOT
Golf made its national TV debut with the final round of the 1953 World Championship of Golf at Tam O'Shanter GC.

TRIVIA QUIZ—
Who's the only player to win two Masters playoffs?

TODAY'S TIP—
In muddy ground you have to strike the ball cleanly. Choke down on your grip and make sure that you hit the ball with little or no divot.

THE 19TH HOLE
"Someone asked if I've noticed much difference between the various courses I've seen on television. 'Not much,' I said. All of them seem to have one of the greatest finishing holes in golf." ——Frank Hannigan

Quiz Answer: Nick Faldo, who defeated Scott Hoch in 1989 and Raymond Floyd in 1990, both on the second hole of sudden death.

N O V E M B E R

TODAY'S THOUGHT:

"Contrary to popular opinion, there are no sadistic motives behind how we set up a golf course for the U.S. Open."

—David Eger, USGA senior director of rules

ON THIS DATE—

In 1992, Fred Couples had the best first day in the history of the Skins Game. Couples won six of nine skins to take home $130,000.

CHIP SHOT

The money Couples won that day boosted his winnings for the *month* to $652,000.

TRIVIA QUIZ—

In 1987, this golfer became the first British woman to win the U.S. Open. Name her.

TODAY'S TIP—

If the glare from the sun bothers your depth perception, have your playing partner hold the flagstick in the hole. It will sharpen your focus.

THE 19TH HOLE

"A golf professional is a fellow who never knows what town he's in till he calls downstairs to the desk clerk in the morning, but can read you the left-to-right break on every green in town from memory."

—Jim Murray, writer

Quiz Answer: Laura Davies.

NOVEMBER

TODAY'S THOUGHT:

"Water creates a neurosis in golfers. The very thought of this harmless fluid robs them of their normal powers of rational thought, turns their legs to jelly, and produces a palsy of the upper limbs."
—Peter Dobereiner, writer

ON THIS DATE—

In 1992, Steve Elkington overcame wet and windy conditions to win the Australian Open. His 8-under-par 280 was enough for a two-stroke win over Peter McWhinney and Duffy Waldorf.

CHIP SHOT

When Tom Watson was asked how he helped the game of Gerald Ford, he replied, "First, hitting the ball. Second, finding it."

TRIVIA QUIZ—

What were the only two majors Bobby Jones didn't win in his career?

TODAY'S TIP—

Don't hit at the ball, swing the clubhead through it. Imagine that the ball isn't there. Learning to feel your follow-through will take your mind off the ball.

THE 19TH HOLE

"Boy, it looked like a Rembrandt up there."
—Lee Trevino, on his shot that fell for an ace in the 1987 Skins Game

Quiz Answer: Jones never won The Masters or the PGA Championship.

N O V E M B E R

TODAY'S THOUGHT:

"I'm the best. I just haven't played yet."
—Muhammad Ali, on his golf game

ON THIS DATE—

In 1991, PGA Championship winner John Daly cleaned up in the first nine holes of the Skins Game. Daly won $120,000 and two automobiles. Jack Nicklaus, Payne Stewart, and Curtis Strange won nothing at all.

CHIP SHOT

In the 1938 movie, *Carefree*, Fred Astaire performed a dance solo in which he hits a row of golf balls while tap-dancing. The solo required almost 1,000 practice shots, 10 days of rehearsal, and 2 days of filming. On-screen, the dance lasted 3 minutes.

TRIVIA QUIZ—

Only one foreign-born player won the U.S. Open during the 1980's. Who was it?

TODAY'S TIP—

Moving your head will cause your eyes to relate incorrectly to the target line and cause you to lose balance. The only cure is practicing to keep your head steady. Sorry.

THE 19TH HOLE

"I regard golf as an expensive way of playing marbles."
—G.K. Chesterton, writer

Quiz Answer: Australian David Graham, who won in 1981.

DECEMBER 1

TODAY'S THOUGHT:

"There's no such thing as natural touch. Touch is something you create by hitting millions of golf balls." —Lee Trevino

ON THIS DATE—

In 1939, Lee Trevino was born. Trevino burst onto the golf scene with a win over Jack Nicklaus in the 1968 U.S. Open. The Hall-of-Famer has won 6 major championships in his career. Also born: Craig Parry (1966).

CHIP SHOT

In '68, Trevino became the first golfer in U.S. Open history to shoot less than 70 in all four rounds. He shot 69, 68, 69, 69 on his way to the title.

TRIVIA QUIZ—

Englishman Ted Ray won the U.S. Open in 1920. The next Englishman to win did so exactly 50 years later. Do you know who it was?

TODAY'S TIP—

Take a minute or two to stretch your hands and fingers before playing your game. Touching a tabletop with only your fingertips, slowly press down and spread them out.

THE 19TH HOLE

"We have three Tours. The Senior Tour, the Supersenior Tour, and the Lee Trevino Tour."
—Chi Chi Rodriguez, on Trevino's dominance

Quiz Answer: Tony Jacklin.

DECEMBER

TODAY'S THOUGHT:

"Golf is a science, the study of a lifetime, in which you can exhaust yourself but never your subject."   —David Forgan, writer

ON THIS DATE—

In 1953, PGA Tour player Jay Haas was born. An NCAA champ and All-American at Wake Forest, Haas has quietly crossed the $4 million mark in career earnings.

CHIP SHOT

Haas is the nephew of 1968 Masters champion Bob Goalby, older brother of fellow Tour player Jerry, and the brother-in-law of another Tour member, Dillard Pruitt.

TRIVIA QUIZ—

In 1993, Greg Norman became the first British Open champion to break 70 in all four rounds of the tournament. But he wasn't the first golfer to do it. Can you name the South African player who finished his final round under 70 before Norman?

TODAY'S TIP—

Ease any pressure by breathing in deeply through your nose and exhaling slowly through your mouth. Avoid the tendency to take short, shallow breaths.

THE 19TH HOLE

"A sick appendix is not as difficult to deal with as a five-foot putt."   —Gene Sarazen

Quiz Answer: Ernie Els, who finished tied for sixth.

3 DECEMBER

TODAY'S THOUGHT:

"Nicklaus loved the pressure. Palmer loved it. They not only loved it, they rose to another level, while guys like me were seeking a level below, just trying to get out of there." —Frank Beard

ON THIS DATE—

In 1972, Jack Nicklaus captured the Walt Disney World Open Invitational and, in the process, became the first golfer to win more than $300,000 in a season.

CHIP SHOT

One year later, Nicklaus won the same tournament. With the win, he became the first golfer to earn more than $2 million in his career.

TRIVIA QUIZ—

When Jack Nicklaus won his sixth Masters in 1986, who was his caddie?

TODAY'S TIP—

For a good wedge shot, you want a minimum of foot movement. Place your weight toward the front foot and keep it there. Use a hand-and-arm type swing.

THE 19TH HOLE

"When I go out in the first round and my heart beats, I chuckle and say, 'Hey, Muffin, it's only Thursday. Your heart's not supposed to beat until Sunday.' "
—Muffin Spencer-Devlin

Quiz Answer: Jack, Jr., his youngest son.

D E C E M B E R

TODAY'S THOUGHT:

"The only way of really finding out a man's true character is to play golf with him. In no other walk of life does the cloven hoof so quickly display itself." —P.G. Wodehouse, writer

ON THIS DATE—

In 1994, Nick Faldo held off Nick Price and Ernie Els to win the Million Dollar Challenge by three shots. Faldo took home golf's richest first prize of $1 million.

CHIP SHOT

Faldo was a runner-up three times in the tournament, played in Sun City, South Africa. The event was staged on the course of the Gary Player Country Club.

TRIVIA QUIZ—

Jerry Pate, Nick Price, Doug Weaver, and Mark Wiebe did something at the 1989 U.S. Open which had been done only 17 times in the history of the tournament. What was it?

TODAY'S TIP—

Under the rules of golf, you are allowed to wrap a towel around your grip while you play. So keep that in mind if you're playing on a rainy day. Your grips won't get soaked.

—THE 19TH HOLE—

"Tranquilizers make it possible for a golfer to relax at his favorite form of relaxation."
—Stephen Baker, writer

Quiz Answer: The four golfers each shot a hole-in-one.

5 DECEMBER

TODAY'S THOUGHT:

"We all choke. You're not human if you haven't. We get just as nervous as the average guy playing for the club championship." —Curtis Strange

ON THIS DATE—

In 1993, Curtis Strange ended a four-year victory drought with a win in the Greg Norman Classic in Sydney, Australia. The last tournament Strange had won prior to this was the 1989 U.S. Open. Born: Lanny Wadkins (1949); Tom Purtzer (1951).

CHIP SHOT

There was no June swoon for Greg Norman in 1995. Playing in four tournaments, Norman earned $781,780 for the month.

TRIVIA QUIZ—

Give the order in which the four majors are played each year.

TODAY'S TIP—

On long putts, decide where you want to leave the ball if you miss. Don't leave yourself with a downhill or sharp breaking putt to finish.

—THE 19TH HOLE—

"The difference between me and an amateur is that I'm not afraid to screw up." —Fuzzy Zoeller

Quiz Answer: The Masters in April, the U.S. Open in June, the British Open in July, and the PGA Championship in August.

D E C E M B E R

TODAY'S THOUGHT:

"In those days, the money was the main thing, the only thing I played for. Championships were something to grow old with."
—Byron Nelson

ON THIS DATE—

In 1992, David Frost became the first three-time winner of the Million Dollar Challenge. Frost fired a 3-under-par 69 to finish four shots ahead of John Cook.

CHIP SHOT

Babe Zaharias was one of the greatest athletes of all time. When asked by sportswriter Paul Gallico if there was anything she didn't play, she replied, "Yeah, dolls."

TRIVIA QUIZ—

True or false: The British Amateur Championship began before the British Open.

TODAY'S TIP—

Don't even think about the hole when you're lining up a pitch shot. Your target should be a landing zone about one-third of the distance to the hole.

THE 19TH HOLE

"Sam doesn't know a damn thing about the golf swing. But he does it better than anyone else."
—Ben Hogan, on Sam Snead

Quiz Answer: False. The Amateur began in 1885, 25 years after the first professional Open.

7 DECEMBER

TODAY'S THOUGHT:

"Golf is the only game where the worst player gets the best of it. They obtain more out of it with regard to both exercise and enjoyment. The good player gets worried over the slightest mistake, whereas the poor player makes too many mistakes to worry over them." —David Lloyd George, writer

ON THIS DATE—

In 1929, Leo Diegel won his second straight PGA Championship with a 6 & 4 win over Johnny Farrell. The previous year, Diegel put an end to Walter Hagen's four-year reign.

CHIP SHOT

The 1929 PGA was the first major championship to be played in California. The matches were held at the Hillcrest CC in Los Angeles.

TRIVIA QUIZ—

How come Bobby Jones never played in the Ryder Cup?

TODAY'S TIP—

If your putts keep missing to the right, move the ball up toward your front foot and make a smooth follow-through.

THE 19TH HOLE

"If the crowd won't applaud for me, I'll do it myself."
—Leonard Thompson, after a good shot

Quiz Answer: Jones was an amateur. The Ryder Cup is for professionals.

DECEMBER 8

TODAY'S THOUGHT:

"A leading difficulty with the average player is that he totally misunderstands what is meant by concentration. He may think he is concentrating hard, when he is merely worrying."

—Bobby Jones

ON THIS DATE—

In 1991, Billy Andrade and Kris Tschetter parred the second playoff hole to beat Ed Humenik and Elaine Crosby and win the J.C. Penney Classic. Born: Steve Elkington (1962).

CHIP SHOT

At 7,252 yards, the links at Carnoustie is the longest course ever played in British Open competition.

TRIVIA QUIZ—

Can you name the four rookies on the PGA Tour who can claim majors as their first victories?

TODAY'S TIP—

Buying a new putter? Make sure it lies flat on the ground when you set up to shoot. If the heel or toe is in the air, your future putts could be twisted off line.

THE 19TH HOLE

"If you swing with grace and ease, then your body will please. But if you swing hard and fast, you will never last." —Bob Toski

---

Quiz Answer: Jack Nicklaus won the U.S. Open in 1962; Jerry Pate won the 1976 U.S. Open; John Daly captured the 1991 PGA Championship; and Ernie Els won the 1994 U.S. Open.

9 DECEMBER

TODAY'S THOUGHT:

"It's an awful empty life hitting golf balls every day. You are not giving much service."
—Willie Auchterlonie, 1893 British Open champ

ON THIS DATE—

In 1991, John Daly won the Charles Bartlett Award for charitable contributions. Daly used money from his PGA Championship prize to start a scholarship fund for the daughters of a spectator killed by lightning during the championship. Born: Orville Moody (1933); Tom Kite (1949).

CHIP SHOT

Samuel Ryder, of Ryder Cup fame, didn't play golf until he was 50. In less than a year, his handicap was in the single digits.

TRIVIA QUIZ—

Who are the only three players to win the British Open in three different decades?

TODAY'S TIP—

Only spend enough time on the practice green before your round to get the feel of your stroke. Bending over for a long period of time can tighten your back muscles and affect your swing.

THE 19TH HOLE

"Golf is a four-letter word. I'm sure a few four-letter words were said out there."
—Greg Norman, after Nick Faldo played the wrong ball

Quiz Answer: Harry Vardon, J.H. Taylor, and Gary Player.

DECEMBER

TODAY'S THOUGHT:

"Golf is the cruelest of sports. Like life, it's unfair. It's a harlot. A trollop. It leads you on. It never lives up to its promises. It's not a sport, it's bondage. An obsession. A boulevard of broken dreams. It plays with men. And runs off with the butcher."

—Jim Murray, writer

ON THIS DATE—

In 1937, Senior PGA Tour player Don Bies was born. Bies played the PGA Tour for 13 years, winning once. After joining the Seniors, Bies won twice in his rookie year and 3 times the following year.

CHIP SHOT

The easiest shot in golf is your fourth putt.

TRIVIA QUIZ—

What PGA Tour player is known as the "Zinger?"

TODAY'S TIP—

If you're in a bunker with no lip and the ball sitting up, you might want to try a bump and run from the sand. Play the ball back in your stance, choke down on the grip, and strike the ball. Take a shallow divot in front of it.

THE 19TH HOLE

"Gary Player is all right if you like to see a grown man dressed up like Black Bart all the time."

—Don Rickles, comedian

Quiz Answer: Paul Azinger.

DECEMBER 11 DECEMBER

TODAY'S THOUGHT:
"All good players have good hands. And I'm afraid you have to be born with them."   —Dave Stockton

ON THIS DATE—
In 1991, the NY State Court of Appeals ruled that a golfer whose tee shot struck a moving car, cannot be sued for the resulting traffic accident. The golfer had watched as his shot sailed off the course and shattered a car's windshield. No word on whether it was a hook or a slice.

CHIP SHOT
Golfer's prayer: May I live long enough to shoot my age.

TRIVIA QUIZ—
It's called the "Saturday Slam." What is it?

TODAY'S TIP—
Yes, you can hit a driver from the fairway. Just make sure that the ball is sitting up so the face of the driver can meet the ball squarely, and take your normal swing.

THE 19TH HOLE
"When I told the career guidance person I wanted to be a golf professional, he said that there's no such thing as a golf professional."   —Bernhard Langer

Quiz Answer: You've won the "Saturday Slam" after leading the all of the majors after three rounds, a la Greg Norman in 1986.

D E C E M B E R

TODAY'S THOUGHT:

"Over the years, I've studied habits of golfers. I know what to look for. Watch their eyes. Fear shows up when there is an enlargement of the pupils. Big pupils lead to big scores."   —Sam Snead

ON THIS DATE—

In 1899, George Grant received a patent for the golf tee. It comes a year after patent rights were granted for the rubber-cored golf ball.

CHIP SHOT

Shinnecock Hills GC was the first golf club in the nation to have a clubhouse. It was built in 1892.

TRIVIA QUIZ—

In 1989, Mark Calcavecchia was the first American to win the British Open in six years. But he had to beat two Australians in a playoff to win the silver jug. Who were they?

TODAY'S TIP—

Bringing the driver back to keep the clubhead low and straight through the ball at impact will give you long, straight drives on a consistent basis. Feel the clubhead chase the ball.

THE 19TH HOLE

"Big league players are the worst. They swing with power, don't ask for advice, and invariably hit to all fields."
—Tommy Bolt, on baseball players

Quiz Answer: Wayne Grady and Greg Norman.

DECEMBER 13

TODAY'S THOUGHT:

"The Ryder Cup is not only about winning, but also about goodwill. There is too little tradition left in the game as it is."
—Dave Marr, U.S. captain in 1981

ON THIS DATE—

In 1992, Raymond Floyd won in convincing fashion in the Senior Tour Championship. Floyd, with a final round 7-under-par 65 beat George Archer and Dale Douglass by five strokes.

CHIP SHOT

Three of the world's greatest golf courses - Royal Melbourne, Muirfield, and Olympic - have no water hazards.

TRIVIA QUIZ—

The oldest player ever to compete in the Ryder Cup sank the winning putt for the United States at the Belfry in 1993. Who was it?

TODAY'S TIP—

Let the Yellow Pages do the swinging for you. Try swinging your left arm while holding a phone book. It will build the muscles of your forearm, shoulder, and wrists to give you a little more power in your left side.

THE 19TH HOLE

"Is it against the rules to carry a bulldozer in your bag?
—Tom Watson**

Quiz Answer: 51-year old Raymond Floyd.

DECEMBER

TODAY'S THOUGHT:

"There are guys who are respected for their long games, and guys who are respected for their short games. But there are also guys who win respect because they know the golf swing and have the ability, even when playing poorly, to make something happen."

—Nick Price

ON THIS DATE—

In 1955, LPGA Tour player Jane Crafter was born. A pharmacist before joining the Tour, it was only appropriate that the Australian won the 1990 Phar-Mor at Inverarry.

CHIP SHOT

More golf is shown at The Masters than any other televised event. Only four minutes of commercials per hour are allowed by Masters' officials.

TRIVIA QUIZ—

What is the biggest possible margin in 18 holes of match play?

TODAY'S TIP—

Prevent a fast backswing by swinging your arms, shoulders, and club back in one piece.

THE 19TH HOLE

"Ian Woosnam, you're from Wales. Is that a village in England?"   —Reporter, at the 1991 Masters

---

Quiz Answer: 10 & 8.

DECEMBER

TODAY'S THOUGHT:
"A tournament goes on for days. It is played at a dangerously high mental pressure. Golf makes its demands on the mind. A golfer is terribly exposed in almost every way."
>—Peter Alliss, writer and commentator

ON THIS DATE—
In 1991, Mike Hill won the Senior Tour Championship to become the leading money-winner on the Senior PGA Tour. He also became the second Senior player to go over $1 million in a season.

CHIP SHOT
The first woman to write a book about golf was Mrs. Edward Kennard. In 1896, she penned the text which was titled *The Sorrows of a Golfer's Wife.*

TRIVIA QUIZ—
Why didn't Nick Faldo receive the green coat from the defending champion after his 1990 Masters victory?

TODAY'S TIP—
Put the pressure on your opponent. You want to hit first onto the green, so use a 3-wood off the tee instead of a driver. He'll feel pressured to match your shot.

THE 19TH HOLE
"The only problem with the Senior Tour is that when you're through here, they put you in a box."
>—J.C. Snead

Quiz Answer: Because Faldo was the defending champion. He had won The Masters in 1989.

D E C E M B E R 16

TODAY'S THOUGHT:
"A match against Bobby Jones is just as though you got your hand caught in a buzz saw."
>—Francis Ouimet, 1913 U.S. Open champion

ON THIS DATE—
In 1930, Bobby Jones received the first Sullivan Award as the nation's outstanding amateur athlete. Jones was honored for completing golf's Grand Slam earlier in the year.

CHIP SHOT
Only 4 of the USGA's 13 national championships are decided at stroke play - the U.S. Open, the U.S. Women's Open, the U.S. Senior Open, and the U.S. Senior Women's Amateur Championship.

TRIVIA QUIZ—
My real first names are Alexander Walter Barr, but you call me "Sandy." Who am I?

TODAY'S TIP—
For a high shot over a tree, play the ball up in your stance with your weight favoring the back foot. Keep the weight there as you swing down and finish high. Don't help the ball up.

THE 19TH HOLE
"Some of the players think it's an illegal aid, that I just aim it at the ground, make my turn around it, and follow through." —Larry Laoretti, on his ever-present cigar

Quiz Answer: 1985 British Open champion and 1988 Masters winner, Sandy Lyle.

DECEMBER

TODAY'S THOUGHT:
"In golf, humiliations are the essence of the game."
—Alistair Cooke, writer

ON THIS DATE—
In 1962, PGA Tour player Rocco Mediate was born. Mediate, who didn't get his first set of clubs until he was 16, had six top-ten finishes in his first seven starts in 1991. Born: Tammie Green (1959).

CHIP SHOT
The last tournament Ben Hogan played in was the 1971 Houston Champion International. The 59-year old Hogan walked off in disgust after hitting three balls into the water on the par-3 fourth hole.

TRIVIA QUIZ—
Has PGA Tour player, Jeff Sluman, ever won a major championship? If so, which one?

TODAY'S TIP—
Usually you'll focus on the whole ball from address to impact. But if you're losing concentration, try focusing on the rear half of the ball for better contact.

THE 19TH HOLE
"They've got the wrong woman playing Wonder Woman on television."
—Judy Rankin, on the play of Nancy Lopez

Quiz Answer: Sluman won the 1988 PGA Championship.

DECEMBER

TODAY'S THOUGHT:

"We were lucky we had Jones for so long, for he had a rare gift for passing ideas and ideals on to other people."

—Herbert Warren Wind, writer

ON THIS DATE—

In 1971, golf lost one of it's true heroes when Bobby Jones died. A supremely graceful and stylish player, Jones qualified for every event he entered and was never beaten twice in match play.

CHIP SHOT

To put the career of Bobby Jones in perspective, only one amateur has won the U.S. Open since his retirement in 1930. Only pros have won the British Open after Jones.

TRIVIA QUIZ—

Two of Europe's top golfers have exactly 11 letters in their surname. One of them is Seve Ballesteros. Can you name the other golfer?

TODAY'S TIP—

You and I know that every course seems to have a par-5 that's a monster hole. In your mind, play it as a par-6. Keep the ball in play so you can be on the green in four. That way, as Ben Hogan said, you'll be able to bring the monster to its knees.

THE 19TH HOLE

"Hell, it ain't like losing a leg!"
——Billy Joe Patton, after losing The Masters

Quiz Answer: Colin Montgomerie, of Scotland.

DECEMBER

TODAY'S THOUGHT:

"Once the golfing champion allows himself to suspect that playing a superb round is not the be-all and end-all of life, he is lost."

—Anonymous

ON THIS DATE—

In 1993, Larry Mize dusted the field at the Johnny Walker Championship, finishing ten strokes ahead of runner-up, Fred Couples. Mize was a last-minute substitute for the vacationing Greg Norman.

CHIP SHOT

The famed Baltusrol GC raised livestock to fight the meat shortage during World War II. Over 50 cows and 140 sheep grazed on its fairways.

TRIVIA QUIZ—

Bernhard Langer, of Germany, has won the same major twice in his career. Which one?

TODAY'S TIP—

If you're stuck in a fairway bunker with a high lip, turn around and play the shot away from the hole. The idea is to leave yourself in a position to recover.

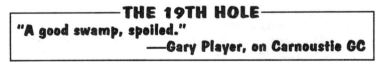

THE 19TH HOLE

"A good swamp, spoiled."

—Gary Player, on Carnoustie GC

Quiz Answer: Langer's two major championship wins have come at The Masters, in 1985 and 1993.

D E C E M B E R

TODAY'S THOUGHT:

"You have the hands, now play with your heart."
—Roberto DeVicenzo, to Seve Ballesteros
before Seve won the '79 British Open

ON THIS DATE—

In 1992, Nick Faldo birdied the last hole to force a playoff with Greg Norman in the World Championship. Par on the first extra hole was enough to give Faldo the win. Born: Don January (1929).

CHIP SHOT

The first tournament Lee Trevino won as a professional was the 1965 Texas State Open.

TRIVIA QUIZ—

What makes the Bob Hope Chrysler Classic different from other events on the PGA Tour?

TODAY'S TIP—

On severe uphill chips, grip the club firmly with your left hand throughout the stroke to stop you from being wristy and hitting the club into the hill behind the ball.

THE 19TH HOLE

"You know what I did at The Masters one year? I was so nervous I drank a fifth of rum before I played. I shot the happiest 83 of my life."　—Chi Chi Rodriguez

Quiz Answer: Though not unique, the Bob Hope Chrysler Classic is played out over 90 holes as opposed to 72 holes.

DECEMBER 21 DECEMBER

TODAY'S THOUGHT:

"All the professionals who have a chance to go after the big money today should say a silent thanks to Walter Hagen each time they stretch a check between their fingers. It was Walter who made professional golf what it is." —Gene Sarazen

ON THIS DATE—

In 1892, one of the game's all-time greats, Walter Hagen, was born. A man with a larger-than-life personality, Hagen played hard on and off the course, winning 40 titles in his career including all four majors at least once.

CHIP SHOT

In 1922, Hagen became the first golf professional to manufacture golf clubs under his own name.

TRIVIA QUIZ—

True or false: Chi Chi Rodriguez has never won a major in his career.

TODAY'S TIP—

When playing a par-3, tee your ball up, and then step on the ground directly behind it. You don't want any grass coming between your club and the ball when you hit.

THE 19TH HOLE

"The Rockies may crumble, Gibraltar may tumble, but St. Andrews isn't going anywhere."
—Frank Deford, writer, on the famed Scottish course

Quiz Answer: True.

D E C E M B E R

TODAY'S THOUGHT:

"Golf is life. If you can't take golf, you can't take life."   —Anonymous

ON THIS DATE—

In 1894, the Amateur Golf Association of the United States was formed in New York. Later changed to the United States Golf Association, its purpose is to promote and conserve the best interests and true spirit of the game of golf. Born: Jan Stephenson (1951).

CHIP SHOT

Jan Stephenson was the first woman golf pro to design golf courses.

TRIVIA QUIZ—

What do you call a golfer with a zero handicap, other than good?

TODAY'S TIP—

If you're ready to hit a shot and are distracted, step away from the ball and gather your thoughts. The same goes for indecision about club selection or alignment.

THE 19TH HOLE

"If USGA people took over the Louvre, they'd paint a mustache on the Mona Lisa."
        —Roger Maltbie, on USGA efforts to make Pebble Beach more difficult for the '92 Open

Quiz Answer: A scratch golfer.

DECEMBER 23

TODAY'S THOUGHT:

"Arnold Palmer usually walks to the first tee quite unlike any other pro on the circuit. He doesn't walk onto it so much as climb into it, almost as though it were a prize ring." —Charles Price, writer

ON THIS DATE—

In 1928, Horton Smith won the Catalina Open with a four-round total of 245. Smith shot rounds of 63, 58, 61, and 63 at the unofficial tournament. Hence, an unofficial record.

CHIP SHOT

Long driver Jimmy Thompson wowed the galleries during the 1935 U.S. Open at Oakmont CC, when he reached the 621-yard 12th green in two. He finished second behind winner Sam Parks.

TRIVIA QUIZ—

If this three-time British Open champion plays his last Open at St. Andrews in the year 2000, it would be the 46th Open championship at which he competed. Can you name him?

TODAY'S TIP—

To hit a fairway wood high, open your stance slightly and take the club back on the outside. The ball will be lifted up naturally from that swing and it will fade slightly.

THE 19TH HOLE

"Golfing excellence goes hand in hand with alcohol, as many an open and amateur champion has shown."
—Henry Longhurst, writer

Quiz Answer: Gary Player.

DECEMBER

TODAY'S THOUGHT:
"Palmer and Player played superbly. But Nicklaus played a game with which I'm not familiar."
> —Bobby Jones, on Nicklaus at the 1965 Masters

ON THIS DATE—
In 1861, the first notable English amateur golfer, John Ball, Jr., was born. Ball ended thirty years of domination by Scottish pros when he won the British Open in 1890. He was the first to win the Open and British Amateur in the same year.

CHIP SHOT
Ben Hogan is the only player to have lost two Masters playoffs. Hogan lost to Byron Nelson in 1942 and Sam Snead in 1954, both times by one stroke in 18-hole playoffs. Hogan won the tournament twice, in 1951 and '53.

TRIVIA QUIZ—
In the 1980's, Europeans won The Masters five times. Can you name the four different players?

TODAY'S TIP—
The one time you don't want to keep your eyes on the ball is on a sand shot. Focus an inch or two behind the ball to help you enter the sand at the perfect spot to lift the ball.

THE 19TH HOLE
"Hitting my drives the right height for the day."
—John Ball, Jr., on how he won the British Open

Quiz Answer: Seve Ballesteros won in 1980 and '83, Bernhard Langer won in 1985, Sandy Lyle in 1988, and Nick Faldo in 1989.

DECEMBER

25

TODAY'S THOUGHT:

"The golfer does not, as a rule, appear at his best at Christmas. A painful alternative is before him. Either he must wholly neglect his duty, fly to a golf course, and leave his wife to hang the Christmas tree and his children to enjoy it alone, or else he must stay at home and go through with it all."   —Bernard Darwin, writer

ON THIS DATE—

In 1875, the youngest winner of the British Open, Tom Morris, Jr., died at the age of 24. Morris captured the Open title in 1868 when he was 18 years old.

CHIP SHOT

Besides being the youngest to win the British Open, Morris is also the only golfer to win it four straight times.

TRIVIA QUIZ—

This golfer played on two US Walker Cup teams, in 1959 and '61, winning all four matches he played. Name him.

TODAY'S TIP—

For a short pitch shot with a lot of backspin, swing the wedge back to your knee. Let your wrists cock fully and then pull your hands down to stroke the ball. Hit the ball crisply so it will "bite" when it hits the green.

THE 19TH HOLE

"The man who can approach does not need to putt."
—J.H. Taylor, five-time British Open champion

Quiz Answer: Jack Nicklaus.

DECEMBER 26

TODAY'S THOUGHT:

"The devoted golfer is an anguished soul who has learned a lot about putting, just as an avalanche victim has learned a lot about snow." —Dan Jenkins, writer

ON THIS DATE—

In 1993, Jack Nicklaus, Raymond Floyd and Chi Chi Rodriguez teamed up to represent the PGA Senior Tour and won the Wendy's Three-Tour Challenge. They earned $100,000 each in the event which was held at the Colleton River Plantation Hotel in Hilton Head, SC.

CHIP SHOT

Television did not impress Horton Smith. Smith, president of the PGA Tour from 1952-54, called it "a gimmick that wouldn't last." In 1994, the PGA Tour broadcast 431 hours of official PGA tournaments.

TRIVIA QUIZ—

In the 19th century, most golf shafts were made of wood. What type of wood?

TODAY'S TIP—

Try using a broken tee to tee your ball up on the par-3's. It will offer less resistance than a full tee (although not less resistance than air).

THE 19TH HOLE

"Everyone has his own choking level. As you get more experienced, your choking level rises."
—Johnny Miller

Quiz Answer: Hickory.

 D E C E M B E R

TODAY'S THOUGHT:

"In the history of American field sports there can be found no outdoor pastime that developed and attained such popularity in such a relatively short period of time as the game of golf."

—New York Times, December 27, 1895

ON THIS DATE—

In 1962, LPGA Tour player Sherri Steinhauer was born. Steinhauer's first victory on the Tour was a major one, coming at the 1992 duMaurier Classic.

CHIP SHOT

Before teeing up for the 1919 U.S. Open playoff, Walter Hagen told opponent Mike Brady to roll down his sleeves. When asked why, Hagen replied, "So the gallery won't see your arms shaking." Hagen won the playoff by one stroke.

TRIVIA QUIZ—

How many European golfers have won the PGA Championship?

TODAY'S TIP—

Hitting the ground behind the ball, or fat, is a result of a quick motion from the top of the swing. Allow your lower body to move left as you start down at the ball.

THE 19TH HOLE

"I am the handicap in golf."

—Boris Becker, tennis pro

Quiz Answer: None.

D E C E M B E R

TODAY'S THOUGHT:
"Golf is the only game in which a precise knowledge of the rules can earn one a reputation for bad sportsmanship."
—Patrick Campbell, writer

ON THIS DATE—
In 1946, Hubert Green was born. Green had nineteen PGA Tour victories and was the winner of the 1977 U.S. Open as well as the 1985 PGA Championship.

CHIP SHOT
Arnold Palmer was the first British Open champion to shoot three rounds under 70. He did it in 1962, scoring 71, 69, 67, 69 on his way to a six-stroke win over Kel Nagle.

TRIVIA QUIZ—
What course played host to the first 12 British Opens?

TODAY'S TIP—
Stay away from trouble if the pin is placed near a trap or water hazard. Play for the fat part of the green and take your chances on a long putt.

THE 19TH HOLE
"In the USA, a number of first class golfers take as long to choose a wife as a club. Sometimes they make the wrong choice in each case."
—Dai Rees, 1937 British Ryder Cup team member

Quiz Answer: Prestwick, in Ayrshire, Scotland.

DECEMBER

TODAY'S THOUGHT:
"Through the ball we are all the same. We just have different ways of getting it there." —Charles Coody

ON THIS DATE—
In 1892, a four-acre apple orchard became the new home of the St. Andrews Club, the golf club recognized as America's first golf club. The course consisted of six holes.

CHIP SHOT
The Ryder Cup, now played in September, was originally played in June. But in 1935, the British team did not want to play in the heat of Ridgewood, NJ so a plan was worked out to put the match back to a cooler month.

TRIVIA QUIZ—
In 1980, this golfer wrote *The Rules of Golf, Explained and Illustrated*. Three months later, he was penalized two shots for giving Lee Trevino a tip during play at the Tournament of Champions. Name him.

TODAY'S TIP—
Use your putter if the fringe near the green is smooth and flat.

THE 19TH HOLE
"Pebble Beach is supposed to be as nasty as a cocktail waitress in a dockside cafe." —Art Spander, writer

Quiz Answer: Tom Watson.

D E C E M B E R

TODAY'S THOUGHT:
"Golf is mostly a game of failures."   —Tommy Aaron

ON THIS DATE—
In 1969, LPGA Tour player Michelle McGann was born. Known more for her fashionable collection of hats than victories, McGann broke through with the first win of her career in 1995. Even without any wins, McGann still had more than $1 million in career earnings. Also born: Kris Tschetter (1964).

CHIP SHOT
In the first 100 years of the U.S. Open, 31 tournaments were decided by playoffs. That's more than double the number of any other major championship.

TRIVIA QUIZ—
Name the only player to score a double-eagle at the U.S. Open.

TODAY'S TIP—
To play better golf, learn the fundamentals of the game and stick to them. Remember, patchwork remedies to get you out of a slump never last.

THE 19TH HOLE
"Why I didn't win the last seven years, who knows? Why I win this week, Lord only knows."
       —Michelle McGann, after her first Tour win

Quiz Answer: T.C. Chen did it at a par-5 hole at the 1985 Open at Oakland Hills CC.

DECEMBER

TODAY'S THOUGHT:

"It is almost impossible to remember how tragic a place the world is when one is playing golf." —Robert Lynd, sociologist

ON THIS DATE—

In 1936, the USGA announced that, effective January 1, 1938, no more than 14 clubs will be allowed in tournament play. Officials said the move was expected to speed up the game.

CHIP SHOT

The first American golf book was published in 1895. It was written by James Lee and titled, simply, *Golf in America*.

TRIVIA QUIZ—

The best finish by an amateur at The Masters, second place, has occurred three times. Ken Venturi was the runner-up in 1956. Do you know the other two golfers?

TODAY'S TIP—

Tomorrow's the start of a new year. Get out and enjoy the game . . . but keep your head steady and your eyes on the ball . . . and your right elbow in . . . and a straight left arm . . .

THE 19TH HOLE

"I like to say I was born on the nineteenth hole -the only one I ever parred."
—George Low, former Tour player

Quiz Answer: Frank Stranahan shared second place with Byron Nelson behind winner Jimmy Demaret in 1947. In 1961, Charlie Coe tied Arnold Palmer for second behind Gary Player.